GEORGE McKAY

Glastonbury

A very English fair

VICTOR GOLLANCZ

LONDON

CONTENTS

For Ran, Freddie and Emy, *con amore*

Festival culture

[Festivals], greater or lesser, each with a peculiar quality, unique and yet related
to those preceding and succeeding, have built up the dance of the year.

Lawrence Whistler, *The English Festivals*, 1947

This is a book about Glastonbury, the town, its landscapes and legends, the festivals
there. It is also about festival culture more widely – the history and development
of popular music festivals, the ways in which they have contributed to alternative
culture, even to alternative history. In spite of the weather, Britain has an extraordinary tradition of festival culture, which, as we will see, takes its inspiration from
sources as diverse as Gypsy horse fairs, American rock festivals, rebirthed pagan
rituals and country fairs. From trad and modern jazzers at Beaulieu in the 1950s to the
New Traveller–Acid House free gathering at Castlemorton Common in 1992, festivals
can be vital spaces, vital moments of cultural difference. They live in the memories of
those who were at them, as experiments in living, in utopia, sometimes gone wrong.
These festivals are about idealism, being young, getting old disgracefully, trying to
find other ways, getting out of it, hearing some great and some truly awful music,
about anarchy and control. Of course, festivals can also be dull, homogenised mass
events, at which crowds worship bad music played too loud in an unconscious echo of
sub-fascist ritual – but mostly those are the heavy metal ones. Key features of festival
culture in Britain include a young or youthful audience, open-air performance, popular music, the development of a lifestyle, camping, local opposition, police distrust,
and even the odd rural riot.

To both chart and to celebrate the counterculture's tribal gatherings, I look in detail
at Glastonbury festival, which has been at the centre of the movement for thirty
years, on and off, and which reflects the changes in music and style, in political

campaigning, in policing and festival legislation over all that time. Its audiences include old and young hippies, punks, folk fans, ravers, neo-pagans, and generations of activists, dreamers, fun-seekers, musicians, pilgrims, as well as the many city-dwellers who come down on Glastonbury for that annual hit of green freedom (within the fences, anyway). The book moves between the micro-perspective of what Somerset dairy farmer and Glastonbury festival organiser Michael Eavis calls his 'regular midsummer festival of joy and celebration of life', and the macro-perspective of what sociologist Tim Jordan has identified as 'the importance of post-1960s festivals to ongoing radical protest'. I make no apologies for positioning my version of festival culture within a political praxis and discourse, however problematic. It is though a politics which admits pleasure, whether of pop and rock music, of temporary (tented) community, of landscape and nature under open skies, of promiscuity, of narcotic. The version of festival culture I offer here contains all these features. Sometimes. In varying degrees. The vibrant adventure that is the social phenomenon of festival culture that has developed since the 1950s in Britain has touched several generations now. I hope you recognise your festival here; it has indeed 'built up the dance of the year'. Be generous and optimistic: remember the good parts, for memory can change the world. (A bit. Sort of.) I hope you recognise your Glastonbury here. Even if you don't remember it.

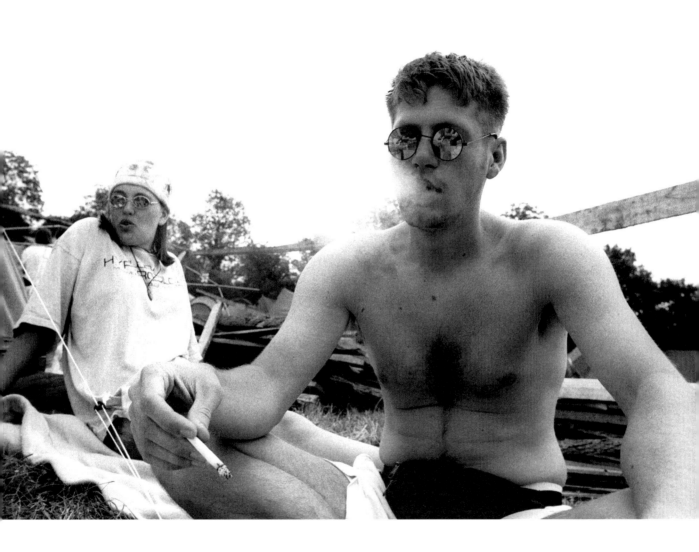

Histories of festival culture

I want to be in that number, when the Saints go marching in

The early roots of British festival culture are found in the jazz festivals run by Edward (Lord) Montagu at Beaulieu (1956–61) and in Harold Pendelton's National Jazz Federation events at Richmond then Reading (from 1961 onwards). They indicate the perhaps surprising extent to which the trad and modern jazz scenes of the 1950s and early 1960s blazed the trail for the hippie festivals of the later 1960s and beyond. After the postwar austerity, the 1950s displayed an increasingly confident and vibrant (sometimes violent) range of youth and anti-Establishment cultures: coffee bars, Teddy Boys, skiffle, beatniks, Angry Young Men, satire, pop art, left-wing journals, Caribbean culture, CND marches, etc., etc. In 1955 and 1956 London cinemas were trashed by rioting Teds inflamed by scenes of, er, Bill Haley and His Comets, in the American films *The Blackboard Jungle* and *Rock Around the Clock*. By 1958 the Teds would be transferring their nasty riotous attentions to London's black community, while by 1960 a series of riots broke out at jazz concerts through the summer, culminating in the trouble at the Beaulieu Festival. According to Christopher Booker, in his study of the cultural revolution of 1950s and 1960s Britain, *The Neophiliacs*:

> For the avant-garde of the teenagers in 1956 and 1957, it was as if they had been caught up in an iridescent bubble, bringing for all those inside it a vision of eternal youth, free- dom and excitement. But over those who remained outside, had fallen a thick veil, which made everything they did or thought important seem suddenly incomprehensible, 'out of date', contemptible and grey.

I asked Lord Montagu about the inspiration behind the first Beaulieu Jazz Festival in the grounds of his stately home in Hampshire: 'It came locally from the Yellow Dog Jazz Club, I think it was named, in Southampton. Yes, I suppose I did have in the back of my mind a British version of the American Newport Jazz Festival, if you like, but I think I saw the festival, ideally, as the Glyndebourne of Jazz, or hoped it might become that.' (Glyndebourne Festival Theatre was opened in 1934 in a private estate in Sussex. Its critically acclaimed opera festivals started again after the Second World War, in 1950.) Interestingly the Beaulieu Jazz Festivals consciously echoed the local Beaulieu fairs of the 1890s, and were seen in some ways as revivals of those lost spring and harvest fairs. According to jazz singer, cultural critic, surrealist and sort of anarchist George Melly, the 1956 Beaulieu festival:

The title page of Jeremy Sandford's and Ron Reid's 1971 *Tomorrow's People*.

. . . was a comparatively small-scale venture: two bands, the Dill Jones trio and us, providing an afternoon and evening session on the palace lawn. Several hundred people

turned up and behaved with enthusiastic decorum . . . There was no local opposition; on the contrary the pub and village shop were delighted with the extra business. We got to know Beaulieu pretty well over the next six years . . . We watched the whole thing grow. The one day became two days . . . A camping ground was available for those who brought their own tents. Beer and hot dog stalls sprang up around the edges of the great lawns. By night the palace was floodlit.

Here, from the mid-1950s, then, are the earliest examples of what we would recognise as festival culture in Britain. For Jeremy Sandford, writing in the first book (alongside Ron Reid's terrific photographs – a project which came about as a result of their meeting high on the Pyramid Stage at the 1971 Glastonbury Fayre) to chronicle the British festival scene, *Tomorrow's People*, the 1958 Beaulieu was 'the first British festival proper, a two-day event that atracted 4000 people'. I asked Lord Montagu about this:

A storage shed burns fiercely in the aftermath of riots at the Beaulieu Jazz Festival, 1960.

Oh yes, we were the first. The rock festivals like Glastonbury and Knebworth followed us. Don't forget that we also had the BBC doing a live broadcast of music from the festival in 1960. My regret is that, when all the trouble started that night, they pulled the plug altogether – they could have stopped broadcasting but kept filming. I've always said that the BBC lost the chance to capture some very very good music indeed that night by turning off the cameras. The worst riots were between the fans of [modernist] Johnny Dankworth and [tradder] Acker Bilk, who was due to come on after poor Johnny's band. But we did feel that 'When the Saints Go Marching In' was always the best number to go out on at the end of the night, so that's why we had put the trad on top billing.

Problems of crowd security, subcultural over-enthusiasm, and a rural invasion, were all seen at Beaulieu, features to become common in the organisation and reporting of, as well as the resistance to, festival culture over the succeeding decades. According to George Melly, who sang at the festival every year with the Mick Mulligan Band and was also an intelligent commentator on pop music and the changing world of Britain:

In 1960 the trad boom was at its height, and a riot occurred at Beaulieu. It wasn't a vicious riot. It was stupid. The traddies in rave gear booing the Dankworth band. A young man climbing up the outside of the palace in the floodlights waving a bowler hat from the battlements. Cheers and scuffles. Then, when the television transmission was going on and Acker playing, the crowd surged forward and began to climb the scaffolding supporting the arc-lights. The few police and the official stewards struggled with them, and the BBC went off the air.

(I wonder whether they were somehow rioting about the site, the Palace House backdrop, rather than the music, but that may only be wishful thinking on my part. In his autobiography Lord Montagu expresses the opinion that 'Beaulieu itself had probably been as much as an attraction to the audience as the music they heard there.') Within five years, the rural festival at Beaulieu became a victim of its own popularity, undoing the very things that had made it so attractive. By 1961, thought Melly, 'The trouble was that there were too many people for the village to absorb, not enough lavatories, too few litter bins. Local feeling rose high, and at midnight Edward Montagu told the press that this was the last festival he would hold at Beaulieu. Trad jazz had outgrown its most typical and happiest occasion'. Mick Farren, self-styled White Panther, leader of the free festival band the Deviants and organiser of the 1970 Phun City free festival, also sees the Beaulieu jazz festivals as significant, describing them as 'primitive mini-Woodstocks that reached media attention when the audience took offence at being filmed as though they were sociological exhibits and turned over BBC TV cameras'. For Farren 'the scarcely plausible figure of Acker Bilk' during the trad craze of the first years of the 1960s could be ignored because, 'Although trad was nowhere as solid as Elvis or Jerry Lee or Little Richard, it did at least bop along in a jolly manner, you could get drunk on cider, and nobody got uptight, although the older patrons did refer to the teenage invaders as "ravers". This was all this group was looking for. It was a collective title, it defined them and they could at last rejoice in a separate identity.' *Melody Maker* had another name for these ravers: 'weirdies'.

Jeremy Sandford recaps the story of festival culture so far:

What sort of people go to pop festivals? To start with the audience were fairly elitist; trad jazz enthusiasts and, later, trad and modern jazz enthusiasts . . . It is no longer like that now. 'Hippy' ideas, ideals, customs and costumes have spread into large areas of the culture of the young, and the influence of the 'alternative society' can very clearly be seen at festivals; the influence of the underground, flower-power scene, head, freaks, bohemians, dropouts, ravers or whatever title you or fashion prefer to call them by, stretches fairly far; furthest in its music, stimulants and clothing, but far also in other ways.

From the beginning of the 1960s, Harold Pendleton's work in particular shows this trajectory of jazz as precursor of festival culture, with his Richmond Jazz Festivals organised under the aegis of the National Jazz Federation at Richmond Showground. These are directly traceable to the Reading Festivals from 1971 onwards, so that Reading can legitimately claim to be the longest-lasting commercial rock festival event in the country. Pendleton showed a skilful ability, learned through his involvement in both the Marquee Club in Soho, London and some of the Beaulieu Jazz Festivals, to identify changing tastes in popular music, and to book newer bands. The Richmond Festivals are particularly interesting as they encapsulate the musical and social transformation of the time; in the space of a few years in the early 1960s, the shift is from retro trad jazz and blues of Acker Bilk, Ken Colyer, Alex Welsh, towards the new pop music – and audience – of the blues-oriented pop bands such as the Rolling Stones, the Yardbirds, Manfred Mann. The 1965 NJF festival at Richmond was the moment when this change in youth consciousness, music, instrumentation and style became most clear, as the festival publicity shows: 'Something unheard of is happening at Richmond . . . for the first time . . . the pure jazz-men are outnumbered by beat and rhythm-and-blues groups who are no stranger to the hit parade . . . [The festival is] something of a teenagers' Ascot, the only social occasion on a national scale when they can "try out" new clothes.' Over 30,000 turned up, many of them girls screaming for the Rolling Stones, and the stage was rushed in the excitement of the loud rock music. In fact, Richmond was the ideal place for the Stones to make their festival splash, since the band had been playing the Crawdaddy club opposite the railway station for two years, building up an audience and a scene there. The band's first review, in *Record Mirror*, was from the Richmond club:

As the trad scene gradually subsides, promoters of all kinds of teen-beat entertainments heave a long sigh of relief that they have found something to take its place . . . At the Station hotel, Kew Road the hip kids throw themselves about to the new 'jungle music' like they never did in the more restrained days of trad. And the combo they writhe and twist to is called the Rolling Stones. Maybe you've never heard of them . . . but by gad you will!!

No one, though, seemed to have told the local press of Richmond, an affluent and eminently respectable town, which described with distaste the seemingly new type of youth (and reinvented elders) who were attracted to the festival lifestyle:

> . . . people of all ages with a penchant for vagrancy, and little use for all the conventional paraphernalia of beds, changes of clothing, soap, razors and so on. Hundreds had come expecting to sleep in a large marquee, as they did last year, but they were told a ban had been put on sleeping on the ground. Everywhere in Richmond with a few yards of green grass claimed a few sleepers.

Of course, the identification of nomadism and dirt as signs of threat is seen in majority culture's attitude to alt.groups across decades, whether urban squatters of the 1960s, New Travellers, Greenham Peace Camp women of the 1980s, or road protesters of the 1990s – consider the whole pejorative terminology of 'crustie', in general. Perhaps if Richmond had allowed an overnight sleeping marquee (a crash tent) and not locked up the public toilets at 10 p.m., the good townspeople would not have had quite so much to get uptight about.

The Richmond Festivals contained familiar elements of festival culture: open air culture and lifestyle, loud music, crowds of young people, camping out, over-indulgence and local opposition. From Richmond, Pendelton's NJF festival moved on to the Berkshire town of Windsor for a couple of years, including the 1967 Summer of Love festival when Donovan, Eric Clapton and the Nice played (and some of the crowd set rubbish alight, threw things at the attendant fire engine, and had battles with security guards). Standing up to criticism from police about the festival encouraging sexual immorality by having mixed-sex crash tents, Pendleton replied, 'I'm not running a morality brigade, and what they get up to is their own affair.' Its most interesting years seemingly behind it, the annual NJF festival moved from its various homes mostly around the Home Counties to a permanent one in Reading, Berkshire in 1971, at the invitation of the local council, which wanted to celebrate a thousand years of the town's existence. After the problems with the authorities at Richmond and Windsor over the past few years, to have a town actually *inviting* this event to come to it must have been a novelty. It was an inspired invitation: in the decades since then, the Reading Festival has become one of the town's, and indeed the country's, annual pop music cultural events, and has indeed opened up the possibly unlikely scenario of the town of Reading being a favoured festival space: Peter

Gabriel's WOMAD (World of Music, Arts and Dance) now holds annual festivals of world music there, too, each July (though it prefers to publicise its site as 'Rivermead' rather than Reading).

Pendleton describes the plans for the first Reading Festival in 1971, which were quite as outlandish as anything being thought up at Worthy Farm for Glastonbury Fayre that same month, June: 'We had the idea of having a floating festival, a floating stage on the Thames . . . then we realised that we'd get a floating traffic jam on the river because of all the holiday-makers who'd stop to listen to the music; so this idea was abandoned.' Yet if they really wanted to hold the festival on water they need not have worried, as Pendleton recalls: 'The [Reading] site was an ex-rubbish dump, and there was terrible weather. The ground became like mass of quaking porridge, we arrived to find a sea of water.' In spite of the fact of the local council's invitation the local paper reported 'signs of an almost hysterical fear building up in the town as the fans stream in'. By 1972, the *Evening Post* was describing the festival crowd favourably in comparison with another mass pop culture phenomenon of the time, football hooliganism: 'It is worth noting that pictures of the faces of pop fans showed nothing but smiles. Those of some football fans were covered in blood.' The programme for the 1979 Reading Festival contains (as well as, curiously, at least two advertisements for Berkshire aluminium replacement window companies) a brief history of the festivals held there through the decade. Recurring bands give a sense of its musical identity: Rory Gallagher, the Faces, Status Quo, Thin Lizzy, Alex Harvey, Genesis.

In one of those conjunctions of festival culture, the late August holiday weekend generally sees the Reading Rock Festival catering for one strand of British youth and music taste, while in London itself the Notting Hill Carnival caters for another. And never the twain shall meet? Mike and Trevor Phillips note in their book *Windrush* that, 'There are a number of different accounts about how the Carnival came into being.' While there are reports of Trinidadian processions and balls going back to the late 1950s in London, I want to concentrate on the account which uncovers some of the roots of Caribbean Carnival in the 1960s counterculture. The London district of Notting Hill itself is significant – by the mid-sixties, a few years after the race riots, it was, according the the Phillipses, 'filling up with social workers, workers from voluntary and religious groups, left-wing activists, housing campaigners, middle-class hippies, pop musicians and academic researchers of every kind. All of these embraced the new festival, seeing it as a moment when, for once in a year, racial barriers could be surmounted and everyone could share the invigorating manna of West Indian *joie de vivre*.'

According to the research of sociologist Abner Cohen, an alternative which connected countercultural utopianism with atavism in the focused moment of a fair is seen in London from the mid-sixties. The small idealistic and political event was held (or thrown) then which exists still today, in a transformed and massively magnified version. The Notting Hill Carnival rivals and, in fact, unquestionably surpasses Glastonbury in terms of tradition, ambition and sheer scale. This event, unlike the massive commercialisation of Glastonbury, despite its partial origins as a free festival, is *still free*, though it is unrecognisable from its original form (or rather from *one* of the stories of its original form) as the revival of an old local English tradition. Like the Reading/Richmond Festival, it is older than Glastonbury festival, and is an annual event combining music and dance, performance, the inclusive expression of the people, frequently an unmissable political edge, and the celebration of community. It was founded by local people including a group of activists in a community arts centre called the London Free School – an organisation which worried the local Mayor, who had originally pledged his support for the event. (Shortly before it was due to take place, writes Cohen, the Mayor withdrew his support 'because he had been told that the Free School was a subversive organization associated with Communists, Fascists, Black Muslims and Provos'.) Mick Farren remembers that the underground scene in London was still developing then: 'I began to see more freaks on the street, but there was still no point of contact, although I heard strange things were happening at something called the Free School in Notting Hill.'

Cohen describes the rationale behind what he identifies as the first Notting Hill event proper in 1966:

> The general cultural form that the carnival was to take was essentially English, i.e., in terms of the symbols of the dominant culture and ideology. There was no suggestion that it would imitate a West Indian or any other foreign form of carnival. It was . . . a revival of the Notting Hill Annual Fayre that had been traditionally held in the area until it was stopped at the turn of the century.

The early Notting Hill Fayre, then, was a community cultural event which crystallised a struggle for 'urban space' – somewhat like the jokey-serious Free States of London squatters or road protesters from Frestonia in 1977 to Wanstonia in 1994, or like a Reclaim the Streets anti-car culture street party of the late-1990s. Unlike many countercultural actions (in spite of their rhetoric of inclusivity), the Notting Hill event *did* in effect mobilise black and white working class alike, though, and, 'Its major impact during the 1966–1970 period was to develop and enhance a united stand of the local population to wage a struggle for housing. The same people who came together to plan, prepare and stage carnival, joined forces on the housing front. Carnival and the housing issue became invisibly intertwined.' Cohen continues:

> As the 1960s drew to an end, the polyethnic character of carnival increasingly gave way to a polarized structure consisting of West Indian cultural formations as opposed to the British dominant culture . . . A dramatic turning point in the form and politics of the carnival was the violent confrontation between the police and West Indian demonstrators . . . in August 1970 . . . Subsequently the carnival became national in scale and almost exclusively West Indian.

For Mike and Trevor Phillips, 'what happened annually in Notting Hill was undoubtedly a British phenomenon . . . That is to say, it was focused around the experience of coming from the Caribbean and coming to a part of British society.' What I find interesting is the extent to which the Caribbean contribution can be seen to merge with white festival culture's efforts at the time to revive or reinvent an alternative festival tradition.

Yet festival culture as largely a rural phenomenon could display the limits of its diversity (off-stage, at least). In his book *Rastaman*, about a religion which, after all, places tremendous importance on the power and authority of popular music, reggae music, Ernest Cashmore reminds us that 'the Rastafarian activity of the 1970s took place not in the geographically isolated wastelands of North Wales or the hippie paradise of Glastonbury, but amidst the heterogeneity and complexity of urban-industrial areas such as London, Birmingham and Liverpool.' The cringe-making neologism of *Glastafari* signals some sort of effort to claim, to relocate music, fashion, lifestyle, spirituality, ganja (but not ethnic identity?) of urban blacks to the Isle of Avalon, which may well seem a bit Babylonian to sorted (nineties) or sussed (seventies) black Britons. After all, as Mike and Trevor Phillips state, 'The story of how the Caribbean migrant came to this country and became British is a story about cities.' And in this simple model of white and black, rural–suburban and urban, British Asian populations do not even fit. The Asian mela that began to be organised on a large scale by local Asian communities in northern cities of England and in Glasgow in the 1980s and 1990s took as its model of festival a traditional gathering imported from the sub-continent. Where budgets permitted, street performers and market traders would even be flown over to give the mela an authentic touch for British Asian festival-goers. It may well be the case that, as Andrew Blake suggests in *The Land Without Music*, one of the few books to deal with festival and national identity, it is the mela, rather than Glastonbury or Stonehenge Free or even Reading which is the truly countercultural festival. British Asian youth have frequently been excluded from subcultural and pop musical scenes (as we will see again later with the Rock Against Racism carnivals of the late 1970s), yet the bhangra soundtrack to some melas has made for some fierce dancing in these urban festivals.

Cultural critic Iain Chambers also draws our attention to the fact that the 1960s and early 1970s were not just about the white middle-class counterculture of the hippie, dropout, rock music worldview. Other groups of young whites were moving along different lines to many of the hippies, were dancing careful steps, not sitting cross-legged. The mods' preference for soul music in the 1960s was one aspect of a 'taste for the exotic in black music [which] found a continuation (and shared sub-

Thousands attended open-air festivals in Hyde Park, London in the late sixties and early seventies.

cultural lineage) in the skinheads and Jamaican ska music of the late 1960s, around the time that the "alternative society" was celebrating its own arrival in [the free concerts in] Hyde Park, and in the energetic dancing and stylized attention to obscure US soul music in the clubs and dance halls of the "Northern Soul" circuit which also sprang up in those years.' The issue of whiteness and festival, and counterculture is one I return to later when exploring the politics of pop festivals. There is a strand running through the book which insists on interrogating the utopian claims of festival culture, and if rural or suburban pop festivals are primarily white events, how exclusive is the utopia which festival culture may claim to be presenting?

The revived traditional English Fayre of Notting Hill in 1966 was inspired by embracing carnival from the Caribbean; the revived traditional East Anglian Fairs of the 1970s were inspired by embracing medieval-style festivals from California, of all places (or: California, naturally). As with the jazz setting of the earliest festivals at Beaulieu and the NJF events at Richmond the energy was sparked by transatlantic cultural exchange. The counterculture was good at such exchange: historian Arthur Marwick goes so far as to suggest that 'In some ways the hippies were the most inter-national of all the phenomena associated with the sixties'. Harry Shapiro maps things as he saw them then:

The Beatles also helped to put London on the psychedelic map and there were many attempts to re-create Haight Ashbury in W10 and NW6. For the *Berkeley Barb* and the *Oracle* read *International Times* and *Oz*; the Roundhouse, UFO and Middle Earth for the Fillmore and the Avalon Ballroom; Ally Pally for the Be-In; Pink Floyd, Soft Machine and Cream for the Dead, Airplane and Quicksilver. Cream and Hendrix straddled both continents . . .

Shapiro implies that the British counterculture is the imitative one, the secondary 're-creation', which is also how George Melly saw it during the Summer of Love: 'San Francisco became the capital of British pop, and British pop became in consequence provincial.' Interestingly, at least one American perspective reverses the transatlantic pop cultural influence. In his 1970 book *Festival! The Book of American Music Celebrations*, *Rolling Stone* writer Jerry Hopkins describes the burgeoning scene in Haight Ashbury in 1965 as follows: 'San Francisco became known as "America's Liverpool".' One of the first rural communes in California was named after a Beatles song, Strawberry Fields, and, of course, one of the San Francisco freak scene's favoured venues for gigs and light shows was the *Avalon* Ballroom. Such small details as these suggest that cultural exchange is a more complex process. Marwick outlines transatlantic festival culture from the 1960s:

> Rock music (and the idolatry it inspired), nature, love, drugs, and mass togetherness – where they all joined hands was in the open-air music festivals, the greatest of all the types of spectacle invented in the sixties. The culminating event of the Summer of Love, 1967, was the pop festival at Monterey, the prototype for the others. From all directions, hippies, fellow-travellers, camp followers, and all descriptions of people filled with a lust for life, converged on the small town on the Californian coast, south of San Francisco. Subsequently, in London, there were several free concerts in Hyde Park, the great British spectacle being the Isle of Wight festival of 1970 – an event French and Italian hippies made a point of attending. But the biggest and best-remembered – great care and preparation went into the filming of it – was the Woodstock Music and Art Fair, held at Bethel in up-state New York, in August 1969.

In October of the same year, a conference was held in New Mexico by festival organisers, members of the counterculture, musicians and other interested parties, to discuss the future of festival in the USA, or 'What comes after Woodstock?' It was called a 'sympowowsium' (since it was held near a hot mineral spring sacred to native Americans in the region). Its conclusions were reported in *Rolling Stone* magazine:

> It was this concept – buying land with festival profits, then turning the land over to a commune – that occupied a great part of the weekend's talk . . . 'We don't have to follow the pop festival any more,' Michael Vosse said. 'We don't need rock and roll to turn each other on. It can be done in other ways. The festival could be a house warming for the earth.'

It is too easy to say that the Rolling Stones' free concert at Altamont only six weeks later, where the security guards of Hell's Angels stabbed a black man to death, put paid to the sense of optimism expressed here. Jumping continents, festival culture could strive to maintain the ambition posited by the New Mexico sympowowsium.

The Aquarius Festival held at Nimbin in the state of New South Wales in Australia in 1973 is one such catalysing moment, where there were concrete steps following the festival itself to maintain and develop some kind of *permanent* alternative space. Clem Gorman, like Richard Neville and Germaine Greer, an Australian player in the British underground of the 1960s and early 1970s, describes what he called at the time 'the major collective event of the past few years in Australia'. There had been for some time an annual Arts Festival of Australian University students, held at a different university each year:

> In 1973 it was decided that this format was no longer satisfying students and a new format evolved [which] would take the form of a rural camping festival, involving rock, video, theatre and other forms of New Consciousness art. The format thus chosen was the rock festival, extended over many weeks and into many other artistic areas. The structure was free and participational, and the organisation was minimal . . . [The] townspeople [of Nimbin] were enlisted as allies. Perhaps surprisingly, they welcomed the event and co-operated with the organisers . . . A paper, the *Nimbin Goodtimes*, communicated news and ideas to the thousands of students, dropouts and freaks who congregated in that small town or in the nearby fields. Film groups, yoga groups, food groups, spiritual groups, were formed all over the valleys and hillsides, and shelters sprang up everywhere.

Festival-goers stayed on in the region, and the nearby town of Mullimbimbi became a centre for alternative types. Posters across Australia asked the question 'After Nimbin – what?' Gorman explains what, in a description that is perhaps glowing because it is written so soon after the project got off the ground, but also because Gorman (as I've said, an Australian) is at pains to balance the patronising view of Australian alternative culture the Brits held. 'After all, the assumption goes, aren't all the adventurous Aussies in London anyway, who cares about Down Under?' he writes wryly. 'It is what happened after the festival that makes Nimbin such a unique experiment in communality. A plan was formulated whereby people could purchase land in the Nimbin or Mullimbimbi areas for a payment of two hundred dollars.'

A 'new land-owning co-operative' was formed which owned the land, and whose members would be any alternative lifestyler who could scrape together that relatively small sum of money. Alan Dearling, chronicler of New Travellers and alternative lifestyles in Britain, saw the Nimbin spirit in 1999 while researching his book *Alternative Australia*. 'A lot of participants stayed on in the Rainbow Region after the festival. Others joined them. Experiments in communal living, rituals, spirituality, a tribal culture and drugs became central to what the very name "Nimbin" meant in the national psyche.' One offshoot was the ConFest movement, founded in 1976 as an eco-festival and conference combined. The wild (feral) ConFest happens biannually, according to Graham St John, writing in *Alternative Australia*:

> ConFest is an open-staged ritual-theatre of the feraliens. Fire dancers, dreadlocked, multi-pierced psy-trance maidens and tribal drummers adorned with feralia – feathers, birds' feet, skulls, and umbilical-cord necklaces – evoke defiance, wildness, otherness, freedom. Spectacular aesthetes, on a diet of tofu and tahini, belonging to anarchist eco-tribes, committed to direct actions, oozing eco-spirituality, these antipodean terra-ists represent an attractive subcultural career for youth disenchanted with their separation from the natural world.

The vision of Nimbin was one of a number of rural cooperative or intentional communities that formed at the time, combining the global Aquarian ideals with the Australian 'bush pioneer' spirit and indigenous tribal practices alike. Setting aside the vast difference in scale of land between Australia and Britain, it would be a bit like using the Glastonbury festival funds to buy up farms and fields in Somerset (like around Nimbin, often dairy land) in order to build a grand, cheap alternative collective of communities and cultural workers. Actually, Glastonbury festival *has* on occasion bought up neighbouring farmland, if for the practical reason of extending the festival site, not for the idealistic purpose of building an alternative community.

Nomadland

> The beauty and mystery of the countryside are being revealed once more to those who will follow the old trackways.
> Janet and Colin Bord, *Mysterious Britain*

The more privileged hippies of the 1960s and 1970s were frequent international travellers (whether London, San Francisco, the hippie trail to India), and festival culture itself benefitted from transatlantic cultural exchange, but there is also a more local, perhaps parochial, version of travel. Following the old trackways meant tracing the ley lines for the Bords in 1972, but it can be equally applicable to (and is often nicely mixed up with) embracing a nomadic lifestyle as a countercultural act. Mobilisation is literal here, which has clear precedents in the countryside. Consider the early Communist or socialist working-class walking groups which campaigned on access, such as the 'Liverpool Hobnailers', or the British Workers' Sports Federation, which organised the 1932 mass trespass on Kinder Scout in the English Peak District. This wasn't the privileged walking of the Romantic poets or of the urban *flâneurs*, but a transgressive, repossessive walking, with political demands such as access and equality that cut across the closed nature of the English countryside – incursions rather than excursions. The direct action of the early walking groups contributed to the formation of organisations like the Youth Hostels Association (founded in 1930) and the Ramblers Association (1935). *If* the justification or measure of worth of direct action is the degree to which it affects public policy, then it is worth acknowledging that associations such as these themselves raised public awareness to the extent of influencing the National Parks and Access to the Countryside Act, 1949. The politics of bordrage echo in the 1990s with direct-action trespass groups such as The Land is Ours. In the 1990s, transport (whether roads or live animal exports, for example) became a central direct action single issue not because of some inherent significance but because it itself contributes to nomadism.

Another version of the moving, now and again dancing, body is a black and white free party collective called, yes, Exodus, based in Luton, bringing 'massive and passive' resistance to DiY community action: the *movement of jah people* matters. (While one of the points for critics is to analyse/historicise/theorise DiY rhetoric and practice, another is to get carried away, to be moved by it.)

Tapping into Gypsy knowledge and modes of living assumed lost to Gorgio culture is a romantic if problematic strategy, but it is one that has been adopted in various forms by dropouts, rural bohemians, back-to-the-landers, the Tipi People of the 1970s, the (always *so-called*) Peace Convoy of the 1980s and the Dongas Tribe of road protestors in the 1990s. One of the attractions of Gypsy living is its perceived atavism, its counter-modernity. Gypsy elder Gordon Boswell recalls his own past in *The Book of Boswell: Autobiography of a Gypsy*:

> In the early days of my great-great-grandfather and his tribes the mode of transport
> was pack donkeys and horses. They lived in tents, which consisted of young ash
> or hazel saplings covered with felts or blankets or suchlike . . . *rods*, as we called
> the saplings. [At school] we got the 'Gypsy, Gypsy, live in a tent, can't afford to
> pay your rent!'

The bender tradition survives as a low impact statement by eco-aware New Travellers. The West Country is a favoured area of alternative lifestyles. Somerset has a number of low-impact communities, where people's lifestyles are centred around a conscious effort to minimise their own impact on the environment, to live in harmony with nature. These include the bender communities of Tinker's Bubble (the name, a Gypsy spring, showing its origins) and King's Hill. Ecology writer and Tinker's Bubble inhabitant Simon Fairlie describes King's Hill:

> About 16 benders, each about the size of a double garage, most of them with windows, are sited in a field, forming a circle around a central garden area. . . . The settlers have planted the site with trees . . . One of the benders is a communal space where guests can sleep, the others are individual or family dwellings . . . Most of the inhabitants are ex-travellers seeking above all a safe place to live.

There are also similarities in the demands or visions put forward by traveller groups, whether traditional Gypsy or dropouts or new travellers. The expressions below are taken respectively from Gypsy elder Gordon Boswell, speaking at a public meeting at Appleby Fair in 1967, and from a high hippie manifesto produced by Albion Free State in 1974.

An early listings and lifestyle magazine for festival culture.

BOSWELL: And what I would like to see is some camps up and down the country. I'd like to see three types: a permanent camp where old people can go and stop and rest and be left in peace; a transit camp where you can come from one town to another and pay to go in and travel the country from the North to the South if you wish; and camps where you can stop in the winter months.

ALBION FREE STATE: The dispossessed people of this country need *Land* – for diverse needs, permanent free festival sites, collectives, and cities of Life and Love, maybe one every fifty miles or so, manned and womaned by people freed from dead-end jobs and from slavery in factories mass-producing non-essential consumer items.

The rhetoric and reasoning differs, but the permanent camp network for traditional travellers and the permanent festival sites for newer nomads have their similiarities, too.

An enterprising stallholder utilises a tree at the second Isle of Wight festival, 1969.

According to underground press writer Nigel Fountain, '1969 was the year that rock festivals took off in Britain.' He cites the two Hyde Park free concerts by Blind Faith in June and the Rolling Stones in July, along with Bob Dylan at the Isle of Wight in August, as constituting 'the summer of festivals'. These events in Britain signalled the continuation of this new mass(ish) movement; the same year in the States Woodstock (August) and Altamont (December) seemed, with hindsight, to signal the end of not just the decade, but the sense of the decade, the idea of the sixties. The death of the sixties at the Altamont Rolling Stones concert is a commonplace observation, but one I'm repeating here in order to stress that this was most certainly not the case in Britain. In fact, in his account of the 1960s underground press, in which he was active, Fountain writes of 'a new army of festival-goers, the latecomers at the 1960s ball'. Arthur Marwick's overdramatic comment in *The Sixties* that Altamont 'seemed to signal the end of the magic of rock, particularly British rock, and of love-in pop concerts' is wide of the mark. As I have also written elsewhere, festival culture, though generally seen as originating with the countercultural project of the 1960s, only began to become a really popular form of social pastime and experimentation at the end of that decade and in the early years of the 1970s. Glastonbury is emblematic of this: not even held until 1970, and on only two other occasions throughout the entire decade of the seventies.

As we have seen, the jazz and blues festivals at Beaulieu, Richmond and Bath from the 1950s onwards combined with film of Monterey and reports of Woodstock in America to inspire the alternative festival culture in Britain. The weekend of 24 July 1970 saw a major (or maybe just ramshackle but somehow documented) free festival in the story of Phun City, thrown in woods near Worthing, in the property belt of Sussex. Nigel Fountain describes it:

> The police arrived, too, to supplement the Hell's Angels security operation. The Drugs Squad attempted to move anonymously amongst the bedraggled crowds . . . Drug dealers became generous in adversity. 'John the Bog' – so named because he usually ran a stall in Middle Earth's lavatories – sold dope until he had covered his costs. Then he gave it away.
>
> Hunger stalked the woods. The Hell's Angels 'liberated' the wretched official caterers' supplies. A people's food stall was established . . . Across the churned earth the message crackled from the PA system. Free food was available. As one, the audience sprang to its feet and ran towards the stall.

Pilton festival (September 1970) and Glastonbury Fayre (the free festival celebrating the summer solstice of June 1971) at Worthy Farm, east of Glastonbury, indicate the origins of Glastonbury festival in the free festival zeitgeist of the early 1970s. The likes of Hawkwind and David Bowie played in 1971 under the first pyramid-shaped stage, while enough locals complained about the 10–12,000 festival-goers to ensure there were no more formally organised gatherings at Glastonbury until the end of the

Upright but not uptight: Glastonbury, 1971

decade. According to one of the Phun City organisers, Mick Farren, in his nicely overwritten book *Watch Out Kids*, 'To a lot of us Phun City, and Glastonbury Fair a year later, were glimpses of the future. Glimpses of a community sharing possessions, living with the environment, maintaining their culture with whatever is naturally available, consuming their needs and little else. It was a powerful vision.' And one contrasting with Fountain's memory of Phun City, above.

Hawkwind were *the* free festival band of the time, and are still going thirty years later. Until the commercial hit of the single 'Silver Machine' in 1972, they were known as the people's band, the last 'true' underground act, and before that, the band that played on a flatback lorry to Desolation Hill fans outside the fences of the final Isle of Wight festival. One critic neatly described their music-message tension as 'like Gandhi backed up by Wagner'. Nik Turner, then of Hawkwind, told me:

> Yeah, I was the guy Hendrix called 'the cat with the silver face' at the Isle of Wight in 1970. Hawkwind played a protest concert outside that festival, in a kind of sausage-shaped dome called Canvas City. The Pink Fairies had vaguely organised it, but we seemed to play for days. I don't have memory loss, but I'm very vague on whether we played Phun City free festival too, organised by Mick Farren and Twink from the Pink Fairies. (In fact, when Farren played with them they were called the Deviants, when he didn't they were the Pink Fairies. That group put a *lot* of energy into building up the free festival movement in the early days.) Hawkwind played the big Bath Blues Festival in 1970, and then Glastonbury '71, too – we're on the album, aren't we?

The triple-album released to commemorate and pay off the debts of the 1971 festival contains liner notes which look forward: 'The most valuable thing is not that the vision of five days in Glastonbury is only remembered, but that the vision is repeated and extended until it becomes reality.' I don't think the vision of Glastonbury festival has been extended, at least not in the ways suggested by some of the hippie activists above, to build a network of free festival sites up and down the country as potential models of an alternative society. But something was happening in the Worthy fields, slow magic.

 National free festivals at Windsor (1972–74) and then Stonehenge (1974–84. Motto: FUCK ALL FOR SALE) dominated the festival scene instead, until 1978 when a semi-organised small-scale Glastonbury occurred again. Alister Sieghart, who lives in Glastonbury and is still involved with the festival, was at the mini-free festival held at Worthy Farm in 1978, after Stonehenge. Sieghart is interested in the ways in which the festival's free nature, its idealism if you like, has been developed over the years (particularly, I suggested, and ironically, as things have become more and more expensive to attend):

> Lookin back at the 1971 event, *that's* where the mystique of the Glastonbury festival today comes from. You know, acid in the mud, the pyramid, its freedom, the film, all those

things. And, in fact, Michael had nothing really to do with that festival, he wasn't even living at the farm then. He just came up each day to milk the cows. I do think he's picked up too much credit for that event, and for the influence it continues to have over the festival. It was much more down to people like Andrew Kerr and Arabella Churchill. Partly it's the media – it's a more interesting angle that a Somerset dairy farmer has put all these events on, rather than the seminal early one being put on by some ex-London hippie dropouts.

The free festival at the farm in 1978 happened when a convoy had left Stonehenge after the solstice to go to another free festival we were planning. It was the early days of making the vision of festivals being a summer-long nomadic culture real. We'd identified a field at Cinnamon Lane in Glastonbury as the site – there had been a small alternative culture settlement there for a number of years: caravans and a tipi. I'd lived there myself. But when we turned up the farmers and police knew about it and had blocked off the access. The police radioed around and eventually came up with the venue of Worthy Farm, so we all headed there under police direction. I remember seeing Andrew Kerr there, and him saying, 'This is better than '71.' I think it was this free festival that rekindled Michael's interest in holding another festival, the '79 Year of the Child one. Actually it was Rebecca, Michael's daughter, and Andrew Kerr – it was *their* interest that was rekindled.

In the early 1980s, while many went to both festivals, relations between Glastonbury and Stonehenge – both held in June each year, round the summer solstice – could be strained, particularly as Glastonbury became a more commercial event and the free-dom of Stonehenge grew bigger and more dangerous. There is a bifurcation in British festival culture at its most utopian or radical edge here, illustrating the different paths taken by its main events which took place at the same time and in the same part of the country: the respectable fund-raising of Glastonbury versus the confrontational anarchy of Stonehenge.

The links between festival culture and nomadic lifestyle are strong, not least in that one of the origins of British festival tradition lies in its connection of traveller culture and traveller gatherings, whether in the form of seasonal celebrations or rural markets. Some of this is American Beat-inspired, of course – going on the road, Kerouac-style, or piling into a converted bus, Merry Prankster-style. The revival of local nomadic gatherings has been a common act of the counterculture, in which lost folkloric tradition is re-presented as contemporary festival. For example, while the first Glastonbury festivals were taking place in the West Country, rural fairs were revived in East Anglia in the early 1970s by a group of countercultural rural activists and community workers. The horse fairs were a central part of the fairs movement of the time, a sort of half-way gathering between a rock festival, a Green event and a village fête, spread over an entire weekend. The attractions of the horse fair for the counterculture were various. The horse fair tapped into tradition, when an atavistic motivation is important in counterculture – the original Charter granting permission to hold the fair could often be traced back hundreds of years. And of course historical reclamation of this kind contributes to the larger theme running through this book: the reconstruction of alternative traditions of Englishness. Also, the revived fairs were generally rural gatherings (though horse fairs and traditional traveller gatherings could take place in cities too), and celebrations of rural culture, whether ploughing, harvests, trees or fertility rituals. This emphasised the counterculture's aim to reclaim contact with nature, to raise a Green consciousness. The involvement of the local community was a vital aspect of the fairs movement, one often seen by fair organisers as distinguishing the fairs from rock or free festivals, and one strengthened by the revival of a local event. There was a romantic attachment to a nomadic way of life, one which seemed to reject or resist dominant culture. There was also, I think, a sense of affiliation with a struggling minority group (perhaps in a way evidenced too with the white Rasta phenomenon of a few years later), but one admiringly seen as capable of generating its own power against authority. Gordon Boswell captures the excitement and edge of a traditional horse fair in a poem about Appleby Fair in the 1950s, the largest extant annual gathering of Gypsies, held in June each year in the Cumbrian market town of Appleby.

> There's Bow-tops and Trailers, Accommodation and Tent.
> And a Whoopee or two that someone's borrowed or lent.
> Both sides of the road – right up to Long Martin
> Horse Dealers and Travellers are having a party . . .
> And now the Fair will soon be over, and will come to an end.
> The Cops are getting needled – they've had enough of my friends.

(Boswell, a Gypsy elder in his seventies at the time, was one of those responsible for saving Appleby Fair from the threat of closure by the local council in the mid-1960s.

Today, rather than the traditional prejudice of signs that say NO GYPSIES, during Fair week in Appleby you will see some shops and businesses with signs saying CLOSED FOR THE WEEK. That's still prejudice in my book.)

That horses were a significant focus of those fairs revived by the counterculture, in terms of dealing, racing and general lifestyle, was a way of defying the overwhelming and alienating technologies of modernity. Among the organisers of the East Anglian fairs there were endless debates about issues such as whether cars should be permitted on site, or whether the fairs themselves should be constructive and living examples of green alternatives. Bearing in mind their approximate contemporaneity, how far were the West Country festivals and the East Anglian fairs connected? Surprisingly little, I think. Mike Weaver was involved in the East Anglian fairs, and he told me:

> As far as I know the '71 Glastonbury was not in the same evolutionary line as the fairs. I don't remember anyone else apart from myself of the core crew who had been at it. The idea for the fairs actually came from California! Two blokes had spent the late sixties out there working with a free radio station which supported itself by holding medieval fairs and 'pan-technical circuses'.
>
> The revival of Glastonbury in '79 we were slightly involved in. A couple of our lot spent late winter and spring '79 walking the ley line which runs from Cornwall to Lowestoft. They stayed with the Glastonbury Fayre people on their way through. At some point (the previous winter) I remember Glastonbury phoning us for advice on how to proceed. We were saying forget the publicity side, do something good for your local residents . . . i.e. copy us. Obviously they weren't taken with our suggestions. They were on a different track. We put the dome up at the '79 one then carried on down to Dartington and Hood Fair, more our scene.

Alister Sieghart from Glastonbury was one of those trying to make the links, though he too sees the East Anglian fairs as largely unrelated both to the Glastonbury festivals and to the Green Gatherings that took place at Worthy Farm in the early 1980s. According to Sieghart, 'I was one of many who with varying success tried to introduce ideas from the East Anglian fairs to Glastonbury. For instance, the tall poles with flags and bunting at the fairs – it took years to bring those uplifting things to Glastonbury. And they are uplifting, literally – they gave a vertical impulse to the visual experience. That attention to detail the fairs were so good at wasn't always appreciated by Michael [Eavis], who is more of a grand gesture, broad brush man.'

In the West Country more generally there have been similar Green impulses, though. Janet and Colin Bord set the scene.

> Until the last century some country districts observed what must have been the remnants of forgotten pagan rites on days which had been converted to Christian holydays . . . A few miles south of Avebury is Tan Hill, sometimes known by its Christian-ized name of St Anne's Hill, where until recently a fair was held every 6 August. Tan was the name of an ancient fire/Sun god, and such syllables as Tin, Tan, Ten and Tein in a name can indicate a former site where their deity was worshipped.

Tan Hill Fayre was revived in 1994 by the Dongas Tribe of self-styled indigenous nomads. The Dongas are a group of ex-road protestors from the direct action campaign to save Twyford Down in Hampshire from the M3 extension, who took to living a low-impact nomadic lifestyle in deepest rural Britain. The Dongas' Amish-style rejection of the grand narrative of technological progress and what they view as its pervasive poisonous symbol of the motor vehicle, of car culture, has led them back to horse and cart for daily transport. The Tribe's aim has been to reclaim lost green lanes and seasonal ceremonies, effectively as a counter-modernist lifestyle of withdrawal or disappearance. It's a neo-pagan project, in keeping with the revived festive celebration of fire and the sun at Tan Hill Fayre, that brings together the various strands of festival, folk culture, nomadism, and Green or countercultural world view, one actually unconsciously echoing the tactics of the 1970s in East Anglia.

Glastonbury 1999

One of the things that sets Glastonbury apart is its continuing engagement with New Travellers – even though Eavis says that they are a major problem for him. This year (in spite or because of the Levellers a few years back?) there's a Travellers' Field a couple of miles down the road – 300 vehicles. Neighbours don't like that much, but it signals Eavis's 'one-to-one' strategy of negotiation or mediation, which is used with both travellers and his neighbours, those opposing the event, anyway. Counterculture's awkward tribes aren't always turned away, they've frequently been given free space at the festival – sure, distancing (two miles) is a way of controlling and codifying. But in a way we're back to the huge, impossible contradiction that is this idealistic, commercial, city in the countryside. The irritant aspects of the counterculture, those difficult to commodify, those resistant to it, are sympathetically treated, given space, green fields (the one thing they really want!), which in turn reflects well on the festival's open, liberal image of inclusivity, of alternatives. Then, no sooner written than in need of qualification, it has to be noted that it's a curious form of inclusion which actually excludes: keeps you two miles down the road, out of sight/off the site. (It may be a necessary form, then, but it still needs expressing.) I think Eavis said something at the press conference like the fact that the festival doesn't want the New Travellers, that the police effectively forced them on Glastonbury post-Stonehenge (1985 and following), to rid them of a social and a traffic problem.

Of course, it is easy and potentially misleading to over-dramatise relations between New Travellers, festival and the authorities, particularly in a focus on negative events, flashpoints between them. Perhaps the most notorious of these are the violent breaking up of Windsor Free Festival in August 1974, and the violent trashing of the Peace Convoy on its way to Stonehenge Free in June 1985, the event known as the Battle of the Beanfield. As I pointed out in *Senseless Acts of Beauty*, both the 1974 and 1985 assaults on alternative festival culture occured in the wake of miners' strikes – police turning to attacks on lifestyle rather than industrial 'enemies within', to use Margaret Thatcher's notorious description of the miners. The cat-and-mouse game by which the authorities thwarted the proposed mega-rave/festival in summer 1995, the Mother Festival (envisioned by organisers as a repeat of the success of Castlemorton in 1992), showed a different tactical approach by police. Significantly, all three events over the three decades, Windsor, Stonehenge and the Mother, were intended to be free festivals, unlicensed, autonomously organised.

Besides, in the earlier days of Stonehenge relations with the authorities could be less confrontational. Police used their car headlights to illuminate the stage when the power failed one year, while during the long hot summer of 1976 the fire brigade sprayed water for the hippies to dance and play in around the stones. A bit part in the clampdown on the Stonehenge Free Festival from 1985 on was played by the new head of one of the organisations responsible for the maintenance and touristic development of the stones themselves, English Heritage. He was Lord Montagu, the very man perhaps most readily identifiable as responsible for birthing festival culture in the first place, organiser of the annual and latterly riotous Beaulieu Jazz Festivals in the 1950s. One of the people involved in arresting the development of festival culture was ironically one of those who had been responsible for getting it going a quarter of a century earlier. I asked him about this.

> Yes, CND and trad jazz, festivals and the counterculture, we were aware of those
> connections at the time, and certainly later. I hoped to resolve the tensions at Stonehenge
> in the 1980s, when I ran English Heritage. But we didn't want people climbing all over
> the stones, and when they did hold the festival it was like a Kosovo refugee camp, and
> we had to pay to clear the mess up afterwards. My desire was to turn the festival into
> some sort of controlled event, which meant it could still have happened. I would have
> loved to have made a sensible event – in fact, one year we offered 400 tickets to the
> alternative community to attend the stones during the solstice, but they said no, we'd
> rather stay outside. I did then think they were anarchists, you see: they'd rather riot,
> really. Were there anarchists at Beaulieu, too, among the trad jazzers, beatniks, and
> CND-ers? Oh yes, quite possibly.

The struggle for the stones continues.

Yet it remains the case that festival culture's energy, edge, enduring rhetoric of freedom, have vital roots in the free festival movement, which Glastonbury still refers back to. The bad reputation of free festivals – bad acid, worse bands, packs of Hell's Angels, junkie travellers, shit everywhere, burnt-out cars – can feel like it is airbrushed out. The great irony in this negotiation between versions of alternative culture which the festivals at Glastonbury and Stonehenge represented in the 1980s is that, while all this was going on, a newer underground movement (of sorts), with its associated sounds, drugs and style, was forming in the invisible landscapes of the post-industrial north and that trapped by the M25 around outer London. In its self-concern with trying to maintain its identity in the face of the sustained assault from the forces of Thatcherism and yuppie culture, alternative festival culture, whether the licenced commercial event of Glastonbury or the autonomous free event of Stonehenge, was losing its edge. As George Berger writes, in his book about the band the Levellers, *Dance Before the Storm*:

> The hippy-punk movement, though, was quiet. Crass had long since gone, as had
> Stonehenge. No one was making waves. All anyone had to cling to, except small,
> badly attended gigs by the remnant-bands of bygone days, were the festivals. Going to
> Glastonbury served as an annual reminder that there were thousands and thousands of

'outsiders' left. [But] seeing the main stage line-ups for Glastonbury also served as a reminder that the music being constantly played said very little to them about their lives.

The Acid House scene, the warehouse parties, free underground raves were all replacing the alternative festival tradition. The massive mobility of convoys of cars driving up motorways the wrong way, the squatted temporary autonomous zones of party venues, the narcotic influence on crowd and music alike, as well as a fluffy luvdup rhetoric of love 'n' peace, makes it tempting to read the so-called Second Summer of Love of 1988 as a weak pastiche of nomadic counterculture. But at least a newer generation were interested, the myth of Thatcher's depoliticised children at least partly punctured. It will take a few years for Glastonbury to throw off its preference for guitars and drum kits over DJs and sound systems, but eventually the Dance Tent at the festival will be the single biggest venue, in the biggest single marquee available in the entire country; for 2000 an open-air Dance Stage was mooted. And, like the 1980s festivals, while Glastonbury offers the commercial side of alternative culture, there is also a thriving free scene. Luton's Exodus Collective (note the nomadic nature of the community implied in the title), for instance, will blend reggae, free parties, a squatted community, and plenty of 'chuffing' (smoking cannabis) in a vibrant and much-discussed example of DiY Culture. A notice on a wall of one of their squatted party venues, addressed TO THE LEASER OF DIS PLACE, illuminates Exodus's project of combining music, youth, party and, yes, the reclamation of space for the construction of an alternative community:

We hope that you are not too mad
Coz of the good time we've just had.
We haven't caused you damage mate,
Even though the dance ran *late*!
Three thousand people were here tonight
Making *use* of this place – right.
It's not a crime to come together
In places sometimes *left forever*.
We come in convoys *five miles long*,
So many thousands *can't* be wrong.
So, once again, we're sorry for

The broken lock on your front door.
But, being truthful, we can't say
That we regret, in any way,
Bringing back community
To a town that's lost it totally.
Thanks
Peace, Love, Unity and Respect
Exodus of Luton
JAH LIVE

Some of the anarchic energy of the Stonehenge Free Festivals can be felt again in events like the urban Reclaim the Streets street parties in, first, London in 1995 and 1996. These shook a moribund festival scene out of itself, by bringing together the energy of the rave scene, the cheek of the direct action road protest movement of the early 1990s, a sense of aesthetics, and a keen if partial interest in the theory and history of revolutionary political culture. In Reclaim the Streets' words:

The great revolutionary moments have all been enormous popular festivals – the storming of the Bastille, the Paris commune and the uprisings in 1968 to name a few. A carnival celebrates temporary liberation from the established order; it marks the suspension of all hierarchy, rank, privileges, norms and prohibitions. Crowds of people on the street seized by a sudden awareness of their power and unification through a celebration of their own ideas and creations. It follows then that carnivals and revolutions are not spectacles seen by other people, but the very opposite in that they involve the active participation of the crowd itself.

2

Old hippie slogan –
'You're never too old for a happy childhood'

Glastonbury and Stonehenge 1970–80s

> It's going to sound corny, [but,] well, it's a kind of utopia, really, something outside
> of the normal world we all live in.
>
> Michael Eavis, on Glastonbury festival, 1995

In what ways, if at all, has the early optimism (or feelgood rhetoric, anyway) of festivals as a space of possible alternatives been maintained? How has policing changed, and the laws tightened over the decades? Festival or carnival traditionally inverts social hierarchy, turns the world upside down. In that special fluid state social experimentation can occur. Is this threatening or exhilarating? Vibrant, or maybe just tired nowadays? Is utopia *meant* to be so disruptive? It is also worth considering the extent to which feelgood alternative culture needs to derive its vision, energy, illusion (take your pick) from narcotic influence, and locating that discussion in the specific context of Glastonbury itself.

Festivals and the law

The invasion of large numbers of young people into the pleasanter parts of the countryside for a weekend or a week in the summer, to camp in the open, listen to music, usually loud, sometimes to consume drugs, and in the context of an espousal of overtly bohemian values, involving attitudes to property and sexuality, for example, that are at gross variance with those of the local population, is inevitably a strong base for opposition.

So writes Michael Clarke in his 1982 book, *The Politics of Pop Festivals*, one of the very few previous book-length studies of festival culture in Britain. Clarke's argument that bohemian values are at gross variance with those of the local rural population may hold less water around the special place of Glastonbury, where incomers are notable for their Avalonian sympathies – some may have first experienced Avalon while attending the festival, so that the festival becomes part of the reason for living or staying there in the first place. The state has veered wildly in its attitudes towards festival culture, from support and donation of land for a national free festival in 1975, to long-term financial backing for a liaison and advisory group called Festival Welfare Services, to periodic clampdowns on festivals with new legislation over the decades. Suspicion of the mass, of music, of festival, is itself not new, of course: Plato's distrust of the place of music in his ideal republic has had long and inglorious reverberations. Folk customs also have been a focus of attack, from church and government alike. This frequently impinged on festival or folk festivities. 'In the thirteenth century, for example, the Bishop of Salisbury . . . forbad all "dances and vile and indecorous games which tempt to unseemliness",' writes Laurence Whistler in *The English Festivals*, and he continues: 'The seventeenth century had unique importance in the history of our festivals. Never before nor since have they been officially denounced and defended, deliberately abolished and restored.'

   While we can all be grateful to the English Civil War for getting rid of the monarchy (if only temporarily), the accompanying cultural revolution also banned the theatre, as well as the observation of Christmas and May Day, and indeed 'all festivals or Holy-Dayes, heretofore superstitiously used and observed'. Further, in a Platonic echo, the distrust of music was espoused: 'the bringing in of musick [is] a cup of poyson to the world', as it was expressed at the time. In the following century, in Wales, the enthusiastic sweep of Christian dissenters had a powerful if less deliberate or explicit impact on festival. Prys Morgan explains the situation there:

> In destroying the old culture the Methodists and other [Anglican] dissenters devised
> a new Welsh way of life which cut the people away from the past. Welsh almanacks
> (of which there were a very large number) mention fewer and fewer saints' days,
> patronal festivals and fairs, as the [eighteenth] century advanced. Rituals and customs
> gradually died away, Maypole dancing, for example, disappeared from Capel Hendre
> (Carmarthenshire) in 1725, lingered at Aberdare (Glamorgan) until 1798.

There is a clear small irony for Michael Eavis, the Methodist organiser of Glastonbury festival, of his own church's historic role in the death of festival. When asked, Eavis has pointed to Methodism's significance in his own background, as a reason for the festival, both musical and social sides: 'Methodists do sing a lot, and heartily. Those Wesley hymns have a lot of go in them … There is a strong non-conformist tradition in Methodism. I was brought up to think that whatever the Establishment is doing needs to be questioned. In a funny sort of way, my Methodist upbringing led straight towards all this.'

Why is festival feared? 'Even the first pop festival [in the United States in 1967], the Fantasy Faire and the Magic Mountain Music Festival, was opposed by the legions of civic "decency", when the Marin County sheriff's office addressed a telegram to state officials in Sacramento saying the promoters woud be held liable for any damage done anywhere in the entire county the weekend of the festival,' writes Jerry Hopkins in *Festival! The Book of American Music Celebrations*, disbelievingly. A few years before this, in England, Lord Montagu could suspect that the local constabulary's refusal to provide adequate police coverage for the large public event of the 1960 Beaulieu Jazz Festival had a darker purpose. Montagu writes: 'I believe it was a deliberate attempt to "kill" the festival. Ours was a potentially combustible national event attended by a number of high spirited and potentially rowdy teenagers. In the same week I saw a large number of police at the New Forest Agricultural Show – an event attended exclusively by the staid and sober.'

Both the temporary claiming of land and the organisation of social space contribute to concerns about order and festival, as Michael Clarke explains:

> In a scout camp or a race meeting, for example, the masses gathered together
> are divided and organized. The camp will have a visible pattern with hierarchical
> control over campers and with each allocated a specific place and series of duties,
> etc, the enactment of which is enforced by the hierarchy. The camp thus reflects the
> bureaucratic order prevailing in the rest of society . . . By contrast the pop festival is
> inherently and deliberately unstructured and even anarchic . . . A gathering without
> a structure, whatever the intentions of the members, is readily categorized as a passive
> mob that might at any moment become violent.

Clarke continues: 'With the exception of clauses in the Isle of Wight Act 1971, there has been no legislation specifically concerned with pop festivals.' He qualifies this by writing of 'other means of control, and of the eventual emergence of a method of regulation which is highly informal and in which, where the law is used, it is existing and often ancient powers that are invoked.' Such powers have frequently been from local rather than national acts. For instance, the Home Counties (Music and Dancing) Licensing Act 1926, and the London Government Act 1963, have each been cited in licensing applications for or rejections of pop festivals in those areas. The second report from the government's Working Group on Pop Festivals, from 1978, *Pop Festivals and Their Problems*, lists planning, food and drugs, public health, control of pollution, and public nuisance as subjects of legislation which could be or have been used to obstruct or prohibit pop festivals.

This raft of legislative possibilities perhaps undercuts Andrew Blake's claim in *The Land Without Music* that, 'Until the passage of the 1994 Criminal Justice Act, in fact, the law was on the side of those who wished to assemble in large numbers and listen to music.' Well, in actual fact, anti-festival legislation has surprisingly frequently been passed by or presented to Parliament. Indeed, if we read the Isle of Wight Act as a cumulative response to the three festivals on the island from 1968 to 1970, each recent decade has seen a legislative attack on festival culture. The Isle of Wight County Council Act 1971 (to give it its full title), was introduced by Mark Woodnutt, Isle of Wight MP, in the wake of the final festival on the island in 1970. Woodnutt explained in Parliament that he had attended the 1970 festival disguised as a hippie for two days to bear witness to the activities. (Did he inhale? Perhaps such an act of disguise is about desire not distaste, or at least both together. And wasn't there a vicar at Phun City free festival the same year who thought it was his Christian duty to check the naked couples out in the woods and report back, shocked, to the authorities?)

Part Two of the Act deals with public order and safety, and introduces the requirement to legislate through licensing the organisation of future festivals. The Act refers only to the island itself, not the rest of the country. A licence will be required for any assembly in the open air 'at which during any period exceeding three hours during the six hours following midnight there are not less than 5000 people present'. Four months' notice is required, the council and Chief Constable must both agree in advance on the site, and a financial bond be left with the council as security. A second overt targeting of youth culture in the Act was a direct attack on what had once been those other youthful spaces of iniquity and deprivation, coffee bars. (I thought coffee bars were a thing of 1950s beats, not 1970s hippies. Maybe Woodnutt's legislation is evidence of the lack of fashion sense and pop music sensibility of Conservative MPs, as anyone who saw pictures of the young Tory leader William Hague in baseball cap at Notting Hill Carnival in 1997 will recognise. Besides, hadn't coffee bars long since been overtaken in the youth music scene by those Mediterranean imports from what George Melly calls 'the Bardot-Sagan moment', *discothèques*?)

A coffee bar can be threatened with closure if:

the persons concerned with the conduct of the premises as a coffee bar are such that
young persons resorting thereto are likely to be depraved or corrupted [or] if a coffee
bar is conducted in a disorderly manner or if any [illegal] drug . . . is sold, supplied
or otherwise distributed on the premises by a person.

From huge festival to tiny coffee bar, the spaces of youth expression, difference, experimentation and music are wished away, disappeared in this extraordinary attack on youth culture. The Conservative government passed the Bill, with little opposition from Labour (a position we'll witness again with another appalling piece of legislation directed at youth culture, the Criminal Justice Act 1994).

The Night Assemblies Bill of 1971–72 was an unsuccessful attempt to introduce further legislation which could have impacted further on festival culture, aimed, as its name suggests, at public gatherings during the hours of darkness. One festival organisation, Great Western Festivals, produced a pamphlet which argued against the Bill: 'all sorts of prejudice against pop music, young people, their long hair and mode of dress, has been allowed to crystallise into a Bill which would not be imposed on, or indeed be tolerated by, any other section of the population.' A decade after that Bill, the fetchingly-titled Local Government (Miscellaneous Provisions) Act 1982 did crack down on festival organisation by giving local authorities the responsibility of issuing public entertainment licences for events like festivals. Licences, available for a fee, can stipulate conditions which have to be met, covering anything from maximum attendance numbers to public health provision to emergency access. Michael Eavis traces the origins of this national Act back to Glastonbury, although he expresses no surprise at the political effort to block an event which had, after all, only really happened twice in the years leading up to the Act (1979 and 1981):

Our local MP spearheaded the Miscellaneous Provisions Act through Parliament in 1981, with the intention of controlling or even stopping most festivals, and which became law the next year. This made life a lot more difficult for us, as festival licensing was now in the hands of the local authority. Glastonbury has played a key role in the development of the principles involved in the licensing of festivals – the local licensing officer in fact received an MBE from the Queen for his involvement with the festival. Ironically, he actually spent most of his time trying to find legal ways to get the festival stopped.

The first Glastonbury festival to be licensed under the act was the 1983 CND festival, and, remarkably, the licence was only granted on May 4 of that year, for a major event which was to take place only six weeks later. There were 24 conditions attached to the licence, 5 of which were raised the following year when Eavis was, following police recommendation, prosecuted by Mendip District Council for alleged breaches at the 1983 festival. The first prosecution of its kind under the new law, the breaches identified included exceeding the maximum attendance number and two concerned with emergency access. Surprisingly, perhaps, Eavis was cleared by local magistrates, opening the way for the 1984 event.

The explosion of Acid House in the late 1980s, the underground rave scene, the new sounds, images and psychoactive experiences of Ecstasy, produced in response a whole series of new laws directed at these latest fearful versions of youth culture. The most notorious of these is, of course, the Criminal Justice and Public Order Act 1994, but there are others. The CJA, as it is usually known, was preceded by the Increased Penalties Act 1990 (known as the Acid House Bill), and followed by the Public Entertainments Licences (Drug Misuse) Act 1997, both of which were seen by dance people as attacks on their culture. The CJA, though, is a different story. 'Rave' is identified and described in the Act, that is, a specific kind of music, of youth social gathering, is pinpointed over all others and, in certain circumstances, made illegal. Writing about it five years on I am still struck by the breathtaking audacity, and the sheer stupidity, *and* the real traces of cultural fascism, of this law. I outlined the implications of the anti-rave aspects of the CJA in *Senseless Acts of Beauty*:

> In an extraordinary passage, music is defined in sub-section 1(b) of section 63 of the Act as follows: '"music" includes sounds wholly or predominantly characterized by the emission of a succession of repetitive beats' . . . There's an element of taste here – the Act has taste inscribed within it, disliking loud music, music that's long in duration, that's

ABOVE & OVER PAGE:
Castlemorton free
festival / rave, 1992.

intended for dancing, that's not purely acoustic . . . – it's the singling out by name of a widespread youth event, style and dance form, and its potential prohibition . . . Much of the anti-rave legislation also applies to free festivals – partly because the free festival scene has been revitalized by rave culture, even moulded into its image: the free festivals of the nineties are arguably less celebrations and demonstrations of alternative values than . . . mega- or mini-raves in themselves, with 24-hour sound systems and so on.

It is important to note that the anti-rave and some of the other public order sections of the CJA are not just about dance music, unlicensed public gatherings (OK, and New Travellers, hunt saboteurs, road protesters), but they are also about an *idealised version of the countryside*, about trying to preserve that special place which is under such threat from a few dancing crowds over the odd summer weekend. The origins of these aspects of the Act, which combine the prohibition of music and festival with a kind

of rural cleansing or exclusion, lie on common ground on the English side of the Welsh Borders. Castlemorton Common in Hereford and Worcester saw a free party-cum-festival over the Spring Bank Holiday weekend (and beyond) in 1992, which signalled the revival of free festival culture in terms of the sheer scale. With 20–25,000 people in attendance, it was the biggest event since the final Stonehenge Free in 1984. A better site could, should, have been chosen: in the middle of this celebration of alternatives on a large common were a few isolated houses in which seven residents had to be provided with 24-hour police protection. On the other hand, the convoys of travellers' vehicles had been moved by different police forces from other perhaps preferable sites where the Avon Free Festival had been held in previous years. Free festival veterans, New Travellers, ravers, all came together at Castlemorton, suddenly realising once again their collective strength and potential, making one of those small legendary moments the British counterculture is punctuated by.

Following the event, a *Report of the Working Party Following Illegal Invasion of Castle-morton Common* was produced by a committee consisting of local councillors, senior police, and representatives from organisations like the Country Landowners' Association and the National Farmers' Union. There were no representatives of travellers or anyone involved with festivals such as Festival Welfare Services on the committee. The report repeated numerous stereotypical attitudes, for instance, expressing 'understandable' 'outrage' at the unroadworthy nature of travellers' vehicles, while buried away in Appendix One is the fact that only 21 vehicles were actually detained – out of the perhaps 2000 vehicles on site. The Working Party's recommendations focused entirely on how to prevent such events happening again through legislative change, and paid little or no attention to the long-term social issue of traveller and festival culture. For instance, the following unsubstantiated claim is made with regard to long-term festival sites.

AVON FREE FESTIVAL

MAY 22–25 1992

No site or contact details whatsoever but it still became the biggest free festival of the nineties.

> 6.3 A further consideration was the provision of a number of national festival sites, to which New Age Travellers could resort. However, from discussions with the Travellers themselves, it appeared that they would be reluctant to be directed to particular sites and would wish to hold their festivals as and when they pleased and without 'interference' or control by others. For this reason it was felt inappropriate to devote themselves to the identification and national servicing of national sites.

Recommendations in the report included some that would become familiar elements

'You're never too old for a happy childhood'

of the CJA two years later, including anti-rave legislation, the criminalisation of trespass, and new laws to seize sound equipment and vehicles and sell them on if need be (though the CJA added a neat and suitably vindictive twist to this demand by taking it further so that the law can *destroy* such property, and charge the owners for such destruction).

Of course, judging by the demonisation and criminalisation of that kind of activity in the mid-1990s, you could be forgiven for thinking that raving, rural or urban, was a/the new thing. It takes an old anarchist and musician like George Melly to correct us here. Between 1951 and 1953, whenever the Mick Mulligan jazz band was in London on a Saturday night, leader Mulligan and his singer George Melly would transform their Gerrard Street basement rehearsal room into an all-night party. Mulligan was then known as 'The King of the Ravers', while Melly recalls in his 1965 memoir of the time, *Owning-Up*:

> Mick and I were the first people to organize all-night raves, and they were an enormous social success, but a financial loss . . . Anyway we didn't really run the all-nighters to make money. Although today the idea of spending a whole night in a crowded airless basement at a small loss appears extraordinary, it was very exciting then . . . [The] all-night sessions were an escape back into the jazz atmosphere of our beginnings. We could dress in shit order, fall about drunk, and tell people who criticized us or our music to get stuffed.

Actually, fifty years on, they still sound like a good night out (if only I could get a babysitter), and not that unfamiliar.

With regard to the practice of policing festivals, and in particular Glastonbury, the Chief Constable of Hampshire's words are worth quoting, since he was the person ultimately responsible for public order at one of the most publicised festivals in Britain, the 1970 Isle of Wight:

> Those who condemn pop festivals out of hand would do well to concern themselves with the motivation of those who patronise these events. Thousands of youngsters are prepared to endure tremendous hardship just to be there. They are ill-equipped and badly trained for such excursions. It is difficult to believe they come for the drugs or the promiscuity – these they can obtain, if they want them, in their home towns. What they seem to be expressing is a sense of unity throughout their age group, a dislike of humbug

and artificial restrictions . . . Nevertheless the atmosphere and conditions of pop festivals must make the young, particularly the weaker characters, susceptible to the evil influences represented by the dropouts and anarchists. That they are evil there can be no doubt, they seek to encourage amorality, perversion, drug addiction and contempt for all forms of law.

The clear recognition that festivals are desirable, fun, social and valid experiences is tempered by a familiar police fear of the anarchist, and worse. The sheer, the repeated *evil* on offer at pop festivals is breathtaking. Yet amorality and perversion? In 1970 I think that referred mostly to public nudity, a few brave souls proclaiming their bare innocence, surrounded by crowds of cameramen and police officers with their truncheons tut-tutting. Drug consumption: frequently, very frequently (festivals are failures if there is a drought of hash at the time), but drug *addiction*? Also, it may be the case that skinheads, football hooligans in every town on every Saturday in the 1970s, showed more violent mob-oriented contempt for the law than any festival crowd. But senior police are like some religious folk, like some Greens come to that: it's their job to talk up apocalypse.

   That's why I was surprised to find the man in charge of policing Glastonbury so reasonable, so sympathetic to the festival. Clearly his close involvement with the event over the past decade has touched him – he's glimpsed the vei, as Avalonian spiritualist Don Fortune puts it, if not through it. In the course of our discussion about policing Glastonbury festival and the surrounding countryside he broke off at one stage and said, 'Well, you've got to remember, we recognise that for a lot of people it *is* the Vale of Avalon, and a special place we're talking about here.' David Jones is the Contingency Planning Officer for the Avon and Somerset Police Force, a retired ('civilianised' in force jargon) police inspector of thirty years' standing. It's his job to have plans in place in case of any major incident in the Avon and Somerset area. As he puts it, in a way which makes very clear both the scale and the demands of the festival, his main responsibilities for planning are for such sites as 'the two international airports, three nuclear power stations – and Glastonbury festival. It's a unique event, and a unique responsibility.' As the festival has become a major event in the region during the 1980s and 1990s, so it has expanded in size: officially 18,000 people attended in 1981; 100,000 in 1999. (My informed guesstimate suggests that this may translate to actual numbers of 20,000 and 150,000 respectively, which may themselves be conservative.) Seemingly like everything else touched by the Glastonbury spirit, nothing is quite certain, though. In David Jones's experience:

> You can't count the numbers with complete accuracy. There was an aerial survey done one
> year, but it could only guess at the numbers of people in tents rather than visible outside
> at the time. For licensing purposes, Mendip District Council does a head count from
> turnstile information each year, and estimates that perhaps 10,000 extra people get in.

The traditional solution to such problems on the Sunday afternoon of festival weekend is for Michael Eavis to open up the gates to the local crowds outside in a spirit
of the free ethos of some of the 1970s events. When I asked Jones about persistent
mutterings I had heard about police saying, 'Let these extra ones in, Michael, take
the pressure off,' he replied: 'No, we don't want to send the wrong signals out that
the festival becomes a free for all. For policing purposes, we'd much sooner have a
properly licensed event, people all with tickets. Lots of people milling around outside
without tickets can make problems for the local community.'

During the early 1980s, the force's activity was largely restricted to policing the
area surrounding the festival site, to controlling traffic, maintaining access, keeping
an eye on public order (that is, moving New Travellers on). The festival itself relied on
private security within its boundaries, which worked up to a point. The legal situation
of the festival changed for 1983, with the introduction of more stringent licensing
requirements under the Local Government (Miscellaneous Provisions) Act 1982,
but Jones identifies 1989 as the watershed year for policing, when police were invited

on-site. This followed a worrying escalation of crime and violence during the festival, which was beginning to see assaults, actual or threatened, with baseball bats and machetes, as well as rising numbers of robberies.

Jones recalls that the police felt 'some trepidation' about being involved on-site, which they countered by adopting a community policing approach to the job. This involved thinking of the festival site as a single large urban area, divided up into smaller sections to be covered by officers on foot patrol rather than in vehicles. Back-up was available if required, and planning ensured that all officers could regroup if necessary. (At Woodstock in 1969, police on-site agreed both to dispense with their usual weaponry and to wear specially designed clothing, as one police chief explained: 'The promoters decided to approach the problem in a non-traditional way. The police wore bright red windbreaker jackets with the word "peace" silk-screened where the badge is usually worn. On the back of the jackets was the emblem of Woodstock Ventures, a guitar with a dove siting on it, which I think is kind of nice.')

Jones sees the fact that there has never been serious disorder during the festival as a vindication of the relaxed festival ethos, the crowd's general sense of responsibility, *and* the police's considered approach over the years. 'There was though – in 1990, was it? – something like a pitched battle between the private security and New Age Travellers, building on antagonism that had been festering all weekend. Maybe the security were from a weightlifting club from Wolverhampton, or something like that, and their macho image couldn't hold it in any more. It happened after the festival was over, on the Monday morning, very close to the farmhouse. We were stuck in the middle, just as we were beginning to unwind and think about going home.'

Nik Turner of Hawkwind and Inner City Unit has been involved in playing at free festivals for thirty years. Yet his strong support of New Travellers doesn't mean he can't be critical. He told me:

Glastonbury is the acceptable face of commercial festivals. It started out small and idealistic, but after the Beanfield things did change. Michael Eavis didn't like the Peace Convoy, and we disagreed on some things, especially the convoy. I remember being in the farmhouse one year and there was a pitched battle going on outside with travellers and security, and Jean, Michael's wife – and, you know, she's dead now, bless her soul – she said, 'The sooner we get rid of them and have a decent festival the better.' Now, that wasn't my approach at all. In other ways, all credit to them for opening the festival up to travellers for as long as they did. If I've got a gig at Glastonbury I've got two hundred people trying to blag their way in, saying, 'I'm with Nik, I'm with Nik,' And some of them have made a nuisance of themselves, using my name and sort of besmirching it. Some travellers do expect a free ride, but the thing with free festivals was everyone had to give something, not nothing. Whether it was a quid in the bucket or me playing for expenses (and less), it's about contributing to make it happen, and that spirit could get lost at a commercial festival or a free one alike.

For the week before and the week after the festival, there is an enhanced police presence in the surrounding countryside. This means that crime drops in the area – Jones tells me that 'in 1999 there was only one reported crime in the town of Glastonbury itself over festival weekend, and that was the theft of a lawnmower', a crime unlikely to be connected with festival-goers. At the festival itself, five miles down the road, there was a spate of crime in 1999, mainly in the form of theft of and from tents. 'Some of it is down to festival-goers, in a way. Lots of young people, just done their A-levels, off to Glastonbury for the first time, a little bit naive, in spite of our constant crime prevention advice – on the Net, in the music press, on Radio Avalon,' says Jones. 'There was a 60 per cent increase on 1998's crime figures, but that was a very wet year, and the weather slowed the thieves down, and maybe us too. Looking at the home addresses of crooks charged with theft in 1999, they've often come down from Merseyside and the South Wales valleys, small gangs specifically targeting the festival.' Jones offers the bald 1999 statistics as follows:

2116 recorded crimes in total
  79 robberies
  26 assaults
 110 arrests on drugs offences
 282 arrests in total

For the size and duration of the event, and its temporary nature ('a bit like a city such as Bath, but without any of the social infrastructure,' says Jones), the numbers of serious crimes compare very favourably indeed. 'There are also lots of little scams going on around the fence,' explains Jones. 'You know: you climb up and then I'll throw your bags over to you. The bags never arrive.' I expressed surprise about the small number of drugs charges considering the size of the crowd (as well as its reputed tastes), especially in the context of wandering round the site myself and seeing what appeared a mass activity of joint-rolling in every section of the crowd. LAND OF DOPE AND GLORY, as *Melody Maker* headlined its festival report in 1994, hinting at a kind of alternative Englishness frequently associated with the festival. When I put it to David Jones that the small number of drugs arrests suggested a clear policy of police overlooking the minor though widespread criminal activity of smoking dope (that is, effectively decriminalising it over the weekend), he replied, and I quote: 'No comment.' (A couple of weeks later Jones got back to me to finesse the official line: 'Drug-dealers are our number one target, but we cannot and do not condone any form of illegal drug-dealing.') I asked Michael Eavis the same question and he said:

Well, they're hardly going to arrest loads of people for smoking a little bit of dope, are they? A lot of people *do* smoke at the festival. I just don't see the need for it myself – being a Methodist I don't drink or smoke anyway. The funny thing is it's the Greens who are the worst of the lot for smoking. For all their preaching about a healthy planet – they don't look after themselves very well, do they? (*Smiles.*) The trouble outside the farm after the 1990 festival, that was a drug thing. On the television it looked like the Middle East or something. Jean and I felt that was the end after that, we really felt it was all over. That's why we had a break in 1991. When I give talks to branches of the Women's Institute or

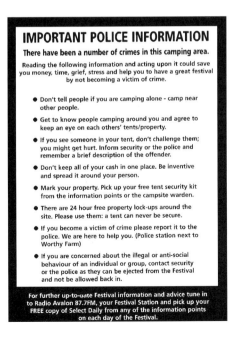

local Christian groups, they often ask me, 'Why don't you stop holding the festival if there are all these drugs being taken there?' But the festival is bigger than the drugs, it's too big to close down just because some people smoke some dope. That's such a small side issue.

The police were keen to tell me that they have recently introduced on-site a machine which tests suspicious substances seized at the festival. This drug-testing facility means that those arrested can be charged and in court within 24 hours. 'We want the message to get across to people that if they are caught on-site they will be charged, convicted and banned from returning to the festival within that space of time,' they said.

The place of drugs in festival culture can be traced at least back to the 1960s, back to the Acid Tests of the Merry Pranksters in the United States (which took place before LSD was made illegal). In his book about drugs and popular music, *Waiting for the Man*, Harry Shapiro shows the early link between the narcotic and nomadic lifestyles of the Pranksters:

> . . . who criss-crossed America through 1964 in a psychedelic thirties bus . . . Back in California, [Ken] Kesey had instigated the Acid Test, forerunner of the 'Be-in', the 'Happening' and eventually the rock festival . . . LSD became a permanent fixture, backstage and front, of all the major rock festivals of the sixties in both Britain and America.

(Shapiro also quotes the pop experts of *Melody Maker* from 1966: 'It is being insinuated in some quarters that drug-taking is widespread among singers and musicians. . . . This is dangerous, irresponsible nonsense.' Yeah, right, guys.) A few years later, and cannabis was the preferred drug – perhaps because of its 'softer' nature, and Class B rather than A legal status. In the advance publicity for Windsor Free Festival in 1974, cannabis was an issue to campaign around, construct your oppositional identity around, whereby the mass phenomenon of the festival began to be used overtly for purposes of breaking the law:

> If two people, while smoking dope, are approached by police, they may well piss in their pants from fright. In a group of say twelve, how much stronger one is. In a crowd of 1000 all smoking dope together, you can tell the police to piss off. We like smoking dope – we know it is against the law – there must be something wrong with the law – because there is nothing wrong with smoking dope.

David Holdsworth, the Chief Constable responsible for public order in the vicinity of Windsor Free, was outraged at what he called the 'gigantic drug-inspired breach of the peace . . . being committed openly under our very noses'. (I suspect that it's the last bit in particular the police didn't like – or is there another reason their noses were so close to the smoke? The police got their revenge in 1975, anyway, when they trashed the festival.) With or without Hawkwind, Nik Turner was always at the Stonehenge Festivals, celebrating the summer solstice. He told me that 'magic mushrooms, ivy and mead were the traditional ways of getting out of it at Stonehenge in the ancient days. Well, just like us, really!' For festival-goers the mass social consumption of drugs, safe from arrest, has very often been one of the reasons for going. For many this confirmation of your own culture means sitting around smoking copious amounts of dope, forming a temporary connection back to the perceived idealism of the sixties counterculture: 'Tune in, turn on, drop out' for a weekend or a week. Michael Clarke identifies drug culture as a key feature of festival lifestyle, arguing that festival-goers of the 1970s and early 1980s viewed their drug consumption as both social experience and social criticism:

> Pop festivals quite rapidly became enclaves where it was possible openly to consume, and even to deal in drugs, without fear of police harassment despite their presence. For this reason festivals became fairly potent symbols of the success of the counter-culture: not only were thousands of apparent adherents assembled together in love and peace, but the forces of straight society were substantially unable to enforce their ridiculous laws against so many.

At Glastonbury, Eavis expresses disapproval at the use of drugs: 'I use to put signs up at the festival saying you don't need to take dope, but I was a bit of a loner in that sense. The young people started to make badges saying "don't tell Michael".' Even here, though, Eavis is carefully delineating the narcotic landscape of Glastonbury, around soft rather than hard drugs, around sociable joint-smoking rather than heavier psychoactive drugs like acid and Ecstasy. Land of Dope and Glory, indeed. For Jeremy Cunningham, bassist with the Levellers, who himself had a painful struggle against heroin addiction, the connection of festival with drugs is misleading anyway: 'You don't just find drugs at festivals. They're a significant part of everyday life, all around us.'

Glastonbury 1999

Select Magazine, which is sponsoring the hospitality tent in the backstage area, and doing a daily free paper, have got a curious slogan. '*Select Magazine,*' it says on these pint beer mugs, these paper cups everyone has, '*Select Magazine* Cos The Drugs Don't Work' . . . And er, that's pretty curious, what's that about, you know, replacing your, er, drugs, er, you know, you're not getting a very good night so you get a bit of excitement from your magazine instead, reading about music and the youth and the kulchur? And, em, that's strange in this place, where there's quite a sort of, well, a rhetoric anyway, of anti-drugs even though, Jesus, everyone all around me is rolling up joints everywhere, all the time, endlessly. But nonetheless it surprised me, that slogan, tapping knowingly into drug culture. (What does Eavis do when he reads that from an official sponsor? Turn a well-practised blind eye?)

The Dance Tent? Em, it's a glorified disco in there really, with flashing lights and a million people. The busiest, the most popular part of the festival by the looks of things – and I can't understand that, but I'm the wrong generation, too old, not old enough. There are all these E-d up youngsters (mostly well dressed, male, early twenties from Henley-on-Thames, they look like), and people wandering by looking over their shoulders saying, 'Want any pills? Es, Es, want any pills?' And – oh, I've just seen someone do something good, which is pick up a glass bottle that someone else was kicking around and put it in a bin. Well done, mate – what I think's interesting is that, just opposite this fucking ginormous tent, with a sound party system thing on in it, there's the Glastonbury Spring Water Company, with their stall, which has got this sort of fake fibreglass rock wall on the front of it, to make it look authentic, like the water's just come out of the ground, though it's in plastic bottles and the limestone's fibreglass. And so there you've got this kind of effort to market itself as a located source, you know, of water, the purest, etc, and it's coming from this area, it's Glastonian, even Avalonian. And they're doing an absolutely roaring trade, queues and queues of people, and it's not cos it's boiling hot, cos it's overcast and was spitting with rain earlier. It's cos everyone's dancing like crazy, and half of them are out of their heads. It's a pointlessly intense atmosphere outside the Dance Tent, just on the verge of something unpleasant. There's a clichéd conjunction there,

of the old image of alternative, fresh, purity, local, even pagan water thing, and then the newer techno thing of E-generated music and narcotic alike. Time to go back to the Green Fields.

Michael Eavis and his girlfriend Jean were first inspired to organise a festival at Worthy Farm after going to the massive Bath Blues Festival in the summer of 1970, just down the road from Pilton village, at the county showground at Shepton Mallet. The showground has a current as well as a historic role to play in the festival: it's here that the police support base is set up each year, a mini-camp and compound of marquees, portablocks, parking, a catering area (though no entertainment I think, nor do many police camp in tents . . .), from which the on-site and traffic police work, to which detainees are taken for processing. The cost of this, a kind of police festival camp, is, of course, charged to Glastonbury festival itself, and so included in the ticket price. That the monies going to policing have often been greater than those going to campaigns or even being spent on bands has been the focus of vehement criticism of the festival: 'a police benefit gig' has been some radicals' dismissive judgement.

The Avon and Somerset Force's expertise in festival policing, developed over the decades at Glastonbury, is in demand from other police up and down the country. In 1999, for instance, David Jones explains, 'Our colleagues attended Reading Festival, and other forces ring as and when necessary. For instance, Devon and Cornwall sought our advice about policing the festivals that were being held on their patch to celebrate the total eclipse. Also, officers from other forces come down to the festival at Glastonbury for a day for training purposes.' For festival-goers across the country, it's a weekend's love and peace, for police it's a nice staff-development opportunity in the West Country. As we will see again through the book, Glastonbury gives you what you want.

No hippies, no bare feet

Glastonbury has done her fair share of stoning the prophets.

Dion Fortune, *Avalon of the Heart*

In *The Land Without Music*, Andrew Blake offers a view of the role of New Travellers in festival culture which presents them as part of the show, to be enjoyed by the wider mainstream or weekend audience. '[Festivals] are patronised both by the comparatively few "New Age" and by the vast numbers of commuter-wage travellers, piling out from the cities to indulge in a touristic creation of paganism, celticism and so on,' writes Blake. There is an unquestionable element of display, of festival crowd gazing at the authentic, for Blake here. Mick Farren traces the traveller ideal back to what he saw as those first few urban beats of the late 1950s and early 1960s, again with an emphasis on the authentic, even heroic. The trajectory Farren maps out, though, may be a sadly familiar one:

> The first home of these pre-Leary dropouts was the romantic conception of being 'on the road'. Declaring themselves the 'true beats', and scorning those with the same ideas but less dedication as 'weekend ravers', they sought a new way of life as spiritual hoboes and rambling bums . . . [But] the clear ideals of roving freedom turned into a degraded bitterness. Jolly dope smoking in the sunshine changed to the furtive use of heroin in an alley or public toilet.

Some were more fortunate, or had more money. (Same thing.) In *The Last of the Hippies*, C.J. Stone describes the transformation of the town and surroundings of Glastonbury itself as traveller culture began to develop and impact.

> [In] the late sixties, everything began to change. First of all it was Sir Mark Palmer, former page of honour to the Queen, with his buckskins, flowers in his hair, living in a horse-drawn cart and accompanied by a ragged band of followers out of Chelsea and Notting Hill. Glastonbury's first hippies. They were all aristocrats, of course . . . More hippies arrived with Andrew Kerr and Arabella Churchill after the 1971 free festival at Pilton. This was the upper middle-class variety. Nearly, but not quite, aristocracy. And they were still coming throughout the seventies. The first hippie/mystical bookshop/head shop, Gothic Image, was opened in 1975.

Glastonbury-based Bruce Garrard writes of some of these early travellers that '[in] the landscape here, and in their own meeting together, they found what to them was a magical atmosphere; one that made living "rough", with very little money, worthwhile. The first hippie camp was in Cinnamon Lane, in 1971'. In the following years Glastonbury developed further as an attraction for new travellers, in part if not directly because of the mystique arising from the 1971 festival then because of the way the event has kept in the mind the connection of the place of Glastonbury with festival culture, peace and freedom. The mystical side of the place has helped too, of course.

Alister Sieghart remembers the anti-hippie sentiment of the early 1970s, when even the BBC Radio 1 DJ Emperor Rosko was refused entry to one Glastobury establishment on account of his appearance. 'There was one pub you could go in, the Lamb I think, but even that had a sign saying SORRY NO FREAKS IN LOUNGE BAR. We were all right to go in the public bar, but not the posh lounge! Cafés were the same, though one greasy spoon-type place was happy to take our money. Pretty soon this got a makeover, reopening as the Temple of the Stars café, with paintings by John Michell.' I also heard a rumour that the American Beat poet Allen Ginsberg, coming to check out the Tor and its mystic vibe, was refused entry to a hotel in town. Patrick Benham was one of the 1970s hippies in Glastonbury setting up an alternative society, which in his case included editing the alternative magazine *Torc* during the four years of its existence. Benham notes that Glastonians, the traditional townspeople – as opposed to the Avalonians, the self-styled Glastafarians and other New Agers – 'have had to put up with all manner of strange and wild specimens of humanity drawn to the place by strange and wild rumours of lines of power and forthcoming cosmic revelations . . . But this is not new; they were all here, looking much the same, in the Middle Ages.' What was needed in the 1970s was some sort of troublemaker to stir things up a bit. Alan Beam appointed himself, flying in from London's BIT information service, one of the main hippie alternative organisations of the time. He recalls in his 1976 self-published memoir, *Rehearsal for the Year 2000*:

We stopped in Glastonbury for a time, and I was aghast at all the signs on the hotels and cafés and shops saying NO HIPPIES ALLOWED. Throughout this trip I'd been wearing long hair, my 20-foot-around-the-waist Arab trousers and my Peruvian multi-coloured bonnet, and looking, in the words of one garage man who called his wife out to gaze at me, 'like an Egyptian tramp'. I decided to test the situaton, and dragged Sylvia into every place where there was a NO HIPPIES sign, and not one refused us service.

Nevertheless, I wrote complaining to the Race Relations Board, pointing out that signs saying no hippies were just as discriminatory as ones saying no gypsies, and that, considering how few pure Romanies there were, 'Hippies' were just as much an ethnic group complete with their own culture; I argued that the signs shold be more specific, e.g. 'no dirty longhairs & druggies' and I urged the Race Relations Board to come up with a cautionary letter that might put some fear into these unchristian trades people. I eventually received this not-very-helpful reply:

Section 6 of the 1968 Race Relations Act makes it unlawful to publish or display advertisements

REHEARSAL FOR THE YEAR 2000

(DRUGS, RELIGIONS, MADNESS, CRIME, COMMUNES, LOVE, VISIONS, FESTIVALS AND LUNAR ENERGY)

THE REBIRTH OF ALBION FREE STATE
(known in the Dark Ages as England)

MEMOIRS OF A MALE MIDWIFE

1966–1976

or notices which could reasonably be understood as indicating an act of discrimination. Discrimination is defined in the Act as less-favoured treatment on the grounds of colour, race or ethnic or national origins.

I do not think that the Board would accept your view that the sign NO HIPPIES ALLOWED *amounts to discrimination against people who, as a group, are ethnically or racially distinguishable. Furthermore, I doubt if such a notice would be generally understood as indicating that hippies would be discriminated against because of their ethnic, or supposed ethnic origins, as distinct from other factors.*

Yours sincerely, C. Fudge

Writing in 1989 in the pamphlet *Travellers in Glastonbury*, Ann Morgan offers a sympathetic view of 'the problems and challenges associated with the growing number of travellers present in and around the town':

In the face of a completely unknown and complex situation, most Establishment voices expressed concern, disquiet, even disgust . . . [But] most of the 'alternative' community are genuinely pleased to see the travellers here, doing their bit towards the rebirth of Glastonbury as a place of planetary service and spiritual renewal . . . Glastonbury is an internationally famous centre of tourism and pilgrimage. The world is looking at us and how we respond to the challenge of the travellers in the life of our community.

As one young traveller put it to Morgan: 'Glastonbury may be seen as a centre where co-operation is working, instead of being a typically boring, stereotyped town where townsfolk and hippies are fighting'. During this period of later Thatcherism, nationally there was a great sense of social and ideological polarisation – do you support the miners or not? Do you sympathise with and secretly admire the Peace Convoy or not? If you are Scottish or Welsh, do you blame the English for voting her government in yet again? In spite of its otherworldly claims and ambitions, Glastonbury could not avoid being touched by the real. Things polarised there, too: on the one hand, a local citizen invested in an old tow-truck for removing travellers' vehicles, presenting it as a community service. In order to cover his costs, he offered £1 shares to citizens sharing his outrage – and the vehicle became known as the Hippy Wrecker. Direct action meets vigilantism, a dangerous shift, especially considering that attacks on isolated travellers were on the increase, by local yobs or men who should have known better after closing time at the village pub. I have written elsewhere of the peace camps of the 1980s that sprung up outside airbases such as Greenham Common, Berkshire and Molesworth, Oxfordshire where American-contolled Cruise missiles were due to be sited. At such peace camps – as also at the rural road protest camps of the 1990s – nomadic lifestyles are overtly politicised, not as a politics of withdrawal or rejection or disappearance, but as a committed politics of obstinate occupation, obstruction. Rainbow Fields Village at Molesworth was set up by anti-nuclear activists and New Travellers. It was evicted early in 1985, and the village went 'on the road', joining up with the larger Peace Convoy of new travellers on the way to the annual Stonehenge Free Festival celebrating the summer solstice. On the way to the stones the convoy was ambushed by police and violently and illegally trashed in what has become known as the Battle of the Beanfield. According to Bruce Garrard, an inhabitant of Rainbow Fields Village, 'many of the [Convoy] came to Glastonbury; bruised and battered, physically and emotionally. Glastonbury was the only place that seemed to offer any kind of sanctuary at all'. They camped up in one of those special West Country landscape features, an orchard, at the aptly named Greenlands Farm. This is the other side of the story, the polar opposite of those championing the Hippy Wrecker. Ann Morgan touches on the difficulty of the post-convoy situation in Glastonbury in the late 1980s with a pragmatic, commercial argument:

> The 'get the hippies out' stance is deliberately promoting local disharmony and unrest. This is bad for trade and local prosperity, and out of harmony with Glastonbury's growing and valuable reputation as a centre of peace and new wave colour and excitement. A more forward looking local establishment figure has admittted that the town was nearly dead on its feet before the 'alternative' activities . . . started a few years ago.

Travellers in Glastonbury

Ann Morgan and Bruce Garrard

A series of articles written during the summer of 1989

THE GLASTONBURY GAZETTE
Unique Publications, 5 High Street, Glastonbury, Somerset.

As we have seen, during the early 1980s the counterculture's twin big events took place at roughly the same time in roughly the same part of the country, each June in Wiltshire and Somerset. Whether they wanted it or not, the Stonehenge free festival and Glastonbury CND festival were entwined, twinned. Bruce Garrard explains the tension between the two neighbouring alternative festivals:

> From the point of view of people who went to Stonehenge, Glastonbury festival was commercial, middle class, a venue for

people who weren't just old hippies but old weekend hippies. The Green Field in '84 was perhaps different, but not different enough. From the point of view of people who went to Glastonbury (CND) festival, Stonehenge was a mess, beer cans and bikers, with no direction or purpose, an unhealthy embarrassment.

Both views were true and both were untrue. But both festivals had their roots in the same spirit, the same culture, even, if you looked carefully, many of the same people; but they'd become divorced. We need to start making more connections, alter our imagery. We need to see Glastonbury once again as a people's festival, and Stonehenge as a peace festival.

Following the crackdown on Stonehenge in 1985, it was no longer possible to make your own choice (frequently people had done both, getting organised music at Glastonbury for the weekend, and a week or two's radical alternative society at Stonehenge before or after). But the demonisation of new travellers impacted on Glastonbury festival as well as on the town of Glastonbury itself. To their shame, Hampshire Social Services were involved with police in a dawn swoop in 1986 on a vestigial convoy of New Travellers vainly hoping to make their way to Stonehenge to hold the festival again that summer. What for? To take forty-seven children into care, as part of the sustained two-year effort on the part of the authorities to break the spirit of the convoy. In the dark hours before the swoop one social worker turned up on the site, as veteran New Traveller Spider recalls:

> I mean it's the middle of the night, the middle of the New Forest, a big travellers' site. For a straight woman to come on like that takes a bit of courage . . . She says, 'Look, I work for Hampshire Social Services, my conscience won't let me live with this. You've got to get your kids away because they're coming on at four o'clock. The police have got care orders for forty-seven kids.' . . .
>
> We got all the kids up and put them all in this big bus and drove straight down to Glastonbury. I went to see Michael Eavis who runs the festival down there, explained what had happened, and he let us park up in this field. So all the kids spent the night there in that bus. It was a very emotional night . . . the thought of what lengths the authorities would go to to drive us down was frightening.

HIPPY

STONEHENGE '86
How it's shaping up

NEW LAWS
How they affect you

LAST SUMMER
Festivals... or refugee camps?

70p

Festivals or refugee camps?

'You're never too old for a happy childhood'

Police home-in on
an old travellers' bus
on the Hampshire –
Wiltshire border,
June 1985.

The peace festival made space for what, with hindsight, was an extraordinarily victimised social group which was being targeted on a scale far out of proportion to its possible threat. (Granted, the convoy's symbolic threat, both as a rejection of yuppie culture and in its sometime celebration of drug culture, was powerful.) As with Greenland Farm the previous year, here was a gesture of sympathy, of practical support for New Travellers, from Worthy Farm, whose annual festival itself tapped into nomadic tradition. National and local press editorials alike expressed sympathy for the travellers in their efforts to re-establish a festival, frequently citing Glastonbury as the example of a positive countercultural tradition. For instance, the *Independent* wrote that, 'The annual festival at Glastonbury . . . demonstrates that it is possible to hold an event acceptable to hippies without it degenerating into an excuse for acts of violence and the systematic abuse of hard drugs.' According to the *Guardian* in 1988: 'Glastonbury festival organiser Michael Eavis has offered to buy a site and stage the [Stonehenge] festival if any Wiltshire landowner – such as the Ministry of Defence – will sell him the land. Nobody seems inclined to and the police still dismiss the idea, recalling the drug problem of the pre-1985 festival which was largely un-organised and attracted 30,000 people.' There was the precedent of Windsor Free in 1975, of course, when the government had supplied a disused airfield for the People's Free Festival to gather. It didn't happen again. But what did happen was the estab-lishment of the Travellers' Field at Glastonbury festival, a space dedicated to New

Travellers, a mini-free festival which soon sprouted its own stages, entertainment, cafés, and to which travellers and their buses and trucks would be directed. For a number of years the festival accommodated the nomadic fringe, rather than attempting to join the clampdown. This didn't stop the Levellers at their 1992 festival appearance dedicating their song 'Battle of the Beanfield' to 'all the people that couldn't get in!' and then calling Michael Eavis 'a cunt' for banning the Travellers' Field after 1990. (When they met him personally, the band rather regretted that insult, and their media person was at pains to stress to me that the Levellers actually think Michael Eavis is a good bloke.) Eavis explained the position regarding travellers today to me at the 1999 press conference:

> We've got loads of space for caravans, we want to encourage more caravans, they're safer, the fourteen-year-olds can't so easily break into a caravan. And we've still got the Travellers' Field, you know, they're in caravans as well, aren't they, but just different sorts of caravans! About one thousand travellers up the road I'm looking after on a daily basis. The festival fence – it only came down in '95, it only came down once – and that was a traveller-instigated thing.
>
> That's another problem with putting on the festival – three hundred vehicles there are, in that Travellers' Field, and they're parked off-site, about two miles away. They're doing their own thing, it's a bit difficult for me to manage, to get the services in there, and to keep the locals happy round about that site. I just manage the travellers who turn up here. We manage them quite well, responsibly, don't go round beating them with baseball bats, just give them a site and we make it work, make it comfortable, and they're reasonably welcome. It's a different approach to English Heritage [responsible for Stonehenge] – but then I've had years of training. It is a drain, it's a very difficult thing, I have to talk one-to-one, with their leaders – you get a dialogue going then it might work. I can't get somebody else to go there. It's a bit of a wordly-wise thing, years and years of history. It's no problem, it's fine, it's just a part of the festival that nobody really knows about.

David Jones of Avon and Somerset Police suggests two reasons for the return to the festival, on that scale, of New Travellers in 1999. First, the annual exclusion zone around Stonehenge in early June had been successfully challenged, with the result that some travellers, as well as druids, pagans, and assorted hedonists, could gather at the stones. Second, the great regional attraction in the South-West of the total eclipse of the sun, and with it a whole spate of festivals to celebrate totality in August. (When I asked him about policing approaches towards travellers and festivals in the region during the 1980s, he replied: 'Perhaps looking back, I don't think the powers we were using then would stand up now. We all learned lessons from the Beanfield and from litigation to do with it in the years afterwards.')

Andrew Blake explores the paradox of the tension between local identity and national even international attraction in our very mobile world: 'Festivals which may have originated in the desire to celebrate localities and work which reflects them, which may be based around local venues and around the talents of local people, cannot be local, cannot be restricted to residents, any more.' Yet one of the points, indeed the aims, of the Glastonbury festival is its continued effort (and success) at maintaining a local identity. As shown earlier, the Caribbean Notting Hill Carnival has developed a huge profile in black British cultural identity, which is still associated with its locale – one of its charms, like Glastonbury, is the extent to which it extends out of itself into a much wider audience without altogether losing its character, its sense of place. It does this by reflecting its community. Glastonbury also reflects (and contributes to) its alternative community (however much that may be resented by some Glastonians). Both Notting Hill and Glastonbury, paradoxically, celebrate or locate themselves within the community by an act of transformation, so much so that the long-term sense of identity of the places of 'Notting Hill' and of 'Glastonbury' have been altered by the temporary weekend annual events held there.

Because of local tensions with, for instance, incoming hippies and new travellers, the organisers of Glastonbury festival have gone to some lengths to ensure that a sense of local identity, of local identification with the event, is felt. Local Somerset charities, such as housing projects and children's community arts organisations, as well as national and international charities and campaign groups, benefit from the funds the festival raises. Also for this reason, the festival website contains quite a detailed breakdown of the monies which pour into the local economy as a direct and indirect result of the festival. In 1994, a specific page called 'local economic benefits' on the website claimed over £2.7 million pounds was brought into the local community. This figure includes sums ranging from £15,000 given to local schools and playgroups from funds raised by the festival to the rather more vague and unquantified £500,000 spent in local shops (excluding cash and carry, supermarkets and garages, in which in total £700,000 was spent). While the figures may be debatable, since no sources are cited, the point that the website feels the need to emphasise the local benefits of the festival is a significant one. Cynics argue that the festival is 'buying off' the opposition; supporters respond with more of a ying–yang argument, that while the local area *is* subject to considerable disruption over one summer's weekend each year, the cultural, touristic, financial and spiritual (not sure about that one) benefits far outweigh that disruption. It's the Glastonian–Avalonian divide again.

Misty, mysterious Avalon:
Glastonbury legend and festival

Right, we're gonna go back.
Mark E. Smith of The Fall

Calling the large 1971 free festival the *Glastonbury* Fayre – despite the greater proximity of the village of Pilton and the well-known festival town of Shepton Mallet alike – was an informed marketing stroke of genius, which tapped into the emerging zeitgeist of Aquarian and later New Age ideals, and lay some of strongest foundations for the festival's longer term claims to having an alternative ethos and atmosphere. The local press has taken umbrage at the festival's name, calling it 'the so-called Glastonbury Festival at Pilton', while locals, of the Glastonbury alternative community, for instance, tend to call it the Pilton Festival anyway. Jeremy Cunningham of the Levellers remembers that, 'Everyone cool and in the know calls it "Pilton" – but I didn't know! I thought they were all talking about a different festival.' Depending on how favourably you view it, the town, the place of Glastonbury itself offers either a cluster or a hotch-potch of utopian and New Age themes and alternative histories. If we buy a ticket for the festival, we buy into a little bit of Glastonbury, its mystical magic, its palimpsestic fictions, its topography. Is Glastonbury possessed of (or by) a *genius loci*? Its legends are interwoven with its landscape, the tor, its wells. Is it a hyperactive text machine, where stories produce stories in a labyrinthine, Borgesian world? Father Aelred Watkin remarked to the Arthurian scholar and Glastonbury resident Geoffrey Ashe: 'You have only to tell some crazy tale at Glastonbury and in ten years' time it'll be an ancient Somerset legend.' You may find that taking a pinch of our daily crystal, salt, can help to clear the mists of Glastonbury.

The early twentieth-century occultist, writer and ethical vegetarian Dion Fortune centred most of her energies around Glastonbury, and was responsible for coining the phrase 'Avalonians' to describe the collection of like-minded souls, eccentrics and believers who congregated there looking for spiritual fulfilment. Geoffrey Ashe recognises the significance of Fortune: 'She foreshadowed the interests of generations after her. She was ahead of her time, for instance, in raising the issue of female spirituality which American feminists began airing about 1975, in protest against "patriarchal" religion.' Fortune saw the duality of the place, the Pagan and Christian Glastonburys as, if not entirely mutually reinforcing, at least mutually invigorating, as she wrote in the curiously powerful (if slightly flaky) *Avalon in the Heart* in 1934:

> Two traditions meet in Avalon – the ancient faith of the Britons, and the creed of Christ. The older, its relics obliterated, its legends bent to a Christian purpose, is shadowy and veiled. Only here and there do we see clearly the lineaments of the ancient creed . . .
> The Abbey holy ground, consecrated by the dust of the saints; but up here, at the foot of the Tor, the Old Gods have their part. So we have two Avalons, 'the holyest erthe in Englande', down among the water-meadows; and upon the green heights the fiery pagan forces that make the heart leap and burn. And some love the one, and some love the other.

Little more than a decade later, Lawrence Whistler was making a similar point about this dualism, but specifically in the context of festival tradition. Whistler's 1947 book *The English Festivals* argued that: 'The festivals of the English people acknowledge their ancestry. One is more pagan in character, another more Christian, but there are few, if we inspect them closely enough, which are not seen to be both.'

Also in this chapter I want to turn again to Glastonbury festival itself – but not so much the bohemian, music-centred Avalonian-touched Glastonbury festival of Michael Eavis in the late twentieth and early twenty-first century, rather the bohemian, music-centred Avalonian-touched Glastonbury festival of Rutland Boughton in the early twentieth century. Hopefully you will have gathered by now that, after glancing through the time-line of festival culture in the centre of the book, I am interested in both the history of Glastonbury and its festival(s) (by its nature a fairly repetitive narrative), and in Glastonbury and the idea of history, the past(s). For, as Dion Fortune, an admirer of Boughton's project, acutely observed in the 1930s (in a remark I'll probably quote again later), 'Glastonbury is not only deep-rooted in the past, but the past lives on at Glastonbury. All about us it stirs and breathes, quiet, but living and watching.'

From Xtianity to the wonderful world of Arthur, to the dawning of the Age of Aquarius. And then the New Age

Glastonbury is fabled to be the place where Joseph of Arimathea brought the Holy Grail to in Britain in AD 63. The Rev. Lionel Smithett Lewis, Vicar of Glastonbury, collated the evidence on this in his 1922 book *St Joseph of Arimathea at Glastonbury*. Joseph founded the first wooden chapel on the Tor and with it introduced the Christian religion to Britain. Maybe. Joseph struck his staff into the ground on Wearyall (Wirral) Hill, where it took root and began to grow, a cutting of which in Glastonbury Abbey produces the Glastonbury 'Holy Thorn' which flowers each winter, or rather flowers each Christmas to commemorate Christ's birth. The Holy Grail may be symbolic, or in different versions it is Christ's plate from the Last Supper, or a cup or chalice in which his blood was caught during the crucifixion. Maybe even Jesus accompanied Joseph to these islands, which is another version of an earlier visit by Joseph, one which leads to (or comes from) William Blake's 'Jerusalem': 'And did those feet in ancient times walk upon England's mountains green?' Glastonbury is then the New Jerusalem too . . . is there no end to the claims? (And on the other hand, mountains aren't usually green as such, they are too high for that. Maybe the spectacle of the grassed Tor rising from the flat valley is Blake's image.) Other West Country scholar-vicars followed the Reverend Lewis's idea up, providing evidence of what John Michell, veteran writer on things mystic and an all-round great believer, calls this 'impressive truth'. In his book, Michell seeks to shed *New Light on the Ancient Mystery of Glastonbury*:

> A legend of St Joseph is that he was a merchant. He may have sailed to Britain for cargoes of Cornish tin, and he may have brought his young nephew, Jesus, with him . . . A popular expression among country people on the Mendips, 'As sure as our Lord was at Priddy!', derived from the local belief that Jesus had passed over those hills on his way to Glastonbury.

Whether during some of the 'lost years' of his youth Jesus travelled, let alone to what we now know of as England, is not *known* – but then not much of this chapter is known, in the sense that it is historically verifiable. Should this surprise us? When you ask people who were at Glastonbury festival a few years or a couple of decades ago, the exceptions are those who can identify which precise year with confidence; even recent personal history is difficult to verify. The place seems to encourage timelessness, of an altogether greater kind than the slower more organic lifestyle we readily associate with the countryside rather than the city. In our postmodern, mediated, fragmented, Western world, timelessness may be part of the Glastonbury attraction. The Tourist Information Centre's impressive Glastonbury website certainly sells that, too, with pages on local legend.

No wonder the Holy Grail is here, too. Consider the competing interpretations and origins of the Holy Grail itself: it is a Christian symbol from the start, the death of Christ; it is an element of a pagan fertility ritual, the horn of plenty; it is mythological Celtic story with roots in Welsh and Breton narratives. The symbolism of the Grail mirrors Glastonbury's own pagan–Christian duality. According to folklorist Bob Stewart, in another example of Christian take-over of earlier belief and ritual, 'The "Holy Grail" extends symbolically to the Celtic or even pre-Celtic "Cauldron", usually connected with the Goddess Kerridwen.' While for Stewart there is something imperial about such encroachment, for others the fact that the Christian church did *not* always seek to suppress earlier belief is significant. Writing of the revived seasonal tradition of well-dressing in the English Peak District, probably with origins in a pre-Roman Celtic ritual to thank or appease the natural water-gods, Roy Christian argues rather contradictorily that 'The early Christian Church handled pagan customs sensitively, absorbing and adapting rather than suppressing. That this was a slow process is clear from a decree of AD 960 expressly forbidding the worship of fountains. As late as 1102, St Anselm was still condemning "this form of idolatry".'

The existence of Glastonbury Abbey itself illustrates that the town was an important Christian centre in the Middle Ages. The abbey predates the tenth century, and is said in the Grail legends to have been founded by Joseph of Arimathea. Some archaeologists and historians have sought to trace the foundation of a Christian sanctuary at Glastonbury back to the period of British rule before the Saxon conquest of the area in the seventh century; others have sought to substantiate what Philip Rahtz calls 'the persistent traditions that Glastonbury was the scene of Christian evangelical activity as early as the first century AD'. The Chalice Well, with its chalybeate waters, is believed by some to be a centre of early Christian activity. Going further, one version of the Holy Grail narrates that Joseph of Arimathea brought the Grail to England and buried it on Chalice Hill, near Chalice Well. Proof? Why else is its water red?

Another Grail, or a Cup of Jesus (there are so many), was the centre of a media storm in the early twentieth century, as reported in the *Daily Express* in July 1907: 'Mystery of a Relic; Finder Believes it to be the Holy Grail; Two Visions; Great Scientists Puzzled; Discovered at Glastonbury.' The mysterious relic is a blue glass bowl with cross-like patterns on it. (Another name for Glastonbury, perhaps a mistranslation: Glastonia, City of Glass – possibly also translatable as, and New Agers love this, City of Crystal. This is according to the twelfth-century writer Caradoc of Llancarvan, whose scholarship may have been touched by the Glastonbury spirit – that is, be dodgy.) The fact that *this* Grail had been bought in Italy twenty years before and also placed in a well (more like a sluice in a field, actually) on the edge of town by a London doctor under the influence of a trance (these were the late *fin-de-siècle* days of great occulture for the fascinated middle and upper classes of England: trances, psychical research, automatic writing, ouija boards, fairies at the bottom of the garden, that sort of thing) was, in what we might begin to see as typical Glastonian fashion, overlooked and blurred. The result: an irrational conflation of the Joseph of Arimathea legend – the saint you'll recall who brought the Grail to Glastonbury following Christ's death – and Dr John Arthur Goodchild, the one who bought his Cup of Jesus in a tailor's shop by the marina in Bordighera, Italy. Patrick Benham, in his book *The Avalonians*, notes the undesired impact this brought on one local farmer:

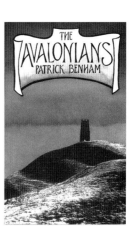

> The people of Glastonbury were somewhat bemused by the national publicity about something of which they had previously been quite unaware. Not the least, farmer James Mapstone, of Northload Bridge, was very put out to learn that someone had found an object on the land he owned at Beckery and had gone off with it without his permission.

With watery eyes, can you begin to see wells, pagan nature worship, Christianity and landscape connecting around Glasto? Pagan academic Graham Harvey offers his contemporary construction of that religion as embracing 'polytheism, seasonal festivals, nature-centred spirituality and lifestyle, recovery of ancestral, indigenous pre-Christian traditions, ecology, self-affirmation, pluralism, and so on'. I like that 'and so on' at the end. It's honest and pragmatic, it confirms paganistic adhockery – and it corresponds to much of the Glastonian – rather, Avalonian – attitude towards local legend too. These Glastonbury stories and the (over-)interpretations of their architecture are very 'and so on' kinds of things.

For Patrick Benham there are 'two linked traditions at Glastonbury. The first is that Christianity came to Britain immediately after the crucifixion, with Glastonbury the chosen site of its foundation. The second is that Glastonbury is the ancient "Isle of Avalon" where, as legend has it, King Arthur and Queen Guinevere lie buried. *The two are connected by the story of the Holy Grail*' (emphasis added). This ancient town in Somerset is near what had once been an Iron Age hill-fort, Cadbury Castle, which, along with Tintagel on the coast of north Cornwall, as well as the hill-fort in North Wales called Caerleon, has claims to be one of the key places of King Arthur. According to the monk and chronicler and a chief early architect of the visionary kingdom, Geoffrey of Monmouth, and others, King Uther Pendragon of Tintagel in Cornwall had a son who became King Arthur, perhaps around AD 470. The standard Arthurian narrative goes roughly as follows. At the end of the Roman Empire, the legendary resistance leader Arthur led a battle against new invaders from Europe, the Angles and the Saxons. (Sounds so anti-European, even though the standard history tells us that the Celts themselves had migrated from overseas a few centuries earlier.) Creating and defending a Celtic heritage with a Romanised version of Christianity, in Wales and the South-West of England, Arthur may have been a real historical figure, or may be a blend of several, or is just as likely a continually rewritten nationalist superhero.

With Arthur, all is fantastically unreliable – so much so that even concrete (well, stone) evidence from eight hundred years ago was quite possibly planted, fictional. According to one story, monks discovered the bodies of Arthur and Guinevere at Glastonbury Abbey in 1190. Was this a cunning plan on the part of Henry II to grab for himself the power of the legend, and to emasculate the Celtic resonance? After all, the Celts of Wales long prophesied Arthur's return from Avalon in the role of avenging chieftain. The report of the dig's findings was suspiciously perfect: a slab of stone and a lead cross inscribed 'HIC IACET SEPULTUS INCLITUS REX ARTURIUS IN INSULA AVALONIA: Here lies buried the renowned King Arthur in the Isle of Avalon.' So Glastonbury has come to declare itself as the Isle of Avalon, burial place of King

Arthur – if indeed the king actually died, and if indeed his grave is there. (*The Black Book of Carmarthen*, written around 1150, says that 'concealed till Doomsday [is] the grave of Arthur'.)

Avalon is one of the 'Fortunate Isles' to which Arthur is carried for healing after his death, according to Geoffrey of Monmouth, in his twelfth-century history of British kings, *Historia Regum Britanniae*. One of the key texts Geoffrey of Monmouth used is a lost 'most ancient book in the British tongue' – scholars ever since have suspected that this book never existed outside Geoffrey's imagination: from the beginnings of Arthurian narrative, fiction is a central ingredient. Geoffrey's writing was pivotal in the literary rebirthing of King Arthur. In a way it's not surprising that Arthur stills attracts today: the fact is that Geoffrey was already reinventing him *600 years* after his apparent life, Tennyson 700 years after that, and Walt Disney a century later again.

Geoffrey of Monmouth was not the first to piece together a story of Arthur at Glastonbury but his version has had, as Geoffrey Ashe notes, 'amazing results' in capturing the imagination of writers and readers. Writing around the same time, one of the first ambitious historians of England to follow the Venerable Bede, William of Malmesbury, was already debunking many of the stories being written about Arthur. There is speculation that William's *De Antiquitate Glastoniensis Ecclesiae* may have been written at Glastonbury itself during the years AD 1129–1139. Either way, such Arthurian texts of the time were soon to be picked up by French and German courtly love writers and transformed into verse romances about the matters of Britain – knights, holy quests, unrequited love for ladies, and so on.

It is telling that referring back to Arthur, to reclaim or reconfigure certain constructions of Britishness, has frequently been a feature of social unrest or change: 'the visionary kingdom [is] pressed in to meet the needs of the real one' is how Geoffrey Ashe explains it. In the fifteenth century Sir Thomas Malory wrote *Le Morte d'Arthur* (actually an Arthurian cycle in *English*, published by Caxton). Characteristically for these well-known but obscured legends, even the exact identity of Malory, the writer, remains in doubt. (*Le Morte d'Arthur* was written in prison, and it is known that one knight named Malory was charged after 1450 with the usual crimes of his class – violence, theft and rape. Alternatively, it is suggested that the French origins of the writing signal that the author was a prisoner in France during the French wars of the time.) Through the social upheaval of the Industrial Revolution early poets from

William Blake to later ones like, most famously, Alfred Tennyson, have used local landscape and legend either as implicit social criticism or as patriotic text for contemporary royalty.

Arthur's multiplicity is commemorated in his influence on British place-names. Ashe observes wryly that, 'Nobody else is commemorated so widely, except the Devil.' Such omnipresence may, of course, rather undercut the claim of the West Country or Wales as especial sites for Arthurian presence. In fact (again, if such a phrase has any place here), Arthur may be buried at Glastonbury – or he may be buried in Snowdonia in Wales, at Arthur's Oon near Stirling in Scotland, or under a stone marked Arthur in the Midlands. In 1999 a car park in Winchester, Hampshire was being dug up to find the poor guy. (And who thought postmodernism invented competing multiple narratives and absent presences?) Yet John Michell insists on a local gaze:

> Among the Glastonbury locations of Arthur's legend are the site of the former Meare Pool where he received Excalibur from the Lady of the Lake; Pomparles Bridge, between

Glastonbury Tor, St Michael's Tower and the surrounding countryside. 'The veil is thin here,' wrote Dion Fortune, 'and the Unseen comes very near to the earth.'

Glastonbury and Street, where the Lady repossessed it; Beckery island where he had a mystical experience in the Chapel Perilous; his fortress on the Tor; the rival fortress of his giant adversary on Bernt Knoll; his palace at South Cadbury and his burial place in the Abbey graveyard.

For Malory, King Arthur's end at 'Glastonbury or Elsewhere' was equivocal. Arthur is *rex quondam rexque futurus*, the once and future king, waiting for some kind of New Age to greet or to spring from his return. Geoffrey Ashe observes that: 'He was like the dying-and-reviving gods of so many cults, whose careers followed the seasonal cycle.' Glastonbury permits us to make a mixture or mix-up of Christian and Arthurian legend. What else have they in common here, apart from the Grail? The central belief in the hero returning from the dead, the promise of a New Age. It is quite a small leap in this context, particularly within the kinds of alternative lifestyles that privilege the intuitive over the historical (I'm not sure that's fair), to map on to such Christian or Arthurian promise the Aquarian rhetoric of the 1960s, the New Age version of that from the 1980s and 1990s.

Glastonbury is a place where, according to Dion Fortune, 'the veil is thin here, and the Unseen comes very near to earth' – a spiritually rich space, a hot spot. In the sixties and seventies Glastonbury attracted a new generation of Aquarians with the hippie movement. This saw some upper-middle class and even aristocratic dropouts move to the area as part of the back-to-the-land movement of the time. That alternative beliefs centred on Glastonbury took off very quickly is illustrated by different editions of Nicholas Saunders' early classic directory of the underground *Alternative London*. (Saunders was later to be re-energised by the rave generation, producing a number of best-selling books about Ecstasy.) The first edition of *Alternative London*, from December 1970, contains a short section on alternative religions, mainly Eastern ones such as Hinduism, Buddhism, Sufism. By the third edition, for the summer solstice of 1972, Saunders is including a section on English mysticism, which explains that, 'There is a current re-awakening of English mysticism – quite apart from the Druids. Over the last few years some quite separate legends and phenomena have begun to be understood as part of the same pattern. To begin with the Glastonbury legends . . .' Other Londoners too were looking for their own spiritual answers, of course. In his book *Rastaman*, Ernest Cashmore suggests that Rastafarianism can be seen in the context of the wide-ranging revival of spiritual exploration also characteristic of the later hippie movement:

> If Ras Tafari was an urban anomaly, then there were others: the revival of occult
> activities in the 1970s, the mystical pursuits of Hare Krishna followers, the emergence
> of the Reverend Sun Myung Moon and his Unification Church, the escalating popularity
> of Scientology, and the persistent fascination with UFOs were all indicative of an effort
> to 're-mystify' the modern social world and incorporate myth into world views . . .

The immediate source for the popularity with the counterculture of the Glastonbury legends, and all things off-beam of those, including mystic numerology and hidden geometry, zodiacs and UFOs, was, of course, John Michell's *The View over Atlantis*, first published in 1969. It was this book, with its discussion of the sacred relation between the dimensions of Stonehenge, the Pyramids of Egypt and Glastonbury Abbey, that inspired the first Pyramid Stage at the festival.

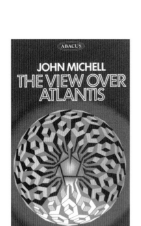

Ah yes, the Pyramid Stage. What an extraordinary thing to do, really: plonk a huge pyramid in the middle of a field in the West Country. What a marvellously hazy gesture that was – so much so, that it's happened with at least three different pyramids over the years. The first was for the 1971 free festival. Glastonbury Fayre, from 20–24 June 1971, is *the* legendary event at Worthy Farm, recognised by Michael Clarke in *The Politics of Pop Festivals* as 'a veritable milestone in the history of free festivals'. It was funded and organised by upper-middle-class dropouts like Andrew Kerr and Winston Churchill's granddaughter Arabella; Kerr had been reading the Bible about redistribution and decided to practise what it preached. Aside from the nudity, it was in other ways quite a pure or strict event: no alcohol on sale on site, food was mostly vegetarian, free food was available from Communal Knead and self-styled 'King of the Hippies' Sid Rawles' Digger Action Movement, and there was a midnight curfew for amplified music. Glastonbury itself and Worthy Farm, a few miles down the road were fast becoming a magnet for the beautiful people, a site of pilgrimage, as C.J. Stone describes in *The Last of the Hippies*:

> All sorts of people were coming and going during the nine months leading up to the
> festival. Hawkwind practised in the barn, as did the Pink Fairies. The cast of *Hair* turned
> up. Members of the Grateful Dead. Friends of John Lennon. Some thieves and plenty of
> phoneys. Even a guru or two.

Andrew Kerr had actually wanted to hold his free festival at Stonehenge, with a circular stage, to celebrate the summer solstice there, as Stonehenge free festival organiser Wally Hope would do in a few years' time. When Kerr was introduced to farmer Michael Eavis, though, plans shifted to the development of Worthy Farm as the site, building on the excitement of the previous September's little festival at the farm. It was to be a free festival in response to the overt commercialism of 1970's Bath Blues Festival (attended by Eavis) and the final Isle of Wight (attended by Kerr). Instead of Stonehenge, then, there was Pilton, with its sweeping views over to Glastonbury Tor down the Vale of Avalon. To give it a further resonance of spirituality, mystique, atavism (which I'm not sure the site even needed) and orientalism, they built a pyramid in the middle of a field. This Pyramid Stage was constructed from KWIKSTAGE scaffolding and plastic sheeting, and situated (so the story goes) over a blind spring on the St Michael ley line, the precise spot chosen by Kerr by dowsing.

The stage was designed by Bill Harkin as a scaled-down model of the Great Pyramid in Egypt. As noted, some of the inspiration must go to Michell's classic hippy book of occult, numbers, ancient buildings and mystical or folkloric practices, *The View Over Atlantis*. In fact, Harkin and Kerr rang Michell from Worthy Farm, and were advised by him to base the proportions of the pyramid on the dimensions of Stonehenge. *The View Over Atlantis* would come to be regarded as a key English text of what

Glastonbury, 1971.

we now recognise as New Age ideas. It's a mishmash of enthusiasm, fragments of text and argument lined up together, energetically sweeping across, sometimes beyond, the globe, embracing regional ideas such as those of Alfred Watkins on ley lines or Bligh Bond on the significance of the dimensions of Glastonbury Abbey. All that and flying saucers and astral projection, too. *The View Over Atlantis* directly links Glastonbury with Giza:

> [The] comparative numbers of, for example, the Great Pyramid, Stonehenge and Glastonbury Abbey do show the same numerical system, and presumably the same principles to which the numbers refer, stretching as an unbroken arcane link over several thousands of years . . . The New Jerusalem was built on earth to patterns and numbers, whose origin lay in divine revelation, which we find at the Great Pyramid, at Stonehenge, at Glastonbury Abbey and everywhere in the great monuments of the former world.

Michell also writes that the Great Pyramid 'was constructed for a magical and sacred purpose, as a vehicle for transcending the material state, for travel in space, through time and into a further dimension.' So Glastonbury had to have one too. During the

The original Pyramid Stage, 1971, constructed with KWIKSTAGE scaffolding and polythene.

festival itself, Guru Maharaji, the thirteen-year-old head of the Divine Light Mission, addressed the crowd from the polythene-covered pyramid-shaped stage. The sound was so poor that few could make out what he said – Arabella Churchill *thinks* he said 'No sects' rather than 'No sex', for instance. Space oddity David Bowie played, as did space ritualists Hawkwind.

William Bloom, Glastonbury-based writer on meditation and ritual, was there in 1971. He described for me *his* memories of a free festival: 'The mixture of very good LSD and very bad scrumpy. Impromptu processions. The frenzy of the underground press to produce newssheets. The good vibe. Bowie waking the crowd playing a foot-pumped organ.'

The fields of Worthy Farm fell kind of quiet for most of the rest of the seventies. Until, that is, the arrival of the second Pyramid Stage in 1978, with a bunch of New Travellers from Stonehenge. Nik Turner, previously of leading free festival stalwarts Hawkwind, has also frequently been seen performing at Glastonbury, from 1971 on. ('I've played there so many times I don't know if I'd get a gig any more! My kids are hoping I get a booking so they can come too, now,' he says.) Turner takes up the story.

In 1978 I was doing my Sphynx project, and I heard the Grateful Dead were planning to play at the Great Pyramid. Well, they were friends of friends, and I wanted to go, to make my music part of that. We were trying all these ways of blagging airline tickets, or better still a plane, to get there, and to get all the gear there. In the meantime we'd made this Pyramid Stage, out of aluminium scaffolding with canvas sides. It was set on a trailer, so the trailer became the stage base, and we used to tow it round from festival to festival on the back of a big furniture lorry we were living in round then. Someone rang me up and said there's going to be a free festival at Worthy Farm, so we went there with it. That Glastonbury in '78 was the first time my Pyramid Stage got used. We never got to the Great Pyramid that year; I remember being struck by hearing Jerry Garcia had tried to use the King's Chamber as an echo chamber for his guitar, but the radio waves wouldn't transmit through the stones of the pyramid. You know, the pyramid sort of saying, 'Right, that's enough.' A few years later I donated my Pyramid Stage to the people, and it got used as the main stage at Stonehenge and other big free festivals.

The third Pyramid Stage was built in 1981 for the first CND festival as a permanent feature, with planning permission for use as a rather elaborate cowshed for the rest of the year. It lasted thirteen years. Alister Sieghart remembers helping to build it, and especially the perspex mini-pyramid that topped it. 'You could climb up there, see the band playing below, and get the most amazing view over the festival site. We got a small crystal pyramid from Gothic Image, I think, and put that at the actual apex of the whole thing, a touch we liked.' A large CND symbol dominated the front of the pyramid for a decade. In June 1994, ten days before the festival was due to start, the Pyramid Stage burned down, and was sadly replaced by a standard outdoor festival rig. The fire seemed ominous: the festival had its first death, a young man from a drugs overdose, while on the Saturday night there was a gun battle in which five people were shot. Since then only the name of the Pyramid Stage survives. Sieghart is still involved with the festival today, running a computer-centred business on Green issues, and doing graphic design work for the festival. When I spoke to him he was working on the materials for the 2000 event: 'I've included a pyramid on the design. There's quite a lot of talk of bringing the Pyramid Stage back for 2000, and a model has been built, costed and approved.'

The various Pyramid Stages are perhaps the most visible sign of the festival's New Age interests. August 1987 witnessed the global Harmonic Convergence, an event to take advantage of a shift in the 'time beam' as the earth enters its final 25-year phase in a 5000-year Mayan cycle. So the New Age will actually start in 2012, since the 14,000 people who hummed together during the Harmonic Convergence around the globe in 1987 have (probably) successfully steered us away from apocalypse and towards a new dawning a dozen years into the new millennium. This saw Glastonbury as one of the world's hot spots for energy, along with Ayers Rock in Australia, the Great Pyramid in Egypt, Machu Picchu in Peru, and quite a few places in California. Shared sunrise ceremonies around the world enabled adherents to 'tune in', and a four-day event in Glastonbury was Somerset's local contribution to global consciousness and the diversion of the apocalypse. A human mandala was formed on the slopes of the Tor, while other believers meditated at sunrise round St Michael's Tower at the top. Dion Fortune has been here before, in 1934 to be precise:

The last thing of interest to happen here was the end of the world, which has now occurred three times. Glastonbury is very

THE HARMONIC CONVERGENCE

Scores of people form a human mandala as they meditate on the lower slopes of Glastonbury Tor on Sunday, as part of the worldwide "harmonic convergence." Photo by Brian Walker.

PRESS CUTTINGS: AUGUST 1987

conveniently situated for this event . . . People have come to live in Glastonbury for this reason, and whenever the date for the end of the world is announced they rush home from their holidays, and pack picnic baskets, and put them handy in the hall.

The contemporary impact of thirty years of New Age activity on Glastonbury itself is celebrated by long-time resident Bruce Garrard, who also looks to a rosy future for today's Avalonians.

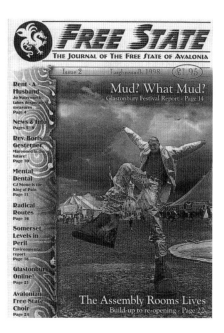

An example of Glastonbury's alternative press.

The community has grown in size to the point where it is beginning to develop its own social structures; it has its own community centre, and business community which is building an economic infrastructure. It has its own distinctive political output, characterised by people with a co-operative ideal, an informed concern about the environment, and an almost patriotic pride in their chosen area of Somerset. It is developing its own religious forms, and its own rights [sic] of passages, with a spontaneous interpretation of ancient ways. It uses music, theatre and the visual arts to explore and communicate these themes, which in turn reinforces the sense of community.

The phenomenon in Glastonbury now consists of two generations, and the younger one is growing up fast. When there are three, when we are the grandparents and the elders, then a community such as this one in Glastonbury should have a wholeness to it . . . With three generations, social structures could become complete, and a 'lifestyle' could become a 'way of life'; and the ancient mysteries could be passed on, renewed.

Sometimes lifestyle is a competition, though. The Jesus Army, for instance, has deliberately targeted the counterculture for its evangelical work, as the book *Fire in our Hearts: The Story of the Jesus Fellowship* makes clear. In the early 1970s, following an American model of evangelism among the hippies, some in Britain saw as their challenge the need to turn on to Jesus a 'mixture of hairies, acid heads, and bikers, ranging from flower power hippies to full-blown Hell's Angels. Most were dropouts, spending their money on dope. There was an openness amongst them, something of a brotherhood.' *New Society* wrote of these evangelicals, in a point that may resonate with Methodist and teetotaller Michael Eavis, 'What Wesley did for gin, the movement does for drugs.' For them Jesus was the original hippie, which meant they had to convert all the hippies to Jesus: 'He would not be acceptable. Few churches would accept his radical lifestyle. It is a shame that the radical, idealistic heart is so readily turned off by our churches.' In the mid-1980s this was advertised as 'a resistance movement of holy rebels' and Glastonbury was one favoured space of recruitment to the Jesus Army from then on:

> Our team went to the [1984] Glastonbury Festival and pitched their tents. As the heavy rock pounded day and night, they moved amongst crowds, chatting with people and sharing the gospel. A Christian lady who lived nearby met them while she was walking her dog. She thought they were marvellous, and opened her home to them. On the last day she gave a farewell buffet where Jesus People, punks and freaks were served cakes, trifles and strawberries by a team of genteel Anglican ladies! . . . At the [1989] Glastonbury festival we joined with the *Hope Now* team to befriend the many seekers, searchers and New Age hippies. We enjoyed the sense of united vision for souls as we worked alongside groups such as British Youth for Christ and Youth With A Mission.

The 'new Christians' looked to alternative youth, and with their communal living, festivals, buses on the road, the rave Xtianity of the Nine O'Clock Service in Sheffield in early 1990s, the *Jesus Lifestyle* (to quote the title of one of their publications) has mimicked many of the characteristic features of the counterculture over the decades. (It's interesting that the music, folk, rock, rave or otherwise, is invariably crap, though: the Devil still has a stranglehold on this aspect of culture, thank God.)

Some New Agers have pointed to festival as a central aspect of their belief system. In 1975 David Spangler published his lectures given at the Findhorn utopian community in Scotland in a book called *Festivals in the New Age*. For Spangler – as for so many New Agers – the social event has greatest meaning only when turned inwards to the self, less as a form of temporary community, more as a route to self-awareness. As with a political ideology like anarchism, there are immense problems with the inward turn to self, the ego in such a view, and it's difficult not to hear an echo of the Me Generation's narrow subjectivity. 'In the New Age', he writes:

> Festivals will again become an important part of human experience, but with this difference, that those who participate in them will do so as an outgrowth of their own recognition and response to *the festival within themselves* and not simply as participants in a ritual, a drama or a dance which has no meaning beyond the activity itself . . . Within each man [sic] is this inner festival, his own unique cycles and rhythms, his own unique place in the dance of creation. It is his dream, his story which he has come into life to externalise, to act out, to give form to.

Yet, interestingly, Spangler connects festival, self, nature and music most strongly in the midsummer festival:

> What we are celebrating when we are celebrating midsummer day, midsummer eve, and this great natural festival of energy, is truly the celebration of Pan . . . Pan lives in rhythm. He is the poet of the earth. He plays his pipes; and if we would share in his festival, then we too must hearken to the poet that is within us and to the dancer that stirs within our limbs.

This is a benevolent Pan – not the other Pan who spreads panic. In conclusion, Spangler re-roots festival in nature and in subjective experience: 'Festivals . . . must move the consciousness into the rhythm of the uplifting streams, the fairy streams, the elfish streams. You have the legends of the fairies dancing about their circle and Pan playing his pipes. Understand the implications of this,' he urges rather than tells.

Glastonbury 1999

It's ever so easy to identify contradiction at Glastonbury. For instance here I am sitting in the Green, no the Sacred Ground, where there are signs around saying SACRED FIELD NO CAMPING, and, em, it's surprisingly unpacked, whereas there are hordes and hordes and hordes of people downby, can see them in the distance, the Pyramid Stage and the Other Stage. And this Sacred Field seems to be filled by people sitting around drinking cans of lager and smoking dope, just like down there, in fact, and there's all sorts of bits of crap and quite a lot of litter but not huge amounts over the floor, empty, empty, erm, what are they called? Cup things, beer cups, with the Glastonbury Festival logo on them. Em, so on the one hand you look down at the, at the earth, the Sacred Field, and it just looks like any other old field with a bunch of people in it, full of rubbish and dump. But then you look up and you see it in the context of, well, you know, all its tents, its flags and poles, there's a big wicker man, more like an angel, staring up to the sky, which might be pretty strange, since I seem to remember the wicker man in the film being quite a paganistically evil thing. Well, this one looks, or is supposed to look, more positive, though the face is ugly. In front of that is the stone circle of maybe twenty quite big – eight-foot, ten-foot, fifteen-foot – stones, with a little dolmen or two in the middle, and some other bits as well, one or two other stones round and about the sides. Uh, that's quite impressive, I don't know when that was done, I'll have to find out, fairly recently anyway, in the last few years, but even there's the idea of sort of reclamation or reinvention of, er, ancient, ancient culture, and the significant thing is its rootedness to the land, it's on a terrific spot, you look down over and a bit along the valley and of course you look down over the valley of what is at this time of year the festival as well.

And when you do mill round and lift your eyes, you do, you see the landscape, you see the Vale of Avalon, and the fields and the trees and the writing of the hedges. At one edge of the site you see a big white cross, erected by one of Eavis's neighbours a few years ago, a dedicated Christian, who sees the festival as a kind of pagan or satanic thing. So at one side there's this big white cross and at the other side of the site, the valley, there's a stone circle, a fake henge, erected by some of the people at the festival a few years ago. So you know you've got Xtianity at one end and you've got paganism at the other, they're competing narratives, discourses underlining it all. (Very dialectic – is the synthesis convincing, though, the festival itself? I did see the Jesus Army tent earlier, near the main drag for easy pickings.) And the thing is, they're both invented, plonked in the middle of fields pretending to be ancient, reaching newly into otherworldly traditions. New cross and new stone circle, ancient religion and then an even older one, grabbing history, the old stories, fighting over them with monuments.

The Glastonbury festivals of Rutland Boughton

Voices: In the Land of Youth
There are pleasant places,
Green joyful woods and fields . . .
(Princess Etain follows in a trancèd ecstasy.)
 Libretto from *The Immortal Hour: A Music-Drama*, 1914

In the early twentieth century a previous Glastonbury festival was organised, a music and theatre event based on local legend and on mystery plays. There was widespread interest at the time in the regional mystery plays and local theatrical groups, such as Nugent Monck's work that led to the Maddermarket Theatre in Norwich, which is still in existence today. These were often supported by significant figures in the arts – supporters and visitors ranging from George Bernard Shaw to Thomas Hardy came to the Glastonbury festival, which ran from 1914 through to 1926 (with an interruption for the First World War). This was an ambitious effort to produce a kind of English Bayreuth, with organiser, energiser and composer Rutland Boughton modelling himself on the achievements of Richard Wagner in provincial Germany in the nineteenth century. Wagner encapsulated in music the German Romantic movement, employing German myth and legend in the construction of a new art, the Music Drama. In his later years he settled in the town of Bayreuth where festivals were held featuring his work in a dedicated *Festspielhaus* (festival theatre), especially the four-evening cycle *The Ring of the Nibelung*. Forty years later, Rutland Boughton elected Glastonbury for his project to produce a cycle of music dramas centred on a national, in this case

Arthurian, legend. Boughton was at least sensitive to the resonance of the place, the Avalonian and Arthurian aspects of Glastonbury. Geoffrey Ashe writes rather waspishly of Boughton:

> At Glastonbury he did a surprising amount with a piano and no orchestra, in a poorly appointed hall. But he was inadequate simply as an artist. His Arthurian music-dramas are dead . . . One of his more disruptive qualities was a left-wing outlook which could take curiously graceless forms (he once refused to conduct at a performance of *The Immortal Hour* because King George V was there). The Arthur cycle, in his hands, kept its Tennysonian panoply yet ended with a peasants' revolt and a red dawn in the east.

It seems that Boughton's upper middle-class bohemianism could unite classes in terms of his alienating them, as Richard Hanlon and Mike Waite note:

> The demise of the Glastonbury series can partly be blamed on such negative reactions as that of one of his chief financial backers who told Boughton bluntly that 'we are not going to have any Communism here' [at Glastonbury]. . . Boughton himself has been remembered by some of the real workers who did have contact with the Workers' Theatre Movement at this time as being 'very aristacratickle' and as being 'up to his neck in money and down to his ass in long hair'.

There are echoes here of class antagonism towards indulgent hippies sixty years later, perhaps. In 1914 the Guild of Glastonbury and Street Festival Players was founded, with the aim of establishing a festival centre in the town, with two main strands of activity. The first was to be an on-going programme of local performances organised by Alice Buckton, a women's activist, new educationalist, writer and dramatist – and, of course, pantheistic spiritual being – from her recently acquired home at the Chalice Well. Buckton wrote that these local plays were 'planned on the lines of the old religious Folk and Mystery Plays, with the aim of celebrating and making beautiful in various ways the Greater Festivals of the year, from Carol Singing to the Festival of the Mid-summer Bon-fire'. Second, there was to be an outdoor annual summer festival of music and drama, organised by composer Boughton.

The impulse towards a seasonal ritual of the celebration of nature is one we'll find again 57 years later, with the next version of a Glastonbury festival, the first held to mark the summer solstice in 1971, of course. Boughton himself had in earlier years sought to connect gathering, music and a kind of nature worship. His ideas for a 1912 'opera for a holiday . . . to be produced in Surrey woods' were reported in the *Daily Mirror* as following:

> Really we are starting a new sort of summer school for grown-ups . . . In a way the work has grown from its surroundings in this lovely country, and the spirit of the free open world is its theme . . . There will be two acts . . . and we have specially chosen the night of August 27th for playing the first act because it is full moon then. A night literally elapses between the acts, Act II being played after breakfast on August 28th. Another novel point about the opera is that each scene will take place in a different part of the woods . . . Performers will be expected to provide their own costumes, which will be of the simplest kind, mostly green in colour.

Boughton's first Glastonbury summer event, a Festival of Music Drama and Mystic Drama, opened the day after the outbreak of World War One, at 8 p.m. on August 5 1914. The company couldn't get hold of an orchestra, so the planned extravagant out-doors performance was reconfigured to the accompaniment of solo grand piano in the Assembly Rooms, down a passage off the High Street. 'In every way the building was unsuitable,' writes Boughton's biographer, Michael Hurd, for performers and audience alike – cramped, functional, uncomfortable, inaccessible. '[Yet] it was here that Boughton, year after year, held his "Festivals of Music and Music Drama".' That first festival saw the premiere of what would remain Boughton's best-known work, *The Immortal Hour*, described by Hurd as 'a very English type of opera'. For Boughton and his supporters, this was to be the beginnings of a national opera.

And it was *in Glastonbury*, which was identified by all interested in Boughton's pro-ject as key to the event. And Boughton's interest was in folksong and legend – King Arthur and Englishness (war had just been declared, after all). Conductor Thomas Beecham wrote, 'I am most interested in your forthcoming production of *Arthur* at Glastonbury, of course an ideal background for the work.' Sixty or seventy years later, at Michael Eavis's Glastonbury festival, classical music would be introduced in a cool blue marquee in a quiet field of the site. The 1986 Classical Stage, organised by John Williams, saw members of Musicians Against Nuclear Arms playing chamber and solo music. In the mid-1990s Eavis returned full circle to Boughton: an alternative Glastonbury festival (yes: alternative to the alternative one) was put on within the grounds of Glastonbury Abbey, an annual classical event for a mostly different English summer festival audience.

While George Bernard Shaw wrote to Boughton: 'do not introduce Glastonbury to Moscow', the development of political pageants during the 1920s and 1930s dramatised the battle over competing versions of English history, of Englishness itself, in a carnival-style ritual celebration. Organised left-wing groups took their own approach, or, rather, adopted for their own political position a tradition of pageantry which had been popularised as a means of celebrating empire and royalty in the early years of the twentieth century. Interestingly, bearing in mind the number of times already we've seen that the Christian church has enclosed or reconfigured older pagan dates, sites and practices, May Day itself became a focus of much socialist and Communist agitation in Britain during the 1920s and especially the 1930s. (Boughton composed a workers' ballet in 1926, the year of the General Strike, called *May Day*, intended for performance at workers' rallies in Hyde Park. It never was.) With pageant there was a practice aimed at combining aspects of political march and demonstration, celebrating local identity as well as the history of class struggle. One Communist organiser of a 20,000-strong pageant that marched through Hyde Park in London in September 1936 reported the event and its rationale as follows:

The Communist Party is learning to speak to the English workers in a language they understand. With new and varied methods of propaganda, based upon the knowledge of history and experience of the English workers . . . [Communism] is revealing itself as the legitimate heir of a generation of great English fighters for freedom and progress. It is preparing and will lead the people forward to a free and merrie England.

The rhetorical touch at the end is perhaps an unusually rustical – definitely not dialectical – one for the baldly stated aim of propaganda, but it worked: 810 people joined the Party at Hyde Park. According to drama historian Mick Wallis:

Historical pageants enacting a celebratory historical narrative offered themselves as one part of that affirmatory culture. Their scale allowed the Party to suggest that it was indeed mobilising the masses, demonstrating Communist muscle at the same time as inviting the participation of non-Communists. They could show the Party as a site of celebration, tradition and community. They were an opportunity to popularise the Party's claim that 'Communism is English', the natural heartbeat of the common people, the proper outcome of their long struggle.

By moving between rural and urban, Arthurian performance in Glastonbury or London, it is possible to see here how cultural events in Glastonbury crystallise actions and debates in wider society, how festival makes its own positive contribution to contemporary political debate, even struggle. My point is partly to address accusations of events like Glastonbury being stuck in some kind of deep countryside backwater or time warp.

Back in Glastonbury, the wealthy Clark family of Quakers from nearby Street, owners of the famous shoe-making factory there, became Rutland Boughton's patrons, and paid him an allowance to live in Glastonbury year-round to ensure the annual festival's longevity and success. Not all Glastonians were enthusiastic though, as a satirical sketch written by George Bernard Shaw and performed at the 1916 festival shows. Shaw mocks both local proprieties and Boughton's reputation as scandalous bohemian, poverty-stricken artist and womaniser. An actor in the audience, playing the role of John Bostock, 'man of Glastonbury', heckles the performance and argues with Boughton.

JOHN BOSTOCK. If you will excuse me saying so, Mr Boughton, you are now talking through your hat.

RUTLAND BOUGHTON. I haven't a hat. Has any man in Glastonbury ever seen me with a hat? I can't even afford a haircut. I spend all my money on music for the people of Glastonbury. And now because Bostock wants his *Maritanas and his Bohemian Girls*—

MR B. I protest. I cannot allow this. I never wanted a Bohemian Girl. I am a respectable married man. I call upon you, Mr Austin, to protect me from Mr Boughton's scandalous insinuations.

MR AUSTIN. I must request you, Mr Boughton, to keep order—

R.B. I won't.

MR A. I shall appeal to the Mayor.

R.B. Not even the Mayor of Glastonbury shall muzzle me.

MR A. I shall call the police.

R.B. I defy the police. No power in heaven or earth shall prevail against Rutland Boughton.

MRS BOUGHTON. Rutland, you are making a fool of yourself. Sit down.

R.B. Yes dear. (Collapses, abjectly.)

Following a break while Boughton did military service during the war, the Festival started again in 1919. There was still local suspicion, sometimes opposition, as Boughton acknowledged: 'A proper festival spirit in any place cannot be enjoyed when the people are divided into "Fors" and "Againsts" as they were at Glastonbury'. Hurd describes what the town was feeling then:

> A quiet, respectable town which had always been thoroughly British and kept its misdemeanours safely behind locked doors and drawn curtains, suddenly found itself exposed four times a year to a horde of young theatricals who made it a point of honour, whatever their inclinations, to appear modern and uninhibited. Rumour had it that they were given to running to the top of the Glastonbury Tor in order to greet the dawn in a state of pagan undress. Then there was Shaw wandering around all the time, doubtless inciting everyone to socialism and free love.

In a letter, Shaw wrote a spoof *Who's Who* entry for Boughton, which gives a further indication of the cluster of lifestyle and mystical facets around Boughton and his chosen festival home: 'Recreation: being seduced by his pupils; Clubs: The Taproom at The George, Glastonbury. Address: Acacia Villa, Glastonbury; Telephone: 1 Glastonbury. Telegraphic address: Arimathea, Glastonbury.'

Spiritualist writer Dion Fortune was struck by the way in which the Assembly Rooms in Glastonbury were creatively transformed for Boughton's productions, even down to the detail of the 'painted paper imitating stained-glass in the gaunt windows of the little hall'. That's a resonant image, connoting spiritual transformation through childlike simplicity, an act of obscuring (of veiling) that permits vision, the shift from the mundane to the eternal – *temporarily*. The same Assembly Rooms in Glastonbury today are a self-organised alternative centre for arts and meetings, and as a symbolic space for alternative culture they recur from Boughton's time onwards. *Torc*, one of the first alternative magazines produced by the late 1960s and early 1970s incomers to the town, describes the events following the summer solstice celebration in 1973. Some of those celebrants would be attracted by the recent reputation of the 1970 and 1971 festivals held nearby at Worthy Farm, Pilton. The recent triple album featuring music from the 1971 Glastonbury Fayre would contribute to the town's reputation, too. As *Torc* put it:

> With no other facilities available in the town over the solstice, a group of visitors decided
> to occupy the disused Assembly Rooms off the High Street, the venue of the Glastonbury
> Festival of Music-Drama in the 1920s. In those bygone days the actors on the stage wore
> curious freaky outfits, the men even having long wigs and headbands. Little did they
> now what spells they were invoking in those years . . . The Avalon Squat, as it came to be
> known, naturally caused quite a stir . . . The internal organisation was spontaneous and
> collective. Food seemed to arrive from nowhere and was supplied to all. In anticipation
> of trouble from angry locals – there were one or two incidents – a defence party was
> conscripted and even a medical room set aside to deal with any injuries.

Alister Sieghart was involved in the Avalon Squat, and remembers it fondly: 'I don't think anyone was aware of Rutland Boughton's tradition. For us it was a music space, lots of guitars and dope-smoking, and a jam-packed crash-pad, where each night, if you got there too late, there'd no space left anywhere on the floor. It was that kind of time when you'd look along the River Brue and see a hippie fresh from India, all ethnic clothing and covered in ash, sitting at the river's edge, meditating. It was all very innocent, really, and I still see that innocence in some of those sitting round the Tor today, in spite of what everyone says.'

 A few years after the Avalon Squat, renovation work on the Assembly Rooms was begun, and in 1987 the Friends of the Assembly Rooms took it over. Julian Lindars, Secretary of the Friends, paid tribute to the unique historic place of the Assembly Rooms in 1990: 'The Assembly Rooms has for a long time had a part to play in [the] unfolding of Glastonbury's spiritual tradition – from the time of Dion Fortune, and Rutland Boughton whose Arthurian opera *The Immortal Hour* was first performed here – right through to the present day gatherings and celebrations of the Celtic festivals that we hold regularly.' August 1998, for instance, was marked by an event to celebrate Lammas (August) and the power of the Goddess, attended by several hundred participants. This combination of pagan earth worship and Harvest Festival (and it is worth noting that Harvest Festival is itself an invented West Country tradition, thought up in 1843 by a Cornish vicar) saw singing, drumming, praying to the ancestors, a first-fruits feast, a procession, and a pagan, feminised Eucharist: according to *Free State*, 'all the participants shaped a small Goddess out of fresh dough, telling their stories as they did so. These were baked . . . and later shared around a blazing Lammas bonfire.' The Assembly Rooms illustrate that, as each group comes to Glastonbury, it embraces the local, it embraces and renews legend and landscape. (And all this time through the century, the Eavis family is farming down the road at Pilton.)

In *The Land Without Music*, Andrew Blake ties together a number of strands which are emerging, and which I will return to through the book:

> Alternative history is part of the agenda here . . . [The] folk-inflected rock festivals of the 1970s and after were proposing a new Albion, a landscape with music which looks 'back' to an imagined pagan Celtic past, to the fire festivals and the celebration of the seasons and to the use of identified and historicised sacred sites, such as Glastonbury [and Stonehenge]. They are thus, like the Glastonbury festivals run by Rutland Boughton . . . involved in a historic imaginary which stretches back through the long history of Arthurian literature and music . . . to propose an imagined rural, mystical and at least semi-pagan Britain . . . The historic agenda is that, like [composers Arnold] Bax and Boughton, they are working with an anti-Anglo-Saxon past; so this may be English in its desire for a certain landscape, but it is against English Establishment history, with its celebration of Empire and Little Englishness.

It should be noted that delving into an imagined rural past for another version of Englishness is not inherently radical: Edward Windsor choosing to call himself the Earl of *Wessex* following his royal wedding in 1999, for instance, hardly shook the Establishment. Similarly, the restructuring of the English–Welsh Borders police force in 1967 led to the founding of the West *Mercia* Constabulary, a reference back to a kingdom from the first millennium, which evoked the response from other police: 'West Mercia – where the fuck is that?' Yet for political pop singer Tom Robinson, too, the Glastonbury festival (of Michael Eavis this time) offers 'an alternative vision of Middle England, not Tony Blair's version, not John Major's, but another, one that recognises dope-smoking, for instance. In the 1980s the continuing growing success of Glastonbury was one of the things working against the tide of jingoistic surface culture. (We saw the dominance of that surface culture again during something like the Diana death madness, when *apparently* there was no dissent in the entire country.) Glastonbury gave voice to what was going on under the surface. And Michael Eavis wandering through it all at festival time – he is like the headmaster. No, he's the Matthew Arnold of the Glastonbury experience.'

Time-line of festival culture

Note: There is a certain randomness to this, both in terms of where it starts and what it includes, and a certain bias in its focus around popular music and left politics, either traditionally organised or lifestyle. Why not add your own entries, too? (Ok, and corrections . . .)

THE FIFTIES

1951

August 26–September 1. Edinburgh. Launch of the first Edinburgh People's Festival, organised by Communists, activists, nationalists and cultural workers in Scotland to balance the élite, frequently non-Scottish Edinburgh International Festival (founded in 1946), and to offer a competing voice to the 1951 Festival of Britain. Theatre, folk music, lectures, a conference 'Towards a People's Culture', a festival club.

1952

August 17–September 7. Edinburgh People's Festival. What we would now recognise as a socialist version of the Fringe, running over three weeks. Because key organisers were Communists and other left activists, the Scottish TUC proscribe it and the Scottish Labour Party bans its members from involvement with it. (Let's hear it for solidarity.) The event, a great success in 1952, fizzles out over next two years, but it's still possible to hear the political echos of the People's Festival in the annual Fringe today.

1954

Rhode Island, USA. First Newport Jazz and Folk Festival.

Sidmouth, Devon. Early, perhaps first, folk music festival, as a part of the Second English Folk Revival, a movement trying to construct a new national tradition of 'radical Englishness'. The radical folk magazine *Sing* launches this year too. Sidmouth Folk Festival still going strong today.

1956

First Beaulieu Jazz Festival, organised by the Southampton Friday Night Traditional Club at Lord Montagu's Palace House. Headlined by the Avon City Jazz Band. Attendance about 600 people, including some who camp the night before in the woods.

Butlins Holiday Camp, Clacton-on-Sea, Essex. Jazz Festival Weekend. Has 'many of the ingredients of a proper festival', according to early festival writer Jeremy Sandford. Ted Heath, Johnny Dankworth, Shirley Bassey, USAF Rock 'n' Roll Group. £5 for a weekend ticket. 2000 people catered for, 800 turn up.

1957

Beaulieu Jazz Festival, with advertising playing on the aristocratic connection (rather downplaying any democratic claims jazz frequently expressed for itself): 'a combination of blue blood and the blues'.

1958

April 4–7. First Campaign for Nuclear Disarmament protest march from London to Aldermaston, Berkshire (the Aldermaston Weapons

Research Establishment) raises the profile of both the issue of peace and the new organisation itself, founded in February 1958. The 53-mile march over four days at Easter means a community of protesters forms, 10,000 strong.

Beaulieu Jazz Festival, the first two-day event, with a large PA and tents for overnight campers. With its combination of outdoors pop music, youth audience and authorised camping, this event is often considered the first proper pop festival in Britain. Note the conjunction with the formation of CND – as George Melly did at the time: 'Beaulieu, like Aldermaston, has become one of the secular festivals of the atheist's year.' Attendance: 4000 people.

Monterey, USA. First Monterey Jazz Festival. Becomes established over the next decade as one of the West Coast's premier jazz festival events.

September. 'Notting Hill race riots', London. 58 arrested in gang fights. A fortnight later 9 white youths are imprisoned for 4 years for 'nigger-hunting'.

1959

January. Notting Hill, London. *West Indies Gazette* organises a Caribbean Carnival.

Easter. CND (now annual) march, now from Aldermaston to London. 3000 do the 50 miles over several days, and are joined for the last part in London, from the Albert Hall to Trafalgar Square, by 12,000 others in a national demonstration on Easter

Monday. All the paraphernalia of a moving festival described in *The CND Story*: . . . 'jazz bands and guitars, songs and slogans, banners, placards and pamphlets . . . luggage vans, banner wagons, litter collectors and Elsan toilet teams; stewards, dispatch riders, first aid teams.'

Beaulieu Jazz Festival. Press reports begin to emphasise what *Melody Maker* called the 'weirdies' element of the audience, as antagonistic youth lifestyles increasingly feature in the burgeoning festival culture.

Paddington Town Hall, London. Mardi Gras, an early carnival-style celebration of West Indian music and dance in Britain.

THE SIXTIES

1960

Easter. Annual CND march over four days from Aldermaston to London. 450 local CND groups nationwide.

Summer. Beaulieu Jazz Festival, televised by BBC, featured riots between trad jazz fans attracted by the likes of Acker Bilk and modernists watching Tubby Hayes and Ronnie Scott. 'The Battle of Beaulieu' it becomes known as. The owner, Lord Montagu, says no more festivals. 10,000 people.

1961

Easter. Annual CND march from Aldermaston to London. 32,000 marchers met by 100,000 supporters in Trafalgar Square on April 3. Up to 900 local CND groups nationwide. Civil disobedience for peace spreads: 826 arrests at Whitehall in May; 1314 arrests in Trafalgar Square, 351 at Holy Loch, in September; 860 arrests in national anti-bomb sit-downs in December.

August. Final Beaulieu Jazz Festival – Montagu changes his mind. Extra police patrol Beaulieu village. Barbed wire and dogs. Further security is supplied by the Eastleigh Boys Boxing Club, hence violence, again between tradders and modernists heckling each other's favourite performers.

August. Richmond, Surrey. First National Jazz Festival, organised by Harold Pendleton of the National Jazz Federation. Pendleton had helped organise some of the Beaulieu Festivals, and also ran the Marquee Club in Soho, London, the birth-place of a number of subsequently famous groups including the Who and the Yardbirds. Trad jazz on the site of the annual Richmond Horse Show.

Easter 1959: 12,000 CND marchers congregate in Trafalgar Square.

1962

Easter. Annual CND march from Aldermaston to London. According to reports in CND's newspaper *Sanity*, this march was 'the biggest of them all . . . 15,000 marchers had to be housed under canvas in Reading', while 150,000 (a *Peace News* estimate) were at the final rally in Hyde Park. Addressed by Hiroshima survivors.

1963

January. Trad jazz all-nighter, from 10 p.m. on Friday until 7 a.m. Saturday morning, at Alexandra Palace, London. George Melly and Diz Disley introduce Acker Bilk, Kenny Ball, Ken Colyer, and other leading British trad bands.

Easter. Annual CND march from Aldermaston to London, which includes a sensational leaflet distributed on Good Friday by a mysterious group called 'Spies for Peace', distributing officially secret information about NATO exercises and government nuclear bunkers.

July 26. Newport Folk Festival, Rhode Island. Bob Dylan, the new folk sensation.

July. Richmond Jazz Festival includes the Rolling Stones on the bill for the first time.

1964

March 29. Clacton-on-Sea, Essex. 97 teenagers arrested in clashes between Mods and Rockers.

Easter. One-day CND march in London. Some loss of initial energy, the optimism engendered by the signing of the Partial Test Ban Treaty in the summer of 1963 and the election of Harold Wilson's Labour government in 1964 – as well as the rise of the Vietnam War as a campaign issue for activists

from 1965 – all contribute to an attenuation of the campaign.

May. First pirate radion stations broadcast from offshore waters. Radio Caroline and Radio Atlanta.

August. Richmond. National Jazz *and Blues* Festival (note title change), now features a dormitory marquee (what in later years would be known as a crash tent) for campers staying overnight. 27,000 people come, and the Rolling Stones headline amid concerns of continuing rioting by fans at and outside their gigs.

1965

April 19. Trafalgar Square rally at end of Aldermaston CND march witnesses 150,000 people, including many bearing anti-Vietnam War banners.

June 11. Albert Hall, London. *Poets of the World / Poets of Our Time* reading of Beat poets, led by Allen Ginsberg. Flowers given to the audience (courtesy of the leftovers from the flower market at Covent Garden the night before) by face-painted women, dope smoke, anti-Vietnam statements, folk music at the end. 7000 people, who would become London's underground constituency, attend. Tom McGrath reviewed it in *Peace News*: 'Even if the poetry reading had turned out to be a giant bore, the audience itself would have been an event.'

The BBC turns off the cameras as jazz fans riot at the Beaulieu Jazz Festival, 1960.

The second National Jazz Festival, held in the grounds of the Royal Athletic Association, Richmond, Surrey, July 1962.

July 26–27. Newport Folk Festival, Rhode Island. Dylan plays electric, and is booed by shocked sections of the audience.

August 8. Richmond, for the last time, National Jazz and Blues Festival. Jazz, but also the Rolling Stones, Yardbirds, Manfred Mann. As the official handout explains: 'Something unheard of is happening at Richmond . . . for the first time . . . the pure jazz-men are outnumbered by beat and rhythm-and-blues groups who are no stranger to the hit parade.' 33,000 attend.

1966

January 21–23. San Francisco. The Trips Festival at the Longshoremen's Hall. Following the first Acid Tests by Ken Kesey and the Merry Pranksters, a major LSD experience is thrown by the American counterculture. According to Tom Wolfe in *The Electric Kool-Aid Acid Test* the Trips Festival 'brought the whole thing full out in the open. "Mixed media" entertainment – this came straight out of the Acid Tests' combination of light and movie projections, strobes, tapes, rock 'n' roll, black light.'

August 1. Windsor, Berkshire. National Jazz and Blues Festival, which has moved from Richmond, where it was no longer welcome. (Councillors and local residents in Windsor try unsuccessfully to have it banned.) The Who incite audience participation in their destructive mode, their riot routine. Eric Clapton, Spencer Davis, the Small Faces. Camping on Windsor racecourse, and police act on the 'immorality' of young people of both sexes being allowed to sleep together in the overnight marquee.

September. London. First Notting Hill Carnival. 'A revival of the Notting Hill Annual Fayre that had been traditionally held in the area until it was stopped at the turn of the present century.' Originates from organisers of an alternative neighbourhood community centre called the London Free School, and embraces local blacks and whites, and the alternative types living in the area. Abner Cohen: 'The general cultural form that the carnival was to take was essentially English . . . There was no suggestion that it would imitate a West Indian or any other foreign form of carnival.'

October 15. *International Times* **launch, Roundhouse, London.** Soft Machine, Pink Floyd, slide shows and psychedelia Brit-style. '*International Times* First All-Night Rave.' 'Bring Your Own Poison,' says the surprisingly unpsychedelic publicity. Sugar cubes handed out on entry. Mick Farren: 'According to legend one in twenty was dosed with acid. Mine

wasn't . . . Paul McCartney came by in an Arab suit. . . . Pink Floyd honked and howled and tweeted. They were very loud with no musical form.'

December. London. Opening of UFO club on Tottenham Court Road, with resident band Pink Floyd. Musical home of the London underground, described by one regular: 'It was a club in the sense that most people knew each other, met there to . . . hatch out issues of *IT*, plans for Arts Labs . . . and various schemes for turning the Thames yellow and removing all the fences in Notting Hill. The activity and energy was thicker than the incense . . .' Early audiences number 150, by July it is ten times that.

1967

January 14. The First Human Be-In, Golden Gate Park, San Francisco, with the Grateful Dead, and Jefferson Airplane. Advertised as a Gathering of the Tribe, and as 'The First American Melah, A Baptism'. Hell's Angels do the security, free food ('It's free because it's yours,' said free commune group the Diggers), free LSD, all is peace and love. (On the strength of the Angels' behaviour, the Grateful Dead's manager will recommend them, two years later, to organise the Rolling Stones' free concert at Altamont.) 'The first rock festival to capture the attention of the media,' says Harry Shapiro. 40,000 people.

March 13. London School of Economics and Political Science (LSE). First British student occupation, lasting six days and involving over 2000 students.

April 29. Alexandra Palace, London. 14-Hour Technicolour Dream. One person remembers: 'It hit you as soon as you walked into the place – lights and films all over the walls and blitzing volume from two stages with two bands playing simultaneously . . . inside this huge time machine were 5000 stoned, tripping, mad, friendly, festive hippies . . .'

The Summer of Love

June 5. Mount Tamalpais, California, near the redwood forests. The Fantasy Faire and Magic Mountain Music Festival. The first major medieval-style event, featuring the non-medieval music of the Doors, Country Joe, the Byrds, Jefferson Airplane, Smokey Robinson, Dionne Warwick. Festival-goers bussed to the site as nearest parking (remember this next time you're grumbling about Glastonbury) is 25 miles away. Profits to go to a local black neighbourhood. Tickets $2. 15,000 people.

June 16–18. Monterey International Pop Festival, California. Country Joe, Jefferson Airplane, Otis

Redding (not long before his death), Jimi Hendrix, the Who, the Grateful Dead, Ravi Shankar, Buffalo Springfield (without Neil Young). Pete Townshend destroys his guitar, Hendrix sets his alight; the Mamas and the Papas close with 'California Dreaming'. D.A. Pennebaker's film of the event, *Monterey Pop*. Until Woodstock two years later this is the festival by which others are judged, partly because many of the musicians were involved in organising it, financing it.

July 15–29. London. International Congress of Dialectics of Liberation is held at the Roundhouse. The counterculture's intellectual wing hears Herbert Marcuse, R.D. Laing, Stokely Carmichael and Ernest Mandel at 'a unique gathering to demystify human violence in all its forms'.

Windsor. NJF National Jazz and Blues Festival, again at Windsor racecourse. Jeremy Sandford describes how the old trad festival has been reinvented by the hippies: 'This was the year of flower power. Hippies completely replaced the familiar beatniks of yesteryear. Beads and bells ousted duffle coats and cider jugs.' Donovan, the Nice, Ten Years After, the Small Faces, while Pink Floyd don't get it together.

August 26–28. Festival of the Flower Children, Woburn Abbey. Marmalade, the Bee Gees, firework displays every night. Free flowers and sparklers.

September. London. Second Notting Hill 'street carnival and the international song and dance festival', a multicultural event, including local black and white residents, and about 2000 hippies. Highlighting the social context and impetus of the event, a performance called *England This England* was described by local *Kensington News* as a 'musical parody of the housing problem'.

October. UFO club closes. Middle Earth, a smaller club for freaks, runs for just over a year.

1968

March 17. The Battle of Grosvenor Square, London. Students and revolutionaries march through London and protest outside the American Embassy against the Vietnam War. Nigel Fountain remembers the drama: 'It was the antithesis of the CND marches. . . [The] issue wasn't peace, it was war: victorious war for Vietnam's National Liberation Front, and class war on the bourgeoisie.'

May, Paris. Following student activism over the past few years in the US, across Europe, and in Japan, connected with anti-Vietnam War protest, spontaneous rioting breaks out around the Sorbonne. A general strike across the entire country, as workers and students agitate in solidarity with each other.

June. Appleby Horse Fair, threatened with closure, is saved by gypsy activists.

August 31. The 'GREAT South Coast Bank holiday POP FESTIVITY'. First Isle of Wight Festival, at Godshill, founded to raise money for a municipal swimming pool for residents. John Peel introduces Tyrannosaurus Rex, the Move, Fairport Convention, and, to give it transatlantic kudos, Jefferson Airplane (who, a few days later, play Parliament Hill Fields). Attendance 10,000.

September. London. Notting Hill 'Carnival of the Poor'. With cunning ingenuity, the early autumn torrential rain is passed off as a 'tropical downpour' in the sympathetic local press.

1969

June. Hyde Park, London. Free concert to launch Blind Faith, a, uh, supergroup featuring Eric Clapton and other '60s luminaries. 100,000 people. Group so super they disband a few months later.

June 25. Bath Blues Festival. First outdoors gig by Led Zeppelin, fourth on the bill behind Fleetwood Mac, John Mayall and Ten Years After. The stage manager says, 'There was so much noise that I thought we had a riot going on. I rushed out of the back stage area to find it was nothing more sinister than the climax of Zeppelin's set.' 30,000 people.

July 3–6. Newport Jazz Festival, Rhode Island. The 16th annual festival, now with heavy rock for the first time. Jethro Tull, John Mayall, Ten Years After, and, on the final night, in spite of pleas from the authorities that they shouldn't play 'in the interests of public safety', Led Zeppelin – as well as more acceptable Newport fare of James Brown and BB King. 80,000 attend.

Donovan performs in the summer of love in front of 20,000 at the National Jazz and Blues Festival, Windsor.

The Great South Coast Bankholiday Pop Festivity

to be held at
Hell Field, Ford Farm, Nr. Godshill
ISLE OF WIGHT

August 31st, 1968 6 p.m. to 10 a.m.
All night

The greatest pop festival ever held in this country

The complete festival will be compered by JOHN PEEL
and opened by JIMMY SAVILLE

Guest Artist from the U.S.A.
The Jefferson Airplane Coming over from America especially for this festival to make their first live appearance in this country

Topping the bill from Gt. Britain
The Crazy World of Arthur Brown

ALSO
The Move   **Plastic Penny**   **Pretty Things**   **Tyrannosaurus Rex**
                              The Mirage   **Orange Bicycle**
Aynsley Dunbar Retaliation   Fairport Convention   Helcyon Order
Blonde on Blonde   The Smile   The Cherokees

Light Show   An incredible multi-screen light show by Students from the R.C.A.
                                                   Refreshment Tents
Free Film Shows   Beer Tents

How to get there
Trains leave Waterloo Station at 6 minutes to every hour for Portsmouth Harbour. By road the A3 runs from London to Portsmouth. Ferries from Portsmouth to Ryde take half an hour and run every half hour. Special Festival buses or coaches will meet all ferries to take passengers to Hell Field

Tickets available from
London Clayman Agency Ltd. Tel. 01 247 5531. 7 8 Aldgate High St. EC3. 154 Bishopsgate, EC2
(opposite Liverpool St. Station)   65 Fenchurch St., E.C.3 (opp. Fenchurch St. Station)
Derek's Records, 8 Aldgate High Street. EC3   Apple Ltd., 94 Baker Street, W1
Isle of Wight Teagues, Newport and Ryde   Youngs, Cowes, Sandown and Shanklin
John Menzies, Ventnor   Photo-Wight. Freshwater
                              Music Box. 23 The Triangle
Bournemouth Minns, 5 7 Gervis Place   Henry's Record Shop, 116 St. Mary's St
Southampton Minns, 158 Above Bar   Planet House. Church Rd., Hove
Brighton 50 West Street and 12 Pavilion Buildings   Bredons Bookshop, 3 Bartholomews
         Television Ltd., 53 North Street   Hove Travel Agency, 123 Fawcett Road, Fratton
Portsmouth & Southsea Portsmouth Radio & Record Centre.
              Minns, 67 Osborne Road
Poole Scetchfields Ltd., 21 High Street   Westbourne Minns, 68 Poole Road
Winchester Whitwams, 70 High Street   Chichester Bagatel Boutique, Crane St
              Worthing Music Shop, 22 New Broadway

Tickets 25s. (or 30s. to include Portsmouth Ryde return ferry fares)

July 5. Hyde Park, London. A free festival thrown by the Rolling Stones (following the success of Blind Faith there last month). Film released, *The Stones in the Park*. 2000 people camp the night before, 250,000 people attend on the day. Jagger reads Shelley poem in memory of Brian Jones, former Stones guitarist who had died two days ago. A sign of eco-consciousness the Glastonbury Rubbish Police would be proud of: at the end, a free Stones record is given in exchange for each full bag of rubbish.

August 15–17. Woodstock Music and Art Fair, New York State. Advertised as 'Three days of peace and music' on 600 acres of dairy farmland near the town of Bethel. A sign in the town says: 'Stop Max's

Hippie Music Festival. No 150,000 Hippies Here. Buy No Milk.' Hendrix, Joan Baez, Janis Joplin, Joe Cocker, Crosby, Stills and Nash, the Who, and 400,000 people (all of who seem to know that Bob Dylan is living a semi-reclusive life nearby). Also three deaths and two births. Halfway through, to avoid a catastrophe, someone says let it be free. Michael Wadleigh's film is influential in maintaining the idealism and actuality of festival culture internationally.

August 29–31. Second Isle of Wight Festival, Woodside Bay, near Ryde.
Bob Dylan, Bonzo Dog Doo-Dah Band, the Nice, the Moody Blues, Indo-Jazz Fusions, Julie Felix, Richie Havens. A state of the art 2000-watt PA system carries the music to Parkhurst prisoners and Quarry monastery monks on the island. Anything between 80,000 and 200,000 people attend (and only 22 drug arrests).

ABOVE LEFT
Wiggin' out to the Stones, Hyde Park, July 5 1969.

LEFT & BELOW
Crowds at the Isle of Wight, 1969.

September 30. Toronto Peace Festival, Canada.
John Lennon and Plastic Ono Band, including Eric Clapton and Yoko Ono, plus rock 'n' roll stars Little Richard, Chuck Berry, Gene Vincent.

December 6. Sears Point Raceway, Altamont, California.
A free festival with stage security courtesy of a Hell's Angels chapter, who kill one festival-goer, a young black man called Meredith Hunter, at the festival with his white girlfriend. Three other deaths: two in their sleeping bags by a hit and run driver, and one drowned in a canal on a bad trip. Originally planned as a free open-air show by the Rolling Stones, it extends into a whole day concert, including Jefferson Airplane, Santana, Crosby, Stills, Nash and Young. If Woodstock is frequently cited as the utopia of the 1960s, Altamont is its nightmare, at its end. Three days later Charles Manson is indicted for the August 1969 murders of Sharon Tate and others. The concert is captured on the film *Gimme Shelter*. 300,000 people.

THE SEVENTIES

1970

March 29. Paris. Evolution Festival at Exhibition Park. A commercial event, featuring Hawkwind, Edgar Broughton Band, Atomic Rooster, Third Ear Band, Kevin Ayers.

Easter. Victoria Park, London. Following the now very small annual Easter CND march, 'Festival for Life' is held for 20,000 people, to protest against war in a conscious development by CND of festival culture. Five stages show rock and jazz bands, poetry, also street theatre, stalls and side shows.

Whitsun. Plumpton, Sussex. NJF festival at the racecourse. Family, Deep Purple, Colosseum. 'There was a row with BIT, the Underground Information Agency, because the NJF wouldn't give them a tent,' writes Jeremy Sandford. 3–5000 people.

Hollywood, near Newcastle-under-Lyme, Staffordshire. A festival which widened out the range of entertainment significantly: rock groups, but also a circus and fun fair, film shows and clothes stalls. 30,000 people.

June 26–27. Shepton Mallet, Somerset. The second Bath Festival of Blues and Progressive Music. A transatlantic bill featuring Led Zeppelin, Johnny Winter, Frank Zappa and the Mothers of Invention, the Byrds (playing an acoustic set), Country Joe, and John Mayall with Peter Green. Jimmy Page dressed as a country yokel. The Pink Fairies play on the back of a lorry to the free festival that's formed outside. Somerset dairy farmers Michael Eavis and his girlfriend Jean – remember this the next time you're broke and want to get in to Glastonbury – sneak in through a hole in a fence, *without paying*. The 212-acre site is planned to cater for 50,000 festival-goers; in the event three times that number turn up, leading to 15-mile traffic jams round the site and overflow campsite.

July 3–5. Atlanta Festival, Georgia USA. Hendrix, Procol Harum, Johnny Winter, BB King, Jethro Tull. State governor attempts to have rock festivals banned following drug-related problems among 200,000 crowd.

July 18. Hyde Park, London. Another free concert by Pink Floyd, also Roy Harper, Edgar Broughton, and experimental jazzers Robert Wyatt and Lol Coxhill.

July 24. Worthing, Sussex. Phun City free festival organised by, among others, self-styled White Panther Mick Farren ('a one man tribe', according to Richard Neville) for underground paper *International Times*. Actually, it originates as a semi-commercial event, but the financial side falls apart before the weekend begins. Camping in the woods. 3000 people (or maybe 10,000, depends who you read / talk to). Publicity in *IT* says: 'Get your end away at Phun City.' The Pink Fairies play onstage in the nude, the MC5 fly over from Detroit. As Farren describes it in *Watch Out, Kids*: 'At night the whole site was bathed in lightshows, free food operations sprung up, the Angels stole beer wholesale and distributed it to the kids, dealers stopped selling dope and gave it away, collections were made to keep the generators going. The thing had become a model of the alternative society, it was nothing like our original concept, but it worked.'

August 14–16. Krumlin Festival, on the edge of the Yorkshire Moors. Catastrophically unseasonal weather in a fairly bleak landscape means there is serious risk of *death by exposure* (this is high summer) for festival-goers. Strong winds, hail, rain and sleet, temperatures in low 40s Fahrenheit. But 25,000 well-hard Yorkshire and Lancashire folk still turn up. Beer tents are requisitioned in the middle of the Saturday night to deal with the flood of exposure cases waiting for fresh ambulances. One of the two main organisers 'last seen walking over the moors in a daze' (according to the report by the Chair of Civil Aid). While other bands haggled and refused to play, Ginger Baker turns up on Sunday and offers to play for nothing, but there is no-one left. The local branch of Civil Aid's pivotal help in saving lives is rewarded with a bounced cheque for the soup kitchen from the organizers.

August 26–30. Third and final Isle of Wight Festival. Kris Kristofferson plays to a poor response, the Freek Press produces a free daily newsletter (as will later happen at Windsor) written by journos from leading underground press papers like *Oz* and *International Times*. The White Panthers and French youth agitate outside, where there is a better view and sound, on Desolation Hill. Hawkwind and the Pink Fairies play free off a lorry outside Canvas City, and eventually all the fences are pulled down. Rory Gallagher, Joni Mitchell, Gilberto Gil, Miles Davis, the Doors (a year before Jim Morrison's death), the Who. On the Sunday the festival is declared free, to see Hendrix (three weeks before his death), Joan Baez and Leonard Cohen. The film of the festival, *Message to Love*, is released 25 years later.

August 30. London. A small bomb explodes outside the home of the Commissioner of the

I didn't have, but he was very good about it and I paid off £100 a month from the milk cheque.' Al Stewart, Quintessence, Amazing Blondel, Sam Apple Pie, Steamhammer, Ian Anderson, Duster Bennet, Keith Christmas and local blues and folk bands play, while the show is compered by one Mad Mick.

The first big Glastonbury, 1971, complete with plastic-covered pyramid stage.

Metropolitan Police. The Angry Brigade takes an alternative route towards social change to that of 'peace and love' festival organisers, being Britain's often overlooked violent direct action campaigners. The counterculture turns to bombing.

September 19–20. Worthy Farm Festival, at Pilton near Glastonbury. A mini-rock festival, organised by Michael Eavis following attendance at the Bath Blues festival earlier in the summer. The *original* Glaston-bury Festival. Similar in idea to the East Anglian fairs that are about to get going, as Eavis says: 'The influence of those late '60s festivals started me off. I thought there might be a way of combining the traditional country fairs with the ideals of the pop festival culture.' £1 entrance fee including free milk. How many people turn up? Between 1000 and 2500. Jimi Hendrix's death the day before the festival casts a large shadow over the good vibes. The Kinks are booked to headline but pull out late on (Eavis thinks because '"Lola" was out and the Kinks were more mega than mini'); Marc Bolan and T. Rex top the bill instead, a month before the release of 'Ride A White Swan'. Eavis: 'I met Marc Bolan halfway down Muddy Lane. He didn't look too pleased going down the bumpy track in his big American car. He went on to play what I swear to this day was the best set I've ever seen at Worthy Farm. I owed him £500, which

1971

Easter. Alexandra Park, London. CND peace festival, with rock music, performance, stalls, etc – as well as a specially written *Passion* play by Edward Bond.

June 20–24. Glastonbury Fayre (or, says Andrew Kerr, F-A-I-R), free festival in response to the overt commercialism of 1970's Bath Blues Festival and final Isle of Wight, and inspired by the excitement of last September's little fair. Again, like the East Anglian fairs, a combination of medievalism and pop culture. Funded and organised by rich hippies like Arabella Churchill and Andrew Kerr, who have been reading the Bible about redistribution and decided to practise what it preached. Midnight curfew for amplified music, no alcohol on sale on site, all food vegetarian, free food from Communal Knead and Digger Action Movement. Pyramid stage built for the first time, out of KWIKSTAGE scaffolding and plastic sheeting, 'close to the Glastonbury Abbey/Stone-henge ley line and over the site of a blind spring'. Andrew Kerr: 'If the Festival has a specific intention it is to create an increase in the power of the Universe, a heightening of consciousness and a recognition of our place in the function of this our tired and molested planet.' An impressive bill for a free festival, indicating the amount of financial clout and organisation that has gone into the event: Pink Fairies, Hawkwind, Edgar Broughton Band, Fairport

Time-line of festival culture

95

Convention, David Bowie, Melanie, Joan Baez, Traffic, Quintesseence, Brinsley Schwarz, Family and Arthur Brown. A 1972 triple album of the show is released, including a side donated by the Grateful Dead, who are supposed to appear but don't. Following the example of Woodstock, a film called *Glastonbury Fayre* is made by David Puttman and Nic Roeg. Attendance 12,000. The legendary one.

June. NJF festival moves to Reading, Berkshire, at the invitation of Reading Council and Chamber of Commerce and Trade, to celebrate the 1000th anniversary of the town. Reading Festival becomes a more-or-less permanent feature of the festival calendar, as a more commercially rock-oriented event, one with considerably less alt.glamour than Glastonbury, but also one that can legitimately lay claim to having roots going back the best part of a decade further.

They turned up to chill and see the NME 'Giants of Tomorrow', but over a hundred fans were treated for exposure and a large marquee was torn down in high winds, Bardney, Lincolnshire, May 1972.

Madison Square Gardens, New York. Ex-Beatle George Harrison organises a benefit for the developing world with a range of pop stars, his Concert for Bangladesh, with accompanying record released on Apple.

August 28–29. Weeley, near Clacton-on-Sea in Essex. Clacton Round Table organises a charitable festival of rock music. But there are predictable clashes between Hell's Angels and other festival-goers, who take revenge by trashing Angels' chopper motorbikes. Mostly British acts: T. Rex, King Crimson, Mott the Hoople, Julie Felix, the Faces, Lindisfarne. Estimates of attendance range from 30,000 to 140,000 people.

September 9. London. Festival of Light holds its inaugural meeting. A collection of fundamentalist Christian groups forming a coalition against what it perceives as the decadence and immorality of the times. Malcolm Muggeridge, Lord Longford, and, representing youth and popular music, er, Cliff Richard. Shouts of 'Praise the Lord!' mingle in London with the co-opted 'One Way' road signals. Some politico hippies have called it the anti-festival, accusing it of trying to steal their festival culture.

September 18. The Oval cricket ground, London. Benefit festival for Bangladesh. The Who, Mott the Hoople, the Faces, Lindisfarne. 15,000 people.

1972

Great Western Festivals try many sites across England to hold two major rock festivals this summer, only to be blocked by local opposition, by police, councils and concerned local residents. Rejected sites in the first few months of the year include Bishopsbourne in Kent, Tollshunt in Essex, Whatlington in Sussex, Bardney in Lincolnshire (where it eventually happens) – and Pilton in Somerset. Is this an early moment where Glastonbury could have gone more commercial?

April 1–3. Puerto Rico. *Mar y Sol* (Sea and Sun) Festival, features the Allman Brothers, Black Sabbath, Emerson, Lake and Palmer. Four people die.

Easter. Falcon Field, Aldermaston. At the end of the revived four-day CND march *to* Aldermaston, a peace festival is held on April 3 in the field opposite the main gate of the nuclear weapons research centre. Hawkwind, Roy Harper, Adrian Henri.

May 5–7. Bickershaw, Lancashire. A commercial rock festival featuring the Grateful Dead, Captain Beefheart, Dr John, Donovan, Incredible String Band and, yes, Hawkwind. The festival site is a disused industrial lot, under pouring rain. An 'Electric Cinema Magic Tent', too. 40,000 people, half of whom pay (the organisers make a loss of £60,000), a third of whom stay, to see the Dead.

May 26-29. Bardney, Lincolnshire. Great Western Express Festival. *NME* sponsors a stage for the 'Giants of Tomorrow', in a failed effort at talent spotting 20 up-and-coming bands, such as, er, Smith, Perkins & Smith, Warhorse, Spreadeagle and Gnidrolog. 40,000 people.

June 22–26. Worthy Farm, Pilton. A small informal free festival on last year's site, featuring Hawkwind. Arabella Churchill recalls: 'Throughout the seventies, I would get phone calls from Michael most Junes: "Bella, I'm not actually having a festival but lots of people seem to be arriving – come and give us a hand." Some very nice, small, unstructured events took place.'

June 28–30. Barnstaple, Devon. Trentishoe Whole Earth Fayre. 1500 people at an overtly eco-friendly event overlooking Bristol Channel. Water supplied in tankers by a group calling themselves Pot Dealers of the South-West. Entertainment from East Anglian commune band Global Village Trucking Company, and free festival stalwarts Hawkwind and the Pink Fairies.

July. Los Angeles. Wattstax '72 concert, featuring Isaac Hayes, Albert King, Rufus and Carla Thomas, and other gospel and soul musicians.

Hyde Park, London. Free concert by the Rolling Stones. 200,000 people, and some loss of crowd control means the government refuses to allow free concert here next year.

August 26. First Windsor People's Free Festival in Windsor Great Park. Electricity is scarce so Hawkwind play lit up by the headlights of an ice cream van, and using power from the van's generator. The smoke that comes from the band's equipment is not a deliberate part of the show. Ubi Dwyer invites 'between one and five million', and anounces that 'the festival will finish when those attending it so decide'. It's short, and maybe 700 people turn up (accompanied by 600 police onlookers).

First Barsham Faire, medieval-style East Anglian festival, at Roos Hall, Beccles, Suffolk. The beginnings of the East Anglian Fair movement, small-scale local alternative festivals, much like the Green Fields at Glastonbury in the 1980s and 1990s (but without the rock megagig down the valley). The fairs of the east thrive for a good decade, another aspect of the rural counterculture.

Festival Welfare Services founded, an umbrella for all voluntary organisations co-ordinating welfare services at festivals. FWS also functions as the lobbying authority of festival culture.

Buxton, Derbyshire. Weekend rock festival attended by 15,000 people. Rumours circulate that this is to be one of the repeated demands/dreams of hippies in Britain: a permanent festival site. If county shows and race meetings can have recognised dedicated spaces, why not festivals?

August 25–27. Reading Festival. The second year of what is to become one of the major annual events in the festival calendar (if one lacking Glastonbury's alternative sheen), though the site is engulfed in mud after heavy rain. Reading Festival's origins in NJF events at Richmond and elsewhere in the very early 1960s make it the longest-lasting regular festival culture in Britain, a decade older than Glastonbury.

September 16. London, The Oval Cricket Ground. Rock at the Oval. Frank Zappa, Arthur Brown, Linda Lewis and Jeff Beck.

1973

Aquarius Festival, Nimbin, New South Wales, Australia. Pivotal free festival in Australian counter-cultural scene, which sparks off a communal experiment in land purchase. Dropouts and other alternative types are able to buy land in the area of the towns of Nimbin and Mullimbimbi for $200, with the aim of creating a regional alternative movement.

Watkins Glen, USA. Claims to be the biggest rock festival ever: 600,000 people watch the Grateful Dead. (Why?)

August 24–26. Reading Festival. Now well established, with smooth liaison between organisers, council and police. 20–30,000 people. Some return to the blues and jazz origins, with George Melly, Chris Barber and Jimmy Witherspoon. The same weekend the other side of festival culture, free, takes place elsewhere in Berkshire, at Windsor:

August 24–26. Windsor People's Free Festival. Thames Valley Police allocate 500 officers to Reading Festival, 292 to Windsor Free, with a helicopter linking the operations. Festival eventually runs for ten days, up to 7–8000 people at the peak.

Buxton, Derbyshire. Second festival on a site which is supposed to be granted ten-year permission. Poor weather again, money lost, though 10,000 people attend.

The 1973 Windsor Free Festival.

The first official report published: *Pop Festivals: Advisory [Stevenson] Committee on Pop Festivals Report and Code of Practice.*

1974

April. California Jam Festival. 200,000 people watch Emerson, Lake and Palmer, Black Sabbath, Deep Purple and the Eagles.

June. First Stonehenge Free Festival, organised by Wally Hope and others, including Jerry Ratter, who will in a few years metamorphose from free festival hippie into leading anarchopunk drummer and spokesperson of Crass, with the new name of Penny Rimbaud. Hope (real name Phil Russell) dreams that 'one day the children of Albion will play again together in the shadow of the great stones'. He was an outlandish hippie, recalls Rimbaud: 'He was yogi of the great purple mountain, carrier of the holy lingam, new age medicine man, yin and yang, light and dark, at least that's what he told me.' A year later, following some kind of breakdown, Hope does indeed die before he grows old.

July. Third and final Buxton Rock Festival. Once more the Peak District plays its part with wind and rain. Up to 20,000 people, money lost.

July 20. First Knebworth Festival, Hertfordshire, the latest of the large commercial events to take place. Held in the grounds of Knebworth stately home, echoing the Beaulieu events of nearly twenty years previous. A 'bucolic frolic', proclaims the posters. Like the Bath Festivals of 1969 and 1970, which he had also promoted, Freddy Bannister presents a transatlantic bill, headlined by the Allman Brothers and Van Morrison, the Doobie Brothers and the Mahavishnu Orchestra. Acccording to Bannister, 'Van Morrison's contract contained a clause stating that he could terminate his performance if he did not like the look of the audience. In the event we couldn't get him off the stage he was having such a good time.'

August. Reading Festival. Police film the crowds for future training film in crowd-handling. (When they lose control at Windsor Free the same weekend, there is no police footage to show the violence.) 110 arrests this year.

28 August–1 September. Windsor Free Festival broken up by police amid violent scenes and public criticism of police actions.

Prescelli Mountains, Dyfedd, Wales. First Meigan Fayre.

1975

July 5. Knebworth. Second Knebworth Festival. Pink Floyd's set accompanied by Second World War Spitfire aeroplanes doing a fly-past. Captain Beefheart, members of Monty Python's Flying Circus, Roy Harper, for some reason with a horse called Trigger (which has a bigger billing on the poster than MC John Peel). Quadrophonic sound introduced. Licensed for 50,000 but double that number turn up. Proximity to the motorway eases access and congestion. Tickets £2.75 for the day.

August. Reading Festival. Lou Reed, Joan Armatrading, Dr Feelgood, Yes, UFO, Judas Priest,

An invitation to multifarious festivities :~

the **FOURTH PEOPLE'S FREE FESTIVAL**

at **WATCHFIELD**, Oxfordshire
from Saturday 23rd August for 9 days.

a celebration of joy to circulate **L**ove, **P**eace
and **A**wareness throughout the **W**orld.

Clowns   **K**ids
Bands and   **F**riends
Artisans   **T**raditions and **T**rends

Wedding ceremony at People's Free Festival, Watchfield, 1975.

Hawkwind. Thousands turn up without tickets to see Yes, and police negotiate with organisers to remove 'House Full' signs and admit crowds. 30,000 limit ignored as 50,000 fans see the show.

August 23–31. Watchfield, Berkshire. People's Free Festival displaced from Windsor Great Park is given a site by the surprisingly sympathetic Labour government, a disused airfield bordering the military college at Shrivenham. Around 5000 people at peak, 95 arrests (66 for drugs), 14 stolen cars cleared from site. (Compare with Reading, also over the August Bank holiday weekend: 115 arrests out of a crowd of 40,000.) Gong and members of Hawkwind jam for free the night after the band had headlined the Reading Festival across the county. Veteran festival photographer Tash recalls: 'At Windsor in 1974 was the first time I was hit with a policeman's stick, and it changed my outlook entirely! We as a "tribe" were much more together at Watchfield. Think this is when I had first thoughts that we had an "alternative" way of doing life and values and stuff. Not a "pop" festival any more.'

September. Wally Hope, founder of Stonehenge Free, dies. RIP.

1976

Tipi Valley founded, South Wales. Tipi People, a self-styled group of alternative nomads, born from and contributing to the vibrant alternative festival scene now taking place each summer.

May 15–16. Mettingham Castle, Suffolk. Bungay May Horse Fair signals a revival in connection with traditional gypsy festival culture of the Horse Fair, last held in 1934. The programme includes the warning: 'Three children were killed at Appleby Fair last year! Look after yours!' The revival of the Horse Fair is a significant development by the East Anglian fair movement, linking to an earlier rural, nomadic, organic, pre-car culture (and deeply romanticised) past.

Free Festivals: First Report of the Working Committee on Pop Festivals published by Department of Environment.

Festival Welfare Services funded by the government to oversee aspects of festival culture. The organisation's origins are as the Festival Branch of drugs/legal rights group Release, and over the next two decades FWS will be involved in advising and supporting free and commercial festival-goers alike. Its funding is withdrawn finally in 1995.

Meigan Fayre. Third event, now on a different site, kept deliberately low-key to make a local rather than national festival. 3–4000 attend, English and Welsh speakers.

Deeply Vale Free Festival, Lancashire. An illegal site, 300–600 people attending this first small event, which will mushroom over the next few years.

August 21. Knebworth Festival, though called Knebworth Fair. 'All the fun of the fair' says the circular poster, which involves 160 clowns, jugglers, fire-eaters, Morris dancers, floodlit trees and even medieval jousting. Licensed for 100,000, but 200,000 turn up to see the Rolling Stones and Lynyrd Skynyrd, making it the main rival to Reading in terms of commercial festivals.

August 26–30. Seasalter. People's Free Festival (the one moved on from Windsor, Watchfield in previous years).

August. Eric Clapton tells audience in Birmingham that he supports the racist policies of Enoch Powell (David Bowie expresses sympathy for fascism in *Playboy* interview in same year). A letter from outraged anti-racist activists in the music press and *Socialist Worker* leads to the founding of Rock Against Racism.

December 10. London, Royal College of Art Students' Union. First Rock Against Racism benefit gig, with blues singer Carol Grimes and reggae band Matumbi.

1977

Punk's long hot summer: There is no future in England's dreaming, according to the Sex Pistols, in punk's popular year, when the two sevens clash. Apocalypse in the air.

Chelmsford. City Rock: one-day punk festival. Alcohol is banned at the venue (the local football stadium), so punks turn up drunk first thing in the morning, naturally.

June 17–22. But the hippies are still sitting around, smoking. Stonehenge Free Festival. Hawkwind, Planet Gong, Richie Havens.

July 6–11. A small free event at Street Hill, Glastonbury, featuring Nik Turner, Here and Now, and celebrating the date 7 / 7 / 77.

August 5–7. Deeply Vale Free Festival, Lancashire. Steve Hillage Band.

August 26–29. The much demonised People's Free Festival eventually finds a temporary home for the tired dedicated few at Chobham Common, Surrey. A nearby gypsy site agrees to give access to a standpipe for water supplies. The local authority's concern over dirt and rubbish is confirmed when it (yes, the authority) refuses to distribute bin bags at the festival site. Maximum attendance: 500 people.

Beaulieu Jazz Festival is revived for a one-off.

September. Whitworth Fair, near Rochdale, is revived. Originally chartered in 1251, it's revived as a cross between a village fête, an alternative festival and a Gypsy horse fair.

1978

April 30. Victoria Park, London. First national Anti-Nazi League/RAR Carnival, following march from Trafalgar Square. Organisers also plan it as a tenth-anniversary tribute to the events of May 1968 in Paris. The Clash, Tom Robinson Band, X-Ray Spex, Patrik Fitzgerald (booed off by the intolerant crowd, which is of course there to demonstrate its tolerance) and Steel Pulse.

Albion Fairs in East Anglia. The first summer of a movable feast across the countryside, from fair to nomadic fair, June to August.

June. The first of two Knebworth Festivals this year. Billed as 'A Midsummer Night's Dream'. Genesis, Jefferson Starship (without lead singer Grace Slick), Tom Petty and Devo.

June. Summer Solstice. Stonehenge. Festival Welfare Services describe this year as 'a model free festival' for 3–5000 people. Local landowner, Lord Pembroke, supplies firewood, and the local Conservative MP writes in *The Times* that: 'Either the festival must be stopped – and I question whether it could be *or should be* – or better arrangements must be made' (emphasis added).

June 24. Knebworth returns. Genesis without ex-singer Peter Gabriel, Jefferson Starship without singer Grace Slick.

June 28 – July 8. Glastonbury. After the Stonehenge Free, a group of what would soon be called New Travellers, in trucks and buses, park up at Worthy Farm for an impromptu, ad hoc, unlicensed free festival. They even bring with them their own Pyramid Stage, with power supplied from an electricity meter in a caravan. Attendance around 500 people.

July 15. Alexandra Park, Manchester. Northern RAR Carnival. The Fall, Steel Pulse, John Cooper Clarke, The Buzzcocks, all the north's finest.

July. Blackbushe Aerodrome, 40 miles west of London. 50,000 show to see Bob Dylan's first festival gig in Britain since Isle of Wight in 1969, supported by Joan Armatrading, Graham Parker and Eric Clapton.

Final official report published: *Pop Festivals and their Problems.*

August 20–25. Deeply Vale Free Festival, Lancashire. Described by local opponents of the event as follows: 'The numbers attracted were beyond anticipation and adequate facilities were not, in the opinion of many observers, provided by the organisers. This led to a great dealt of environ-

Hill dancing at the Summer Solstice, Stonehenge 1978.

mental despoliation due to lack of toilets and means of rubbish disposal, and the destruction of dry stone walls and trees to provide camping facilities. Many "visitors" had stayed on in the area, living in tents and makeshift shelters without proper facilities and despoliation had continued.' Up to 8000 people attend, and Steve Hillage Band and Sphynx play.

August. The much demonised People's Free Festival eventually finds a final, temporary home for the tired dedicated few at Caesar's Camp, near Bracknell, Berkshire. Acoustic music only. Maximum attendance 300 people.

September 9. Knebworth Festival II, advertised by a poster which said 'Oh God, not another boring old Knebworth'. Some of punk's more respectable energy on show, such as the Tubes and Boomtown Rats, as well as Zappa, Peter Gabriel and Wilko Johnson.

September 14–16. Giza, Egypt. The Grateful Dead play in front of the Egyptian Pyramids, and on the third night there is an eclipse of the moon. Hundreds of West Coast Americans fly in for the ancient and cosmic vibe. (British hippies have a stage in the shape of a pyramid; Californian ones fly to the real thing.)

September 24. Hyde Park to Brockwell Park, Brixton. RAR Carnival 2. Elvis Costello, Misty, Aswad and Stiff Little Fingers playing instead of Sham 69 (too many skinhead fans). 150,000 dance against racism – while the National Front marches through Brick Lane on the same afternoon less than hindered.

1979

Festival Welfare Services identifies at least 24 summer rock festivals across the country.

June 21–23. Glastonbury. Did the small free event of last year inspire a revived Glastonbury Fayre? The first official, commercial event, but already a fund-raising ethos: profits to go to UN Year of the Child. (Aptly, Eavis's youngest daughter Emily born this summer.) Eavis backs the project financially with the deeds from his farm, while Arabella Churchill, Pyramid Stage man Bill Harkin, musician Steve Hillage and Andrew Kerr also contribute to the collective organisation. A special area is set aside for children, and money goes to found Children's World charity, still going under Churchill's director-ship in Somerset and Avon, working with children in special schools. Also a Theatre Area, at which groups like Incubus and Footsbarn performed. The main stage is provided by Genesis (and *not* pyramid-

shaped). Peter Gabriel, Steve Hillage, Tom Robinson, SAHB, John Martyn, the Only Ones, the UK Subs, the Leyton Buzzards, Nona Hendryx and Sky. Attendance 12,000. £5 for weekend tickets. Large financial loss, though charities still funded.

Albion Fairs through East Anglia: a movable feast in the countryside, from weekend to weekend.

August. Knebworth Festival, headlined by Led Zeppelin two Saturdays running, playing their first gig for nearly two years; first UK gigs for four years.

August. Reading Festival. Some punk bands are added to the bill, including (bad choice) Sham 69, which means that hundreds of skinheads turn up. (Crap band with a crap following.) Sham's lead singer Jimmy Pursey and unreconstructed hippie guitarist Steve Hillage appear onstage together to appeal for cross-subcultural unity and understanding. Not the wisest move from the punk perspective; for them, so the slogan went, 'The only good hippie is a dead hippie.'

THE EIGHTIES

1980

June. Stonehenge Free. Bikers trash punks at Stonehenge Free; punks have turned up to see Crass, whose Penny Rimbaud had been involved in setting up the Stonehenge Festival in the first place. Barbed wire round the stones, hippies complain when they are strip-searched in public. The line-up is surprisingly impressive (so an obscure website database tells me): reggae and ska bands Misty in Roots and Selector, pop band the Thompson Twins, new wavers Flux of Pink Indians, as well as old stalwarts like Hawkwind and Nik Turner's Inner City Unit.

ABOVE Punk situationists declare apocalypse, 1978–79.

TOP LEFT Glastonbury poster featuring the chalice and the Tor.

TOP RIGHT The misty vale of Avalon. Glastonbury festival and Tor, 1979.

Time-line of festival culture

101

June 21. Knebworth. Unimpressed with the antics of Led Zeppelin's manager last year, the organisers only agree to run another festival with a change of musical direction. Capital Radio sponsors a middle of the road festival: Beach Boys (Brian Wilson slumped over the piano), Mike Oldfield, Santana, Elkie Brooks. 5000 ping pong balls are dropped on the crowd from a B17 Flying Fortress bomber plane (I don't know why); the wind blew them into another field.

No Glastonbury festival, following last year's financial loss.

Instead, in July: Worthy Farm is host to the first Ecology Party Summer Gathering, a mix of greens (without the official backing of the Ecology Party, which would become the Green Party) and festival-goers. In a nearby barn amplified music is supplied by Roy Harper and Inner City Unit. Around 500 people.

Albion Fairs through East Anglia: a movable feast in the countryside, from one weekend to the next.

New Age Gypsy Fair, Inglestone Common, Avon. One of 47 alternative fairs and festivals this summer identified by FWS. Through the early years of the decade festival culture as an alternative to the yuppie culture of Thatcherism spreads, from the Albion Fairs in East Anglia, to free festivals in Wales and Norwich, to the peace-oriented Moon Fairs at Nenthead in Cumbria.

16 August. Castle Donington, Derbyshire. First Monsters of Rock festival, featuring Ritchie Blackmore's Rainbow.

Reading, Berkshire. August Bank Holiday weekend. The old National Jazz and Blues Festival still going strong as the Reading Festival, though dominated by heavy rock. UFO, Def Leppard, Iron Maiden and Whitesnake. (Didn't anyone ever tell these people that punk happened a few years back? Some punk bands were booked at Reading in 1978 or 1979, but the music's speedy aggression was generally less than convincing *en plein air*. DJ John Peel refuses to MC because it is 'too heavy metal'.)

World of Music, Arts and Dance (WOMAD) formed. The organisation founded by Peter Gabriel will, after a shaky start, be central in presenting world music to festival audiences in Britain and overseas.

1981

February. Greenham Common Peace Camp declares itself a female zone. In March, at a CND rally there, Inner City Unit play free.

June 19–21. A change of name, from 'Fayre' to 'Festival'. Glastonbury CND Festival, the first time CND is involved. The formation of Mid-Somerset CND early in 1981 sparked greater interest locally. Old hippie stalwarts like Ginger Baker, Gong, Hawkwind, Taj Mahal, Judy Tzuke, Rab Noakes, Roy Harper and Supercharge – as well as newer acts like Aswad, New Order, John Cooper Clarke, the Jazz Sluts, the Sound, and Matumbi. Speakers included E P Thompson. Worthy Farm puts up the money, books the acts, organises the actual event, while National CND handles publicity and sells tickets. The Pyramid Stage returns, this time as a permanent structure, with planning permission as a cow shed when not in use by the festival (ironically its metal sheeting was army surplus). Attendance: 18,000 people, paying £8 for weekend tickets, and £20,000 raised for CND.

June. Stonehenge Free. Over one hundred arrests, some fighting with police. Again, line-up quite impressive, and reflecting more recent changes in pop music taste, with reggae and punk featuring prominently: Black Slate, the Damned, the Ruts.

July. Worthy Farm. Six-day Ecology Party Summer Gathering. Acoustic music only this time, as a matter of policy. Around 1500 people. Though it is mainly advertised through the Ecology Party, at the end of the gathering activists decide that future events will be *Green Gatherings*, to attract people from all parts of the movement. Green CND is formed here.

Albion Fairs through East Anglia: a movable feast in the countryside, from weekend to weekend.

July. Chapeltown, Leeds. RAR Carnival. Misty in Roots, the Specials, the Au Pairs.

July 8–12. Inglestone Common, Avon Free Festival.

July 25–26. Knebworth. Another change of musical direction. George Wein, of Newport Jazz Festival, books the bands for the Capital Radio Jazz Festival at Knebworth.

September 4–14. Psilocybin Fayre, Devil's Bridge, Wales. Landscape, (legal) drugs and free festival culture come together at a magic mushroom harvest event.

September 6. Winchester Fayre, another revived event from an ancient charter.

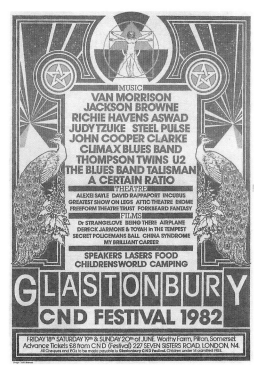

September to November. USA. The original Earth First! Road Show tours coast-to-coast across America, raising the profile of the new direct action local radical environmentalist organisation. EF!'s use of the term 'Road Show' later ironically dropped in light of massive anti-roads protest by British Earth First! in 1990s.

24 October. London. Biggest national CND demonstration to date.

1982

June 6. Hyde Park, London. Estimated 250,000 people demonstrating at a CND march and carnival.

June 18–20. Glastonbury Festival. CND more involved in the organisation of the festival, West Region CND doing the gates and Mid-Somerset CND responsible for the information stalls. Van Morrison sings 'Summertime in England', reggae bands Aswad and Steel Pulse, veterans Roy Harper and Judy Tzuke, Alexei Sayle in the Theatre Area, and films by (as CND's national publicity put it) directors like 'Dereck Jarmone'. Pouring rain and muddy fields at the end of the festival. From the USA (signalling the international profile the festival, as part of the peace campaign is beginning to receive) come Richie Havens and Jackson Browne. Attendance 25,000 people. Tickets £8.

June. Stonehenge Free. Around 20,000 come, 125 arrests (mainly for drugs and shoplifting from local stores). New Travellers leave *en masse* and head for Greenham Common to hold a 'Cosmic Counter-Cruise Carnival'. In the wake of hippie groups like the Tipi People and the Tibetan-Ukrainian mountain troupe, the nomadic festival-centred lifestyle is now represented by this group, the Peace Convoy.

July 27–August 1. The first Green Gathering, a development of the Ecology Party Summer Gatherings, still at Worthy Farm. 5000 people attend, including feminist peace group Women For Life On Earth with a dedicated women-only marquee. 'For the first time we began to feel like a movement . . . We all feel the Gatherings have generated a very specal energy, an Avalon energy which we are now taking to all parts of the world. It was the 1982 Gathering though that had the most magical quality. It was the first *Green* Gathering,' writes one organiser.

Albion Fairs through East Anglia: a movable feast in the countryside, from weekend to weekend.

August 21. Castle Donington, Monsters of Rock Festival. Maybe that should have been Dinosaurs of Rock: Saxon, Uriah Heep, Status Quo, Gillan . . .

Shepton Mallett, Somerset. The first WOMAD festival, held on the showground site of the early Bath blues festivals, a few miles from Worthy Farm. According to one person who was there, 'due in part to a train strike, the very few who attended had a large amount of money spent on them, with bands on five separate stages'.

August 27–30. Knebworth. Yet another change in approach. Knebworth hosts the Green Belt festival, a Christian gathering that had grown larger over the previous eight years and now needed a more ambitious space.

October. Milton Keynes Bowl. Peter Gabriel reunites with Genesis, explaining: 'the motivation is to pay off the WOMAD debts'.

1983

May. Brockwell Park, London. CND carnival. Paul Weller's new Style Council contribute some of the entertainment for the large crowd.

June 17–19. Glastonbury Festival. A public entertainment licence needed for the festival, as a result of the recently passed Local Government (Miscellaneous Provisions) Act, 1982. The licence costs £300 from Mendip District Council, and specifies a limit of 30,000 people (so, unsurprisingly, the official website states 30,000 as number of people attending), along with 23 other conditions. First appearance of the festival's own radio station, Radio Avalon. World music beginning to appear: King Sunny Ade, the Chieftains, Incantation; alongside Curtis Mayfield, the Fun Boy Three, the Beat, UB40, A Certain Ratio, Melanie and Marillion. £3000 raised for local charities. From 1981 to 1983 £133,000 raised for CND. Tickets £12, programmes 80 pence.

June 16–22. Stonehenge Free. Followng a free festival appearance for bikers at a Motorcycle Action Group event in Somerset in early June, Hawkwind play a two-hour sunrise performance on solstice morning with the stones as backdrop, recalling their Atomhenge stage set of 1976. Over the course of the festival, three people die: a four-year-old girl from burns, a woman hitch-hiker in an accident, and one drugs overdose.

July 27–29. Glastonbury Green Gathering moves from Worthy Farm to Lambert's Hill Farm, near Shepton Mallet. The Peace Convoy makes an appearance, a contribution, and a large-scale police operation (felt by Greens to be considerably over-the-top, though the Convoy is used to it) involves searches and taking details from New Travellers and Greens alike. A naked protest march ensues. This is the Children's Gathering, with entertainments and worshops based around their needs and desires. Also features the largest tipi circle seen to date outside North America.

July–August. Regular commercial summer festival circuit offers variety of music and culture: Elephant Fayre at St Germans, Monsters of Rock at Castle Donington, Reading Festival, and the big free urban event, the Notting Hill Carnival in London.

1984

June 22–24. Glastonbury Festival. Eavis successfully defends himself in magistrates court against five charges brought by Mendip District Council of contravening conditions of last year's festival, and permission is granted again, for 35,000 people. (Council officials however note large numbers of festival-goers without wristbands.) Dedicated fields for parking cars are stewarded by the PTA of West Pennard School. The blatant sale of drugs is an issue, with many signs posted saying SALE AND DISPLAY OF DRUGS FORBIDDEN (note this doesn't even try to proscribe consumption), and the organisers even having their own undercover anti-drugs operation. Speakers include Bruce Kent of CND and Paddy Ashdown. Joan Baez, Ian Dury, Fairport Convention, Weather Report, the Smiths, the Waterboys, Howard Jones, Black Uhuru and Nigerian superstar and rebel Fela Kuti. CND hot air balloon sails over the festival site. In part because of the trouble at last year's Glastonbury Green Gathering, the first Green Field is introduced at the festival, with eco-issues signalling a growing awareness and shift of perspective towards the environment. £60,000 raised for CND. Tickets £13, programmes 80 pence.

June. What turns out to be the last Stonehenge Free Festival (yet). 25,000 people turn up over the month of June. One man dies. Hawkwind perform *Earth Ritual* over two days, and The Enid do a set that feels two days long. Punks and hippies, difficult to tell them apart by now.

August. Green Gathering at RAF Molesworth, Cambridgeshire. Perhaps radicalised by police treatment at last year's Glastonbury Green Gathering, the Green Collective decides to organise an altogether more provocative squatted event,

Serious mud years at Glastonbury, 1985 (TOP) and 1997.

RIGHT New travellers try to keep the free festival vibe alive after the Battle of the Beanfield, summer 1985

which leads to the formation of Rainbow Fields Village peace camp.

1985

May 27. Proposed festival at Long Marston Airfield, Stratford-upon-Avon, cancelled. A decade later the site will be used for the short-lived Phoenix Festivals. (From Watchfield to Blackbushe to Phoenix: don't people realise that you need more than the land of an airfield to make a successful festival?)

June. Battle of the Beanfield, as New Travellers on their way to hold Stonehenge Free Festival are set upon by police a few miles from the stones. It is, as one Traveller admits, the beginning of the end for the Convoy. Some find their way to the welcoming orchard of Greenland's Farm, Glastonbury.

June 21–23. Glastonbury Festival, on an enlarged site due to the purchase of extra 100 acres from neighbouring Cockmill Farm. The programme includes an interview with anarcho-punks the Poison Girls. Roger Chapman returns to the pyramid stage he'd last played in 1971. Rain and mega-mud, as in 1982. The Boomtown Rats play, with singer Bob Geldof performing just a few weeks before Live Aid. Echo and the Bunnymen headline. The Pogues, Ian Dury, Aswad, Hugh Masekela, Working Week, James, The Men They Couldn't Hang, Microdisney, Joe Cocker and the Style Council. Tractors work overtime at the end to tow vehicles off site. 40,000 people. Tickets £16, programme 90 pence. £100,000 raised for CND and local charities.

July 10. New Zealand. French Secret Service blow up the Greenpeace ship *Rainbow Warrior*, which was protesting about French nuclear testing in the South Pacific. One Greenpeace activist killed.

July. London and Philadelphia, simultaneously forming what organiser Bob Geldof calls a 'global jukebox'. Live Aid, at which David Bowie and Eric Clapton turn their backs on their rhetoric of 1976. 28 global superstars (though not many African or reggae musicians) in a 12-hour transatlantic festival transmitted live worldwide. Live Aid raises money for famine in Ethiopia, inspired by the success of the Christmas 1984 charity single 'Do They Know it's Christmas' and the American 'We are the World'. (By the time it finally closes its accounts in 1992, Band Aid will have raised £110 million.)

Essex. Recovered from the debt crisis, Peter Gabriel holds the second WOMAD Festival, Thomas Mapfumo, Toots and the Maytals, samba, country, etc.

Reading Festival cancelled at the last moment.

August. Bramdean Common. First Torpedo Town free festival on the South Coast, featuring Hawkwind.

August 24. London, Crystal Palace. Anti-Heroin Festival, with the Enid, Comsat Angels, Hawkwind. Alternative culture taking a stand on hard drugs.

1986

26 April. Chernobyl, Ukraine. Nuclear plant explodes, twice in the space of a few seconds, and catches fire. Fallout drifts across much of the continent of Europe, and today in Britain some upland areas of North Wales and Cumbria are *still* contaminated by radiation and subject to government restrictions on livestock. The apocalyptic combination prophesied by some campaigners of nuclear and green issues together thus comes to pass.

Some of the Peace Convoy of New Travellers, who would normally have gone to Stonehenge Free, turn up at Pilton in early June, following their mass eviction in a dawn swoop from Stoney Cross in the

The Cure take to stage just before the heavens open, June 1986.

New Forest. They move off so as not to make life difficult for CND and Glastonbury – or, Eavis evicts them so as not to invalidate his insurance (take your pick). Later, Eavis involves himself in trying to find an alternative site for the Stonehenge event.

June 20–22. Glastonbury Festival. Another major expansion – 60,000 people attending now. The rate of growth through the 1980s begins to worry some of those involved in organising the event, though communications, welfare and medical provisions are extended, and the developing market areas relocated too. The Classical Tent introduced. Bands include the Cure, the Pogues, the Waterboys, Madness, Simply Red, the Housemartins, the June Brides, the Go-Betweens, the Psychedelic Furs, the Nightingales, the Dream Syndicate, Half Man Half Biscuit, Microdisney, the Woodentops and Level 42,

alongside Ted Chippington, Fuzzbox, Billy Bragg and Ruby Turner. Tickets £17, programme £1. £130,000 raised for CND and local charities.

July. Manchester. A festival to celebrate ten years of punk, with the Smiths, New Order, the Fall and newcomers Happy Mondays.

Note the limited range of free and alternative festivals over the past couple of years: a result of the Thatcher government's crackdown on New Travellers and unlicensed gatherings. Cantlin Stone Free Festival, Avon Free, Elephant Fayre and Meigan Fayre are among the few that manage to survive around now. The East Anglian Fairs also run out of energy, having too many hassles trying to accommodate local needs with national problems.

1987

In a local referendum, Pilton villagers vote against the Glastonbury Festival continuing. Mendip Council ignores the result.

June 6–14. Smarden. Green Gathering.

June 19–21. Glastonbury Festival takes place, confirmed following annual licence wrangles with the local council as late as May. Described by *NME* as 'an annual blend of mysticism, music and mild mayhem'. In something of a stylistic throwback, 'the brightest spark' at this year's festival, according to *NME*, is Michelle Shocked, voice and acoustic guitar, managing to make a campfire atmosphere in spite of the rain. Also: Van Morrison, Elvis Costello, New Order, Julian Cope, Billy Bragg, Hüsker Dü, Green on Red, the Woodentops, the Triffids, the Weather Prophets, Gaye Bikers on Acid, the Soup Dragons, Felt, Courtney Pine, Trouble Funk, the Communards, Pop Will Eat Itself, That Petrol Emotion and the WOMAD stage for the first time. 60,000 people, tickets £21. £130,000 raised for CND and local charities.

August 16–17. Harmonic Convergence. Centres of spiritual energy round the world are the focus of believers trying to divert us from global apocalypse.

Groups of New Agers meditate and 'tune in' together at, among other places, Ayers Rock in Australia, Machu Picchu in Peru, the Great Pyramid in Egypt – and Glastonbury Tor. An alternative local–global peace movement to the one of the CND Festival. As the *Central Somerset Gazette* concluded its preview article: 'Anyone who can help should contact Andy on the following Glastonbury number . . . '

August 28–31. First Ribblehead Viaduct Free Festival, near Settle in Cumbria.

1988

Acid House declares the Second Summer of Love. British dancefloors get the beat from DJs mixing Chicago house music with Balearic tourist beat, and the club scene trances out on constant bpm and the new drug Ecsatsy.

No Glastonbury Festival. Eavis suggests that problems may be traceable to Stonehenge, since the 30,000 people who used to go to the free festival there have often, since 1984, been going to Glastonbury. The fact that the festival's attendance has grown more than three-fold through the decade is also a factor in everyone having a break. A plea from New Travellers to New Travellers in the alternative press: 'This year there is *no* Glastonbury festival. If any policemen tell us to head for Worthy Farm they are simply trying to stir up trouble down in Somerset where the local right-wing opposition (anti-CND, anti-hippie, anti-festival of any sort) are beginning to froth at the mouth. This year it's essential that we don't go to Worthy Farm – the place does need a rest. It's time to go back to the stones.'

11 June. Wembley Stadium, London. Inspired by Live Aid, Jerry Dammers organises a superstar benefit concert for imprisoned South African activist Nelson Mandela's 70th birthday party. Whitney Houston, veteran civil rights activist and calypso singer Harry Belafonte, Dire Straits, Eric Clapton, Stevie Wonder, Hugh Masekela and Miriam Makeba. Screened a few hours later in the USA, as *A Concert for the Freedom of the World* rather than *for* Nelson Mandela, many of the political comments from the stage and references to the anti-apartheid movement are edited out.

June. Stonehenge. Riot before midsummer dawn. Fighting between an estimated 3500–4500 hippies and 1000 police near the stones. Hippies beaten back before they reach the stones, apart from a small group who manage to climb the Heel Stone.

No one seems to have told the hippies (above) or the heavy metal fans (below) that it's the Second Summer of Love, though.

August. Castle Donington Monsters of Rock festival attracts its biggest crowd of 100,000 people, hundreds of whom are injured and two killed during slam-dancing.

September. Reading Festival. Iggy Pop, the Ramones, Uriah Heep, Squeeze. Numerous bands blown off stage by crowd trouble: Bonnie Tyler, Deacon Blue, even Meatloaf.

September. Athens, Greece. 'Greek Free Festival' deteriorates with serious crowd trouble, damages of over £1.5 million, and busy hospital wards. Rioting seems to have flared up when Public Image Limited postpone their set for security reasons – what chance such a reaction if they'd actually played? The only free festival that lasts less time than it is supposed to (one out of three days).

1989

June. European elections in Britain. To general amazement the Green Party wins 15% of the vote (but no seats).

June 16–18. Glastonbury Festival, again in spite of planning wrangles with the council. Glorious sunshine all weekend. Sponsored by *New Musical Express.* Suzanne Vega plays despite a death threat, Van Morrison, Elvis Costello, Black Uhuru, Youssou N'Dour, Fela Kuti, the Pixies, Throwing

Muses, the Bhundu Boys, the Wonder Stuff and the Waterboys. Rave is introduced to Glastonbury by Sugar Lump sound system, who play nonstop 24-hour dance music behind the market stalls. The police are brought into the organisation and planning of the festival for the first time, with around 300 arrests, mainly for minor drugs offences (though local police say the event is 'a great success considering the numbers involved'). 60–65,000 attend (elsewhere, 100,000 is the number given). £100,000 raised for CND. Tickets £28, programme £2.

June 16–18. Morecambe, Lancashire. WOMAD comes to an old-fashioned seaside resort.

July 27–August 2. Liskeard, Cornwall. Treworgey Tree Fayre. A commercial event, though heavily alternative music: Hawkwind, Here and Now, Ozric Tentacles, Misty in Roots, the Levellers.

August. Free festival scene begins to pick up again, with events like Cantlin Stone, Ridgeway, Cissbury Ring, Rough Tor, Ribblehead through the summer. Free festival-goers get their summer hit of landscape and liberation.

Tribal Gathering begins round now, a commercial festival-style event to cater for the rave generation.

THE NINETIES

1990

June 3. Finsbury Park, London. Gaelic culture comes to festival, with the Fleadh, featuring Van Morrison, Rory Gallagher.

June 22–24. Glastonbury Festival, the twentieth-anniversary event. Retitled as 'Glastonbury Festival of Contemporary Performing Arts' to reflect diversity of attractions. 'Europe's most effective anti-nuclear fund-raising event,' says the publicity. The Green Fields quadruple in size to 60 acres, and include Mind, Body and Spirit Healing Area, Earth Mysteries, as well as a green small business trade show. Again sponsored by *NME* which describes the festival as 'held with all its usual attendant problems of drug busts, muddy, quagmire-like fields, and crush-related injuries'. Confrontations on the Monday morning between on-site security teams and groups of travellers cause £50,000 worth of damage to equipment and facilities. Ry Cooder, Aswad, the Cure, Sinead O'Connor, Happy Mondays, Galaxie 500, the Pale Saints, Lush, James, De La Soul. Also circus, theatre, cabaret and comedy. Tickets £38, programmes £3. 70,000 people. £100,000 raised for CND and local charities.

June 29–July 1. Brighton Urban Festival, featuring up-and-coming local lads The Levellers.

July 20–22. WOMAD comes to the epicentre of British festival culture – Reading, that is. WOMAD rebrands the Berkshire town site as Rivermead. Van Morrison, Radical Dance Faction.

1991

Earth First! founded in Britain, following eco-activist model of direct action from USA. Summer gatherings will form a major part of EF!'s consciousness-raising activity, a little like a festival in the countryside, but explicitly stating that they are not festivals. The emphasis is on the social solidarity and the education and energising/chilling rather than on music and entertainment.

June 2. Finsbury Park, London. The Fleadh, with the Pogues, Christy Moore, the Chieftains, That Petrol Emotion.

No Glastonbury Festival of Contemporary Performing Arts, following disturbances last year.

June 20–25. Longstock Free Festival, featuring radical sound system Spiral Tribe.

June-August. Regular commercial summer festival circuit offers full variety of music and culture: WOMAD at Rivermead, Cambridge Folk Festival, Monsters of Rock at Castle Donington, Reading Festival, Notting Hill Carnival in London.

1992

May 22–29. Castlemorton, Hereford and Worcester. The annual Avon Free Festival moved from various possible sites ends up on common land in the next county. The biggest free festival /

Crowds at Glastonbury, June 1990.

rave event to date signals a revival of alt. lifestyle, with New Traveller/acid house/free party crossover. Attendance officially estimated at 20,000. Sound systems like Spiral Tribe, DiY, Bedlam play. Locals living in isolated houses surrounded by it all feel 'invaded', 'bombarded', 'intimidated', and their working party's report after the event leads to some of the anti-rave and criminalisation of trespass clauses of the Criminal Justice Act two years later.

New Travellers, ravers, road protesters find new strength to be direct

June 26–28. Glastonbury Festival of Contemporary Performing Arts. With the end of the Cold War and the rise in Green consciousness, Eavis feels that the time is right to widen out the beneficiaries of the funds raised from just the anti-nuclear movement. Greenpeace (which was originally anti-nuclear) and Oxfam (with its campaigning against the arms trade) benefit with local charities to the sum of £250,000. Event is linked to National Music Day. The Levellers, Carter USM, Primal Scream, Blur, James, the Breeders, PJ Harvey, Billy Bragg, Van Morrison – the line-up needed a surprise, and a Glastonbury tradition is invented, that of hosting a veteran performer, this year Tom Jones. Also Curve, Kitchens of Distinction, Television, The Fall, Spiritualized, the Shamen, and the Jazz World stage is introduced as a focus for world music, and some jazz. 70,000 people. Prices have nearly doubled in the space of three years: tickets £49, programme £4.

Luton, Bedfordshire. DiY group Exodus Collective forms from local black and white youth, holds first free party/rave.

1993

June 25–27. Glastonbury Festival of Contemporary Performing Arts. 'Golden Oldie' Rolf Harris with didj reinvents himself as world music elder. Velvet Underground on a reunion tour, the Orb, Lenny

Kravitz, Robert Plant, Galliano, Belly, Come, Sebadoh, American Music Club, Teenage Fanclub, Superchunk, Ultramarine, Baaba Maal, Suede, and the Lemonheads. 80,000 people. Tickets £58, programmes £4. £250,000 raised for Greenpeace, Oxfam, and local charities. In the early 1990s admission prices are rising by around £10 per year, which is 20–25 per cent annual inflation – even so, this year's festival sells out well in advance.

June–August. Free festivals organised by a lager company to promote its product. Heineken Festivals take place in Brighton, Preston, Nottingham, Swansea and Portsmouth, offering free rock and world music in marquees in public parks. The free festival movement develops a respectable edge?

Brighton Urban Free Festival (BUFF) is stopped by the council after eleven years of the annual event.

1994

June 24–26. Glastonbury Festival of Contemporary Performing Arts. Ten days beforehand the Pyramid Stage burns down, and is sadly replaced by a standard outdoor festival rig. The fire is ominous; the festival has its first death, a young man from a drugs overdose, while on Saturday night someone fires a gun in the crowd. Five people are shot. (*Melody Maker* notes that Glastonbury 'isn't Compton, but it's not Utopia, either'.) Practising what they greenpreach, a wind turbine provides 150kW of power for the main stage area. Channel 4 broadcasts live on television. Manic Street Preachers suggest during their set that we could 'have some more by-passes through this fucking shithole'. Elvis Costello, Bjork, Orbital are more polite, Oasis, Blur (with Phil Daniels), the Lemonheads, Ride, Beastie Boys, the Boo Radleys, Nick Cave, M People, Senser, Paul Weller, Tindersticks, Pulp, Inspiral Carpets, Radiohead, plus Golden Oldie Johnny Cash. DiY sound systems blast out techno through the night. 80,000 people. Tickets £59, programme £5. £300,000 donated to Greenpeace, Oxfam and local causes.

Glastonbury, June 1992.

June–August. Regular commercial summer festival circuit offers full variety of music and culture: WOMAD at Rivermead, Cambridge Folk Festival, Monsters of Rock at Castle Donington, Reading Festival, Notting Hill Carnival in London.

July 14–17. Long Marston, Stratford-upon-Avon. The disused airfield. The Phoenix Festival arrives, organised by the Mean Fiddler Organisation, sponsored by *Melody Maker* and Carlsberg.

July 30–31. T in the Park, near Glasgow. T is for Tennent's – like Heineken last year, Carlsberg with the Phoenix and Guinness with the Fleadh in a couple of years' time, breweries are tapping into festival culture for promotion. Headlining are Rage

1995

May 5–7. Fairmile, Devon. Beltane Festival, organised on site of the road protest camps against the development of the A30 trunk road.

May 14. London. First Reclaim the Streets anti-car culture free street party blocks off Camden High Street for a dance party protest.

June 23–25. Glastonbury Festival of Contemporary Performing Arts. In an echo of Woodstock and Isle of Wight festivals of a quarter of a century before (this is the twenty-fifth anniversary of the first festival), fences are pulled down by some sections of the crowd to make a free festival. The Cure, Portishead, Simple Minds, Oasis, Prodigy, Dodgy,

Against the Machine and Del Amitri, while in King Tut's Wah Wah Tent you can see Blur, Pulp, Oasis and Manic Street Preachers.

New York State. Woodstock 2. 300,000 people believe the publicity. They then get rained on while listening to the contemporary sounds of Santana, the Allman Brothers. 'Woodstock 94. Live it. Love, Pepsi,' say the sponsors. Sad.

November. Criminal Justice and Public Order Act becomes law. A sustained attack on alternative lifestyles and politics in Britain, including almost unprecedented laws directed specifically against pop music and culture: the notorious anti-rave sections, identifying 'music characterised by a succession of repetitive beats'.

Shed Seven, Supergrass, Zion Train, Dread Zone, Gene, Elastica and Goldie. The Stone Roses pull out from their headlining slot at short notice, and Pulp, in one of those Glastonbury moments, step in with a legendary pop performance for the common people. The new Dance Tent is a real crowd-pleaser, featuring Massive Attack, Tricky, Red Snapper, Earthling, Richie Hawtin, Autechre, System 7 and Eat Static. 80,000 people. Tickets £65, programme £5. £400,000 raised for Greenpeace, Oxfam, and local causes.

June–August. Regular commercial summer festival circuit offers full variety of music and culture: the Fleadh in London, WOMAD at Rivermead, Cambridge Folk Festival, Monsters of Rock at Castle Donington, Reading Festival, Notting Hill Carnival in London.

Brighton Festival of Freedom. Following the end of the Brighton Urban Free Festival a couple years back, and the recent introduction of the CJA with its anti-rave clauses, a group of admirable trouble-makers decides to throw a *new* free festival in the town. 10,000 party politically.

July 7–9. The Mother megarave, somewhere in southern England, conceived by free party activists as Castlemorton II, fails to materialise following cat and mouse game with police from site to site.

July 23. London. RTS 2. Street party in blocked-off street: sand covers tarmac, deck chairs are brought out as a summer beach party takes over London and thousands dance.

1996

May. Tribal Gathering, a *commercial* dance festival, has major problems getting permission to happen. Underground organisers the Advance Party see this, after the CJA in 1994 and the banning of the Mother megarave/free party in 1995, as evidence that 'the authorities are out to crush the whole movement, be it legal, illegal, large or small'.

June. Finsbury Park, London, seems to become a semi-permanent festival venue for the month. A series of one-day events, all commercial: on the 8th the Fleadh with Christy Moore and Clannad; the next day, 'A Lazy Sunday Afternoon' with Paul Weller; a fortnight later, Saturday at the Park is 'Madstock',

Noel Gallagher, Jarvis Cocker, Richard Ashcroft, Massive Attack's Daddy G, Damon Albarn and the Chemical Brothers – all stars of Glastonbury '95–'97. Along with Johnny Cash, who represents the Glastonbury tradition of embracing a veteran performer.

August 5–7. Tan Hill Fayre, Avebury, Wiltshire. A revived ancient charter fair, by Dongas Tribe eco-protestors, now living a low-impact nomadic lifestyle reclaiming the green lanes of the English countryside.

September 3. London. Newham Unity Festival. A response to organisers' previous criticism of 'the "ANL syndrome"': passing off anti-racist concerts in black areas, attracting thousands of people, but leaving little lasting effect, as huge anti-racist mobilisations. The Unity Festival is different.'

September 22–24. Clunie Dam, Scotland. A free festival for the very brave: Midge Death Festival.

featuring a reunited Madness, and Sunday is, sadly, a reunited Sex Pistols day.

June 12–18. North Wales. Earth First! Summer Gathering of radical environmentalists and other direct activists. Advance publicity clarifies the distinction between it and (a slightly jaundiced view of) festival culture: 'Please note that this is NOT a festival. It is a gathering of those involved or interested in direct action in defence of the earth. There will be no sound systems, but there will be acoustic bands in the evening. If you just want to sit around getting pissed up and listening to music we can provide you with a list of festivals where you can do just that.'

RIGHT Festival and gatherings reflect the rise of eco-protest in the 1990s.

No Glastonbury Festival of Contemporary Performing Arts, after last year's crowds and crowd trouble. Instead, festival organisers branch out, to offer the first Classical Extravaganza, an open-air concert in the grounds of Glastonbury Abbey. There is a clear and conscious echo here of Rutland Boughton's Glastonbury Festivals of the early twentieth century.

13 July. London. RTS 3 hit the motorway! A street party blocks off the M41, and 8000 people do the party & protest.

July 18–21. Long Marston, Stratford-upon-Avon. A disused airfield. Hoping to pick up Glastonbury's crowds, the Phoenix Festival features David Bowie, Neil Young and the Sex Pistols.

August 10. Stanmer Park, Brighton. Festival of Freedom. 30,000 come to this free festival of DiY Culture, with eight stages featuring live bands and all sorts of alternative stalls.

1997

June 27–29. Glastonbury Festival of Contemporary Performing Arts. One of the mud years following torrential rain just prior to the festival, which leads to the Other Stage threatening to collapse and performances there being cancelled as a precaution. Sting, Ray Davies, Prodigy, Radiohead, Massive Attack, Dodgy, Pavement, Super Furry Animals, the Chemical Brothers, Ocean Colour Scene, Smashing Pumpkins, Mansun, the Bluetones, Beck, Echo and the Bunnymen, Kula Shaker and Stereolab, but overall fewer big names, more variety. Site now covers a huge 800 acres, and has a daily newspaper and live television broadcasts on BBC2. A 'dubhenge' made from upended VW beetles and campervans, the first Greenpeace field with a reconstructed *Rainbow Warrior* (the boat blown up by French secret service

in New Zealand in 1985). Greenpeace, Oxfam, and a local homeless charity are among main beneficiaries. 95,000 people. Tickets £75 with no charge for programme.

June–August. Regular commercial summer festival circuit offers full variety of music and culture: the Fleadh in Finsbury Park, Phoenix Festival, Cambridge Folk Festival, WOMAD at Rivermead, Monsters of Rock at Castle Donington, Reading Festival, Notting Hill Carnival in London.

August 16–17. Leeds and Chelmsford. V97. Virgin V Festival continues its innovative festival structure: it is split on two sites up and down the country, with the line-ups swapping overnight. Blur headline.

August Bank Holiday Weekend. Luton, Bedfordshire. First annual 'Free the Spirit' free festival, organised by leading DiY-ers, Exodus Collective, on their Long Meadow Community Free Farm.

Tribal Gathering, the longstanding commercial festival of the dance generation, is involved in an acrimonious legal battle with commercial partner, Mean Fiddler Organisation, over the increasing commercialisation of the festival.

RIGHT Theatre, comedy and cabaret are by 1997 Glastonbury staples.

1998

June 26–28. Glastonbury Festival of Contemporary Performing Arts. Bob Dylan, Robbie Williams, Tony Bennett wearing the only white suit in Somerset in June, play for anything between 85,000 and 100,000 people. Tickets £80, plus £3 booking fee, £20 extra for coming in a campervan. Another one of the mud years, and a small outbreak of gastral infection spreads through the mud. 1000 different performances on 17 stages, including the Lightning Seeds, Primal Scream, Underworld, Tricky, Blur, Sonic Youth, Bernard Butler, Nick Cave, Cornershop, Fatboy Slim, Prodigy, Spiritualized, Asian Dub Foundation, Pulp, Roni Size. Over £500,000 raised for Greenpeace, Oxfam, Water Aid and many local organisations.

June 20. Milton Keynes Bowl. Ozzfest '98. Ozzy Osbourne and Black Sabbath reunite. Advertised unassumingly as follows: 'Ozzfest takes a big wet bite out of the arse of every other festival . . . You haven't seen jackshit . . . the event of the millennium!'

July 11–12. T in the Park, near Glasgow. Prodigy, Spiritualized, Asian Dub Foundation, in case you missed them a couple of weeks back in Somerset.

Mud, sunshine and sunsets, Glastonbury '98.

Dance music goes from strength to strength at Glastonbury: an impromptu rave and Norman Cook.

July 16–19. Phoenix Festival, Britain's only four-day commercial event. Bands booked include Prodigy, Spiritualized, Asian Dub Foundation, in case you missed them at T in the Park last weekend. The event is cancelled late on due to poor ticket sales. Along with last year's Tribal Gathering struggle, a crisis in the development of commercial festival culture in the 1990s is taking place, with many proclaiming the death of festival. A number of smaller festivals are also hit by lack of demand, by the oversupply each summer.

1999

June 25–27. Glastonbury Festival of Contemporary Performing Arts, 'supporting Greenpeace, Oxfam, Water Aid, and worthwhile local causes'. Hundreds of acts, including REM, Manic Street Preachers (who bring their own portaloo), Beautiful South, Hole, Underworld, Beth Orton, Mogwas, Mercury Rev, Pavement, Sebadoh, Tindersticks, Lonnie Donegan, Suzanne Vega, the Chemical Brothers, Fatboy Slim, David Holmes, Paul Oakenfold, Jurassic 5, Travis, Optical & Ed Rush, Fabio & Grooverider, DJ Krust, Baaba Maal, Natasha Atlas, Squarepusher, Junior Delgado, Patti Smith, Joe Strummer, Texas, Blondie, the Glastonbury Town Band and the Avalonian Free State Choir. Ian Dury is too ill to perform. Tickets £83 plus handling charge. Attendance stable at 85,000–100,000 people. Sponsored by *Select* magazine, the *Guardian,* Orange mobile phones, BBC 2 and Radio 1. The sun shines again.

June-August. Some of the regular commercial summer festivals happen as usual: Cambridge Folk Festival, T in the Park, the Fleadh at Finsbury Park,

WOMAD at Rivermead, V99, Notting Hill Carnival in London.

Phoenix Festival doesn't rise from the ashes.

July 31–1 August. Someone has the bright idea to revive the Buxton Festival of the 1970s, an event called BADAM '99. An unashamedly retro bill was to feature Hawkwind, The Crazy World of Arthur Brown (last seen – when? *Decades* ago?), and Daevid Allen from Gong. Ticket prices from another era too: £20 in advance. Was this event cancelled?

August 11. Total eclipse of the sun. Line of totality includes some of the West Country, so a number of tribal gatherings and commercial festivals are held. Those advertised in Devon and Cornwall include Lizard Festival, Lynx Voodoo Eclipse Festival, Moonshadow Eclipse Festival, Total Eclipse Festival, Cornish Eclipse Stone Festival, and a free festival at Men-an-Toll. All of the commercial events lose money.

August 28–29. Reading Festival. Picking up on the Virgin Festivals of the past few years, 'The Carling Weekend' Reading offers a north-south split. Friday and Saturday see the bands at Reading, Saturday and Sunday the same bands at Leeds.

October 9. London, New York, Geneva. Net Aid benefit to alleviate poverty in the developing world. A bit like Live Aid from the previous decade – with many of the same 'superstar' acts: Bowie, George Michael, Eurythmics – and a smattering of '90s talent like Wyclef Jean, Puff Daddy and Robbie Williams. The difference is that these transatlantic simultaneous performances are broadcast live on the Internet.

et cetera . . .

'Fields are our lost history':

countryside and landscape

> The fact which makes Glastonbury a unique experience among the major rock
> festivals in this country is that the site itself is miles from anywhere. It's not tacked
> on to a dormitory town like Reading, nor in a purpose-built area like the Milton
> Keynes Bowl . . . Glastonbury offers no such cosy links with civilisation . . .
> The challenge of how to get there is the same for pop star and punter alike . . .
> The real Glastonbury experience comes from all of us being in it together.
>
>   Billy Bragg, 1995

It is almost easy to overlook the fact that Glastonbury festival takes place on a *farm*, a working dairy farm at that. (There are practical reasons for it being a dairy farm, at least as a midsummer event: if the land was arable, for instance, crops would be growing at that time of the year. Many of the East Anglian fairs took place on stubble fields just after harvest, but that would be later summer rather than June. What does need harvesting is the silage, grass feed for the cows, which is usually done by June 11, leaving a very tight fortnight to transform fields into festival.) This in spite of the marketing of the festival as being on farmland – the herds of photogenic Friesian cows against green backdrop has been used by the festival and by television broadcasts of the festival alike. Partly here we're being presented with the promise of a rural idyll (though maybe not for vegans), partly a story of transformation (where have all the cows gone?). Michael Eavis told me that 'the farm is important to people's perceptions of the festival – it's a real, working dairy farm, with very attractive, small fields that haven't been turned into prairie-style agribusiness. The layout of the fields remains much as it was in medieval times, in fact.' Jeremy Sandford quotes someone

In a field, framed by trees, and used as a cowshed: a pastoral pyramid

(maybe himself) in *Tomorrow's People* on the 1971 Glastonbury Fayre: 'It was one of the most ideal places you could have for a festival. The low wooded hills and hedges and slopes with the stage right at the bottom and the little eighteenth century farm buildings made a perfect environment.'

Other festival sites have been on racecourses (some of the pre-Reading National Jazz Federation festivals, like Plumpton, Windsor, in the 1960s), or old airfields (the 1975 People's Free Festival at Watchfield, Bob Dylan's Blackbushe concert, the Phoenix Festival in the 1990s), even ex-rubbish dumps (Reading started like that in 1971 – no jokes, please). Not Glastonbury. The earthy and ancient day job contributes to Eavis's authentic aura, as he himself notes: 'We're a real farming family, and the farm still comes first, even now, but people who come to the festival know that I'm real, too.' How is this authenticity transmitted, in image and marketing terms? 'Oh no, we don't do all that marketing, all that image stuff. Well, maybe subconsciously, we might prefer an image of the countryside, but then I am a farmer, it is a farm.' (He is a farmer, but he has also been a merchant seaman, and even worked for a time in the Somerset coal fields, facts which do not always make the press reports: the media prefers the dairy farmer milking his cows to the sounds of new pop music.)

Comparing the dairy farm setting of Glastonbury with another strand of festival culture will perhaps further highlight the agricultural contribution. The stately home of Beaulieu is better known for its motor museum than for its early flourish of festival culture. Yet Beaulieu, like Woburn in the 1960s and the better-known Knebworth Festivals of the 1970s, began a connection of aristocratic privilege and pop music, of private means and mass entertainment, that characterised a certain social stratum of those swinging times. 'A combination of blue blood and the blues' was the 1957 Beaulieu

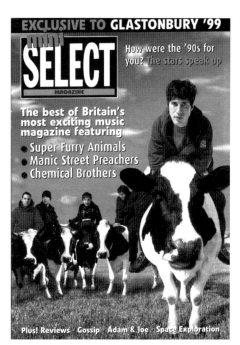

Dairy cows and grass contribute to the Glastonbury experience.

motto. Partly it was generational (Montagu was around thirty years old at the time of the first Beaulieu Jazz Festival), partly a social shift, as Christopher Booker recognises: there was 'intimate cooperation between members of the crumbing old order and of the rising new – each fascinated by the powerful image of the other: the insecure lower or less "established" group longing for the style and stability of culture and breeding, the insecure upper group mesmerised by the life and vitality of the *arriviste*.' Symptoms of this apparent class blurring ranged from the new satire movement calling its London comedy club *The Establishment* to Lord Snowdon, society photographer and brother-in-law of the Queen, holding swinging celebrity-packed parties at Kensington Palace, from Teddy Boys ironically adorning themselves in upper-class Edwardian-style long jackets in the 1950s to Albert Finney and John Lennon swapping their E-Type Jaguars for Rolls-Royces in the 1960s. At pop festivals in the grounds of stately homes the aristos got to feel secure in uncertain times, with the added attraction of making some much needed hard cash, while the bands got to be flattered that they really were going somewhere in the world. Not much of an alternative England in these festival moments, at first sight.

Richard Neville, as befits his outsider status as an Australian, acutely observed this mixture of 'blue blood and the blues' at the Rolling Stones' free concert in Hyde Park in July 1969. Neville sneered in *Play Power* at the new aristocracy of rock, the hierarchy of the counterculture:

> Pop's swing-swing version of Prince Charles's Investiture which had dazzled a different generation a few days earlier; similar solemn pageantry and shallow circumstance at a Welsh castle, the same prostrate media and indoctrinated crowds, the medieval-bedecked flunkeys matching the Hell's Angels; Prince Charles's over-praised eloquence with a useless dialect no less a gilded sham than Jagger stumbling over Shelley in the sun. Pop's own institutions become like Buckingham Palace without the efficiency, like [the Beatles's record company] Apple, collapsing in a confusion of crooked accountants, straw-clutching stunts, snivelling celebrity-fuckers.

Chrissie Lytton Cobbold, owner of Knebworth House, recalls one of the 1978 festivals there, where another sneering outsider, American Frank Zappa, could also be commendably rude in the face of English class privilege.

> Frank Zappa came to the house before going down to the stage. He arrived with a six-foot, bald-headed, coloured bodyguard who will always be remembered at Knebworth House as the man who ate all [my husband] David's favourite Swiss liqueur chocolates, a present from Zurich . . . Zappa went out of his way to be disagreeable; he looked at our Long Picture Gallery Drawing Room, festooned with gilt-framed ancestors, and remarked, 'Hmmm – this could be quite a nice room if you got rid of all those pictures.' He asked for some coffee. I was in a rush to get back to the arena, so I made him some Nescafé. He took one sip . . . 'Instant coffee, how disgusting.'

My point is that Michael Eavis at Worthy Farm projects a quite different image to these aristocratic festival organisers, a benevolent, productive, in his own word, 'real' persona (he'd say person), outside the framework of excess and privilege which the upper class and the rock aristocracy alike may present.

I think the dairy farming aspect of Glastonbury also echoes the great mythic festival of them all, Woodstock Music and Art Fair in 1969, the year before the very first Pilton Pop Festival at Worthy Farm (which, of course, included free milk from the farm in the ticket price). The festival was never even planned for the town of Woodstock, of course, but for nearby Wallkill – an unfortunate name during the time of the Vietnam War, and one also lacking the resonance of nature and farming of Woodstock itself. (Because of local opposition, the festival eventually took place even further from Woodstock.) Max Yasgur's dairy farm witnessed a transformation familiar to all who have been at Glastonbury ever since. DON'T BOTHER MAX'S COWS. LET THEM MOO IN PEACE, said one sign. LOVE YOUR ANIMAL FRIENDS, DON'T EAT THEM, said someone's placard. The promise of the countryside was expressed in the advertisements for Woodstock, which seem directed at city-dwellers:

> Three days of peace and music. Hundreds of acres to roam on. Walk around for three days without seeing a skyscraper or a traffic light. Fly a kite, sun yourself. Cook your own food and breathe unspoiled air.

Of course, our dominant narrative of the contemporary British countryside is that it is too white, too straight, really too *slow*, and it may well be all of these. But it is, too, like Max Yasgur's dairy farm of the Woodstock festival, or Michael Eavis's dairy farm of the Glastonbury festival, an escape from the urban. Keith Halfacree writes of the British countryside that 'the rural provides an "escape" from an uncertain, multiracial and crime-ridden urban world into the "timeless" countryside, with its social quietude, peace and beauty', and he further identifies 'rurality's role as a "refuge from modernity" in the guise of the city.'

   Yet, after all, it is important also to recognise that the countryside is a deeply politicised space. There is so much to campaign about there: public access, animal husbandry and animal rights, hunting, peace, food production, organic farming, genetically manipulated crops, development (roads, housing, etc). And, surely non-coincidentally, a gamut of alt.culture is there, from ciderpunks to crop circles. In Britain, the countryside has itself been reconfigured, perhaps reclaimed, certainly reinvigorated as a public site of contestation in recent years, not only by the peace campaigners and eco-protesters, but by belief groups and organisations as varied as neo-pagans, eco-feminists, mythopoetic men's groups, land and animal rights activists, the Black Environmental Network and the Conservative government which thought up the Criminal Justice and Public Order Act, 1994, to name a very few. What interests me here, as elsewhere, is the legacy of Thatcherism's underbelly, the reverse yuppie culture that saw the Peace Convoy, anarchopunk, Greenham Common and the other peace camps, Stonehenge and the free festival movement, Acid House, etc., re/invent themselves as anti-authoritarian spectacles, disappearances, confrontations. Many of these moral panics have been located in or by the countryside, and, since as conservationist group Common Ground notes, '[fields] . . . are our unwritten history', that's where I go, too. (It's important to bear in mind though that fields are not just magical repositories of lost history, the places where the West Anglian Romantic poet John Clare 'found' his poems, but also that they codify control, intervention, property.) Even the Countryside Alliance of recent years uses mass mobilisations and threats of other direct action tactics to defend 'traditional' country life – ironically enough in response towards proposed legislation in Parliament to ban fox-hunting. (Gamekeeper turned poacher.) As Newbury road protester Merrick expressed the situation, while sitting in a cell in Newbury police station in '95 or '96: 'There's hunters and hunt saboteurs on the same side! If we don't save this land, there won't be any countryside here to argue about.'

And all the while these arguments and confrontations have been going on, there in the background, in those fields, over those walls, those hedges, has been Glastonbury festival, constant, constantly changing.

Like Prime Ministers from Stanley Baldwin to John Major, I *love* the countryside (and don't live there). They presented it for its spurious, retrogressive national iconicity of, in Major's case, warm beer and cricket, or, in Baldwin's, the 1926 collection of sounds that was already retrospective as he spoke it: 'the tinkle of the hammer on the anvil in the country smithy, the corncrake on a dewy morning, the sound of the scythe against the whetstone'. I prefer an alternative form of nostalgia – to echo Walter Benjamin, a critical nostalgia, or, more suitably situated, Fraser Harrison's explorations of 'positive nostalgia' in his writings about Suffolk. For Harrison, 'a society which is addicted to nostalgic longings for a lost and largely invented countryside is probably sick, but a society which feels no longing for its countryside is sicker still'. Nostalgia is pivotal in constructions of the countryside: the place of the child – or, indeed, of the retiree, often the same person fifty years on (nostalgia is homesickness, after all) – makes it a site of memory, fantasy, even sentimentality. The past is a different countryside. (Or is it the same? I can never work it out.) It's significant that Dion Fortune's psychic classic (believe me, I've never written that phrase before) *Avalon of the Heart* opens with a description of her journey from London to Glastonbury, explicitly from the contemporary commercial city in the east to the atavistic spiritual countryside in the west: 'The long road from London spans the breadth of England and leads from one world to another.' On this journey landscape and self are transformed. Fortune passes the stone circles, our pins of the past in the land, of Stonehenge and Avebury:

Stonehenge stands grey and ominous, dominating the wide grey lands … All around their grim circle the air is heavy and cold with ancient fear. The sun shines grey upon them and the earth feels full of death. They belong to the end of the ancient race, when its light was spent and its vision darkened. Very different is Avebury, the great sun-temple of its glory. Here an invisible sun, formed by the magic of the priests, shines ever into the hearts of men. Here is healing and joy, and a wisdom which is not of this age.

Debbie Harry in 1999.

Glastonbury 1999

The countryside. These fields, hedges, trees, the grand mellow sweep of the valley itself. A couple of years ago wasn't an image of the dairy cows used to promote the festival, the event marketing itself through its rural product, land use? The Green and Avalon bits, they're called – Fields. And with all the male pissing that goes on in the brook and hedges, you need, like the giant wicker man/angel in the Sacred Ground, to look up – up from the detritus to the horizon, from the valley floor to the hillsides, from the stages, scaffolded and transitory, to the Tor, hazy but solid.

And anyway it meant I had to walk from where I'd parked the car, and you drive along this kind of aluminium rack, track which is put down in the fields, right, so there's a roadway that's put down of aluminium, and that goes on and on and on, of aluminium strips joined together, a bit like a pontoon bridge or something over the grass. As I was driving along there I was thinking, Jesus, you know, in this whackingly huge car park driving on aluminium, you know, all this stuff I've been writing about festival – communing with nature, celebrating the solstice, the Arthurian past thing, all that – it's like forget it, man. It's just a mass, mass, mass, mass event. Metal cars on metal roads.

So, em, what else, I've been wandering, yeah, so, I had to go back to the car about an hour later, and it's getting dark by then, and, er, to pick up, you know, the clothes, my rucksack with clothes and sleeping stuff and food and things like that. And I walked along the old railway line that runs through the site, and then, where it runs through this particularly sort of ugly bit, in the middle of which is like a little scar, a sort of a waste land, and ironically this is right next to some of the Green Fields, and in there there was kind of old dead wood around and stuff, and people were pulling that off, and there were a few dead trees, and loads of people were hovering around, and it stank of sort of damp dead wood and piss and things like that, and there were loads of people in there pulling it all off to get a big batch of wood so that they could have a big fire when they drag it back to their tent, you know, three-quarters of a mile away or fucking two miles away, Jesus. That was a bit grotty actually, it was all dusty and dry and smelly and horrible, and all these people sort of beavering away in this dark little space, pulling bits off dead trees (better than live ones, I suppose), scavenging, scavenging a temporary identity.

At the Pyramid Stage. Debbie Harry of Blondie – see? The past again – says, 'We're out here in this beautiful aspect of nature,' as an introduction to a song, and there's a legitimacy in that, especially coming from an American, recognising a little local wilderness myth. The song they do is a ballad, a slow piece, nobody's very interested, but the band seem to have the idea that it reflects, uh, some sense of the landscape, as though slowing down can capture it. I guess the only thing spoiling the landscape is the electricity pylons, you know, especially in this sort of atavistic space, where frankly the quick perspective of the future should not run! There's an atavism about this place which, even if it doesn't go back to medieval times it goes back, oooh thirty years, which is a fuck of a long time for a terminally amnesiac culture like ours, and that's why you see all the press photographers congregating up in the Sacred Ground round the stone circle for their faux-past images. You know, even the pylons, when I was last night gazing at the Tor, for a while they seemed to direct themselves towards the Tor, even if they veered off afterwards like insecure ley lines.

The rural landscape contributes massively to our experiences of Glastonbury. In *Avalonian Quest*, Geoffrey Ashe writes compellingly of 'the eye-cheating perspectives, the sudden appearances and vanishings of the Tor, the inconsistency of the hills and the plain' around the town of Glastonbury. From his own daily routine of living there, Ashe suggests that the experience of landscape, what we generally think of as *terra firma*, solid ground, is here a much more uncertain and ambiguous experience. John Michell concurs, quickly blurring the distinction between geography and mythology:

Everything about Glastonbury, the landscape, the light and atmosphere, its archaeological relics and its accumulation of unique legends, contributes to the mystery of the place. Its special quality is made obvious at first sight by its most prominent feature, Glastonbury Tor, the central pivot of its mythological landscape.

The uncertainty of the landscape makes it, like some curious ancient text scholars argue over, ripe for interpretation. I want to look at both the local landscape itself around the fields of the festival and at ways in which it is charted – not charted in Ordnance Survey terms, but in those ways we recognise now as characteristic of the area, that is, intuitive or spiritual cartography. How is Avalon mapped on to Glastonbury?

For all, as noted, the most striking aspect of their common landscapes is Glaston-bury Tor. The Tor is that extraordinary natural (not man-made, though it *eye-cheatingly* looks like it ought to be) feature, a shapely 500-foot mound rising suddenly from meadows and green vales below, which is one of the most dramatic markers of the Somerset landscape. In a county more famed for its eponymous landscape feature of

the Somerset Levels, that is flat land, the achievement of the Tor appears perhaps all the more dramatic. In *Avalon of the Heart*, Dion Fortune wrote of the Tor that 'it has that subtle thing which, strange as the word may seem when applied to a hill, we cannot call other than personality'. Such anthropomorphic impulses make greater sense when considering the etymology of the word 'Tor'; one suggestion is that it derives from the Old Welsh word *twrr*, meaning 'belly'. Its obvious male and female symbolism – the phallic tower, the breast of the hill – appeals to the yin and yang New Age constituency.

As befits its strangeness, the Tor too has its legends. It is the home in Welsh tradition of a fairy king, or king 'under the hill', Gwyn ap Nudd. Entry via a secret door leads to a wondrous palace, where Gwyn sits on a golden throne. The Tor has visible terraces once assumed to be the remains of farming activity, but (naturally enough) more recently it has been suggested that they are part of an elaborate ancient maze, or, more accurately, a three-dimensional labyrinth. This interpretation was put forward by an Irishman, Geoffrey Russell, in 1964. Russell had experienced a vision twenty years earlier, which revealed to him the importance of labyrinths to the conscious and unconscious minds (my conjecture is that he was reading Joyce's recently published *Finnegans Wake* at the time). John Michell explains:

> The hill is presumed natural, but anyone can see that at one time it has been shaped.
> Around its sides are several tiers of well defined terraces . . . [The] rings [are] seven
> in number and joined up to form a continuous pathway towards the top of the Tor,
> accurately reproducing the twists and turns of the seven-layered labyrinth which
> symbolized the classical Mysteries.

The sole tower that crowns the Tor today, and emphasises its bare otherness, is what is left of the medieval church of St Michael, itself built on an earlier monastic settlement, which in turn had replaced a significant settlement. This earliest, possibly of Arthurian or Celtic or pagan times, dates for Dion Fortune from the era 'when the worship of the Son supplanted that of the Sun'. Folk-singer Bob Stewart has observed on Christianity taking over older sites of worship or veneration that 'pagan hill-top sites were rededicated to Michael, to guard against pagan infiltration'. Comparing the 1960s countercultures of America and Britain, Iain Chambers is altogether less convinced by the power of the Tor. Yet even Chambers pinpoints landscape – and, perhaps more importantly, its mythologisation – as an essential factor in the hippie

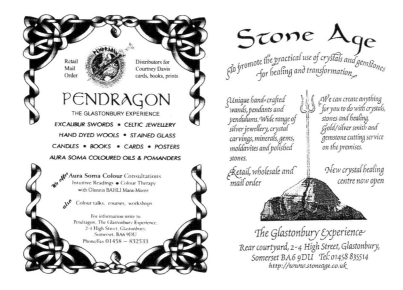
movement. Where American youth looked to the West Coast, British youth have turned to the West Country, right?:

> This 'alternative reality', laconically fixed in the distinctive style of the hippy,
> came to fruition in the mythological land of perpetual sun and endless surf where
> the wave of youth never breaks: California . . . In Britain, all this tended to occur
> on a different scale . . . The green mound of Somerset's Glastonbury Tor, for astrological
> and mythological reasons a favoured hippy site, has little in common with the dramatic
> nature of southern California where various communes (including Charles Manson's
> Family) camped out on the edge of the desert and strange scenarios were rehearsed.

The scenarios around the Tor are never as extreme as those Chambers slightly mis-leadingly refers to, never the murderous frenzy of Charles Manson and his followers, but (like many of the American communes, in fact) altogether quieter, less spectac-ular, personal affairs. Not that C.J. Stone, in his trawls around Glastonbury for his book *The Last of the Hippies*, finds much peace there. For Stone, the Tor is spoilt by the crowds of 'mystical tourists': 'People dowsing. People praying. People meditating. People playing the drums or the didgeridoo. It's always busy, Glastonbury Tor. It's the spaghetti junction of the spiritual journey,' he concludes, with an unsympathetic metaphor, if an unsurprising one for a Brummie.

Glastonbury 1999

I've been having a close look at the hedges on the outskirts of Shepton Mallet. I can see several different sorts of ivy, brambles, thorns, blackthorn perhaps, Ican see some high trees there, like elder maybe, I can see a rowan tree, I can see cow . . . cow . . . whatever that stuff's called, cow parsley, and stinging nettles, of course, and we can also see just on the other side there some lovely purple wild geraniums, and wild wheat. I can do all this while I'm waiting and have been waiting for one hour now, in the queue outside Shepton Mallet, the traffic jam, to get through Shepton Mallet, to get on the Glastonbury road, to stop at Pilton, on Thursday, oh God, evening now, it was afternoon when I got to Bristol, it's evening now when I'm twenty miles down the road, serves me right for coming in the car. Listening to Wimbledon on Radio 5, another green England. One brilliant thing I just saw a minute ago, in one of the rare moments when the traffic moved, I glimpsed through the hedge, and it's sort of flat the landscape, green, green, fantastically green, shades of it, and then voomph out of nowhere on the horizon there's this really extraordinary rump, bump, mound in the landscape, with the Tor on top of it, with er St Michael's Tower on top of it. That's Glastonbury Tor, up out of a flat haze. First time I've seen that. It's an impressive sight, more so in glimpses.

Four days later, leaving. And the Tor, coming from the festival to Glastonbury is so spectacular, it's just the way to see it, it's its perfect frame. It's so confident, the way it presents itself, free-standing. The festival does the Tor and St Michael's Tower such a favour: the contrast between our temporary noisy mass event and its fixed silent solo power was worth, worth all the crappier bands and their overbearing volumes. When you see the Tor from the other side, from the west of the town, it's just a church tower on a hill. But from the east side, looking down the Vale of Avalon, moving along it in fact, it's so isolated in its splendour, and the isolation contributes to that splendour. And when you hit Glastonbury town, at the roadside, the town sign says WELCOME TO GLASTONBURY, ANCIENT ISLE OF AVALON. I must get a photo of that.

In other obvious ways, the local landscape simply does not fit the legend. For instance, surely it is a significant obstacle for the so-called Isle of Avalon that the town is far from sea-, lake- or large river-water, is in no way an island? I certainly thought so. Yet all is explained by Philip Rahtz in *The Quest for Arthur's Britain*:

Towards the end of the Roman period [circa AD 400], there were changes in the relative sea and land levels, which brought the sea (at the highest tide, at any rate) to the 18-feet contour. Such a level would cause most of the north Somerset plain to be flooded, leaving Glastonbury isolated except for the higher ground to the east linking it with the Shepton Mallet area.

The remains of lake villages – communities consisting of houses on stilts – to the north of the town are evidence of the older watery surroundings. On the official festival website Michael Eavis indulges in one of those seemingly irresistible correspondences when he writes that 'Recent archaeological digs have suggested that there were regular midsummer festivals in the Lake Villages near Glastonbury as early as 500 BC. Beads and other artefacts have been found at sites only free of flood water at the height of summer.' With this casual two-and-a-half-thousand year leap of Eavis's, it's possible to witness once more that knack Glastonbury has of supplying you with what you want in order to believe, of presenting you with just enough for you to confirm whatever idea or position you hold, whether fantasy, religion, legend, cod history. A leap of faith, of intuition, reliant on the sort of 'proof' that makes the objective academic's heart sink. Verb-free scholarship. (John Michell: 'Like all discoveries at Glastonbury, it came through revelation, which is not a popular medium among the professors.') At Glastonbury, people are leaping all over the place, maan. I suspect I'm even doing a bit of it myself in this writing – or perhaps I'm editing it out, embarrassed. Because of its 'eye-cheating' qualities, perhaps it should not be surprising that the landscape around Glastonbury has been subject to layer on layer of interpretation. Many souls have designs on Glastoscape.

Alfred Watkins was a photographer, businessman and writer of the best-selling *Watkins' Manual of Photographic Exposure and Development* during the late nineteenth and early twentieth century. His family roots were in the Welsh Borders brewing trade, and Watkins was a familiar figure, man and boy crossing the local countryside for pleasure and business alike. During high summer 1921 he began the 'rush of revelations' which was to open up the perception of landscape of a country man in his mid-sixties. It is fair to say that what Watkins saw on June 30 blew his mind, to adopt a more recent phrase – he talked of 'the amazement' of it, of time rushing by, 'scarcely realizing that half the year had gone', of 'a most surprising fact'. The power for him may have come as much from its simplicity as from the revelation itself: ancient sites on the English landscape are aligned with one another.

John Michell describes Watkins's moment of vision: 'He pulled up his horse to look over the landscape below. At that moment he became aware of a network of lines, standing out like glowing wires all over the surface of the country, intersecting at the sites of churches, old stones and other spots of sanctity.' Ley lines offered Watkins the opportunity to align a number of his enthusiasms: scopophilia, the technology of photography, rambling, naturalism, the study of antiquity and mystery, and interpretation of map and land alike – it all had to *mean* something to Watkins. Here is an extraordinary way in which an apparatus of modernity, the camera and its technologies (by its ninth edition *Watkins' Manual* had sold 80,000 copies to other camera enthusiasts) led to a new way of seeing the ancient, the landscape and its textualisation. In his 1922 self-published lecture *Early British Trackways, Moats, Mounds, Camps and Sites*, Watkins connects the country landscape, ley line and the English language itself in an ambitious interpretation (which he modestly describes as 'a mere framework for a new knowledge'):

Title page from Alfred Watkins's *Early British Trackways*.

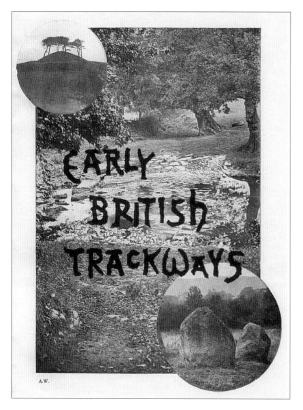

A.W.

The fact of the ley is embedded in the rural mind . . .
It was once absolutely necessary to 'keep straight on' in the ley, for if you did not you would be de-leyed on your journey. This is not said as a pun, but as in some succeeding sentences, to point out the place of the ley in the evolution of our language.

Where the ley laid in a wood [it] became a glade . . .
Where the ley had lain for a time often became a lane. This last noun became a verb used in the 18th century enclosure acts, where ground was 'laned out'. Where it was so laned out it became land.

The etymology may be questionable, but I confess an admiration for this chap who, a bit like Russell Hoban's post-holocaust boy-hero, Riddley Walker, walks his riddles on the landscape. (And I, who wrote a doctoral thesis in part on Hoban's brilliant novel, had never noticed until right now the word *ley* in Riddley's name, Hoban's novel's title.)

The West Country, rich in ancient sites and markers, has been fertile ground for ley charting. Glastonbury town is said to be criss-crossed with ley lines, connecting the holy places of the Tor, the Abbey, the Chalice Well. Geoffrey Ashe, following a sceptical description of leys, concedes that, 'While the ley theory is most decidedly Not Proven, it must be conceded that one of the few lines which do impress passes through Glastonbury. John Michell drew attention to it and called it the St Michael Line.' (I did wonder whether the last sentence is a subtle comment by Ashe on the egocentricity of students and teachers of the ancient mysteries . . .) This is a ley line from St Michael's Mount, Marazion in Cornwall all the way over to the east coast near Lowestoft, Suffolk, on its route touching many hills and churches dedicated to St Michael – including the tower on Glastonbury Tor, as well as the stone circle village of Avebury (but not Stonehenge). So, Michell called it the Michael line (yes, and the farmer, landowner and festival organiser is *Michael* Eavis. Stop already). During festival time, though, looking west along the valley, the Vale of Avalon, toward the Tor, more noticeable energy lines are supplied by the vast intrusive electricity pylons, where runs what the thirties poet Stephen Spender called 'the quick perspective of the future'. While himself seeming to prefer the more landscape-oriented 'winding paths respecting local topography', pagan academic Graham Harvey notes the connection of ley lines to Aboriginal 'song lines' in Australia, as well as to 'dragon lines' of energy in China (including Feng Shui). For Watkins, leys were simply the residual evidence of ancient trackways, but according to Janet and Colin Bord's rather seventies book *Mysterious Britain*:

> Later researchers believe that this is only part of the answer, and that the leys may in fact follow invisible lines of power criss-crossing the countryside . . . It is thought by some people that leys are used, possibly as a power source or navigational aid, by flying saucers or UFOs as they move around our skies.

And the 1990s me-generation has come up with another altogether more *ad hominem* explanation. According to Harvey, in his study of contemporary paganism, ley lines 'are human artefacts created to image the shaman's out-of-body flight across the land'.

The crop circle phenomenon of the south and west of England provides more recent evidence of the sheer appetite of the British public's desire for mystery, the appeal of what Theodor Adorno damningly called 'the metaphysic of dunces' –

occultism. Crop circles have been found in corn and grass for silage alike, a kind of invented mystery of landscape and pre-harvest celebration combined. Like the fairies at the bottom of the garden that so entranced Sir Arthur Conan Doyle in the 1920s – or rather like the *photographs* of fairies that so entranced him – and like the photographic mind of Alfred Watkins when he saw ley lines for the first time in the hot summer of 1921, the crop circle combines mystery and visual technology. As Pat Delgado and Colin Andrews point out with apparently straight faces in their book *Circular Evidence*, 'the circles are very photogenic . . . The dramatic symmetry of the circles is seen at its best from an aircraft and good detail is picked out with the powerful zoom lens.' The camera, or in Watkins's case, the camera-focused mind, *lies* for us, to us, gives us what we want: aerial shots of circles in corn or silage grass not stone. In the pseudo-scientific language common to New Age-style discourses, Delgado and Andrews place their circles in the context of Watkins's lines:

> Detectable lines of some unnamed force exist and are traceable along either long or short distances by various forms of dowsing. This force, which is probably in the form of a network, may have static and variable lines . . . [There] may be a random or ordained intersection of lines. Should this occur under specific conditions, a short-lived rotating spiral force may be formed with sufficient energy to create a flattened circle. Ley lines may be considered as a surface force . . .

To move finally from an aerial to a heavenly view, Glastonbury has other astral projections. In fact (again a turn of phrase), mapped on to Glastonbury are the heavens: the Glastonbury zodiac, Temple of the Stars. The connection of starscape and landscape is a tradition that goes back at least as far as Fu Hsi, the early Chinese ruler and geomancer. Like most such esoterica, it eventually made its way to Glastonbury, as Janet and Colin Bord describe:

> This enigma was rediscovered in 1929 by Katherine Maltwood, a sensitive and erudite woman who, by reading the earliest known accounts of the Arthurian Grail Quest, was able to transpose the knights' journeys from Camelot (South Cadbury Castle, 11 miles south-east of Glastonbury) on to the surrounding countryside, beside the Isle of Avalon . . . When a map of the heavens is placed upon the map of the ground and the major stars in the signs of the zodiac are marked through, they are found to fall within the areas of the figures.

POSITIVE EARTH ISSUE • RISING FROM THE ASHES • £ 1

FESTIVAL EYE
SUMMER **92**

- Media Madness
- Glastonbury City!
- On safari in the UK
- Crop circles
- Music
- Reincarnation-Rubbish?

I've perused drawings of the zodiac on the landscape around Glastonbury and they look to me like random squiggly areas – but then, to me, beyond Orion's belt, there's not too much of the actual stars in the sky that resemble their mythical beings, either. (I'm having problems freeing myself totally of my materialist prejudices here. Sitting at my desk rattling the bars of the iron cage of rationalism. Whatever.) Writing forty years after Maltwood's 'rediscovery', John Michell kindly suggested in *The View Over Atlantis* that 'the existence of the Glastonbury zodiac must for the present be accepted as a poetic rather than a scientific truth'. To Katharine Maltwood, on the other hand, the zodiac may also have been the topographical version of Arthur's round table! The town is centred, of course, upon the sign of Aquarius, and the Bords excitedly extrapolate:

> Thus the three major features of Glastonbury [the Tor, the Chalice Well and the Abbey] are seen to lie within the outline of the figure that has the greatest significance for these times. As our jaded civilization moves restlessly on, ever seeking fresh sensations and novelties, the figure of Aquarius, which is the phoenix, is an apt symbol for the coming Aquarian Age when mankind must rise again from the ashes of his past stupidities, and all things will be made anew.

Heavy, or what? Now Glastonbury is Ground Zero. A quarter of a century later we are still – or have given up – waiting to escape our past stupidities. (The unkind thought occurs that maybe this belief is one of them.) While even Michell accords that the Glastonbury zodiac is an aesthetic or intuitive projection, that may be because he has his own, better astral connection with Glastonbury landscape and legend. Now, this one begins with King Arthur, the star Arcturus, and the constellation the Great Bear . . .

So. Legend and landscape. Switching between the everyday Glastonian and the infinite Avalonian. King Arthur's burial site, the Celtic otherworld, Isle of Avalon, an early space of Christianity, the Holy Grail, the surrounding land all dotted with circles and crossed with ley lines, marked with labyrinth and zodiac alike, the end of the world every few years: not bad going for a little market town in deepest Somerset. And that's all before the two festivals at opposite ends of the twentieth century kick in (let alone the summer lakeside raves of 500 BC). The multiple spaces of Glastonbury are fictions and interpretations. The controversial Victorian historian E.A. Freeman, not renowned for his sympathetic consideration of medieval myth, pointed out that, 'We need not believe that the Glastonbury legends are records of facts; but the existence of those legends is a very great fact.' In his classic *The Time of the Tribes* sociologist Michel Maffesoli offers an explanation for what he sees as a widespread symptom of contemporary life:

> We may well ask ourselves if the harking back to the past (folklore, the revaluing of popular festivals, the return of sociability, a fascination with local history) is a way of escaping from the dictatorship of finalized, progressive history and thus a way to live in the present.

There is a frequent impulse, probably bred by the very narratives I have presented here, to romanticise Glastonbury, to present it as a utopia. This is seen in the title of one of the most recent magazines from Glastonbury's alternative community, *Free State* (as in Free State of Avalonia). In the *Free State* Peter Please contributes a nicely balanced paean – not to the town itself, but to the misty, mysterious idea of the town: 'Glastonbury gives people permission to be unique, to be dignified when they are poor and own nothing, to trust in their process of renewal, wholeness even when they cannot recognise it. Glastonbury is a sacred dustbin.'

But – and here in conclusion I have to sound ungraciously unAvalonian – dustbins are for rubbish, aren't they? I have found in researching this chapter in particular that common sense is a far from valuable or even valued commodity in the versions of Glastonbury presented here. In fact, for those who champion intuition and revelation, common sense may be part of the problem, a cloak of the banal that obstructs our pure vision. Depending on your position (which may itself be largely intuitive) this view can be refreshing, or it can be exasperating. Here are two brief examples of a lack of critical distance from believers, of what New Agers with their shaky grasp on contemporary science might celebrate as fuzzy logic. First, John Michell writes in *New Light on the Ancient Mystery of Glastonbury* that 'the old thorn tree, whose descendant stands today on Wearyall Hill, provides solid evidence for those who like to believe that Joseph of Arimathea actually came to Glastonbury'. What? *Solid evidence for those who like to believe?* That is an elegantly casual Jesuitical phrase. Second, Janet and Colin Bord write in *Mysterious Britain* that 'leys customarily touch the edges of earthworks and do not pass through their centres'. What? You mean the old straight track doesn't actually align very often? The ley line is really a ley curve? Come on!

In 1934, Dion Fortune nicely described her book about Glastonbury, *Avalon of the Heart*, as 'speculation, not history; modern myth-making, not research'. This book, mine, is, though, in part a history of speculation, research on modern myth-making. Writing it has its difficulties, but at least I am in good company. James Carley, the Glastonbury historian, has identified 'a disease which attacks most scholars who deal with the history of Glastonbury Abbey, a kind of galloping gullibility'. Carley has even experienced 'early symptoms of this malady' himself. So have I! The unreliable, hidden, plural, lost stories and invented truths of legend, the temporary experience of the countryside, the intuited images imposed on or springing from the landscape – these problematic and energising narratives have required more than a pinch of salt, more like an hourglass – sign of ancient time, mostly computerised today: ⧗ 's worth.

Fluffy Glastonbury festival.

Let me entertain you!

Next time was '89 with the raggle taggle band
We were jamming jigs and reels in a backstage transit van
I wore a wedding suit, sang 'When ye go away'
Sharon Shannon's accordion was the soundtrack of the day.

    Mike Scott, 'Going back to Glasters'

The range of popular music styles presented at Glastonbury illustrates the way in which the festival aims to renew, refresh itself. The festival has managed to become established and yet also regularly transforms itself – to an extent at least (though not without problems). Other festivals have stuck more with one type of music (generally some rock or rock variation, as at Knebworth for a decade, or Reading for, well, longer), or specialised from the start (WOMAD, for instance). The Glastonbury formula has been characterised by change, which may be all the more surprising since for the past two decades it has been solely identified with a middle-aged (now approaching elderly) Christian farmer. The bill over the three decades of the festival reflects changing subcultural interests: folk, hippy, punk (a little bit, in the indie mould), reggae, jazz and world music, dance culture and so on. Not much blues. For instance, 1970 had Marc Bolan and T. Rex (though the Kinks were originally lined up as headliners; that Marc Bolan ended up headlining makes the Pilton Pop Festival more cool, more of its age, partly because of the Bolan young death myth), 1982 featured the Thompson Twins, 1986 featured Level 42, 1990 featured Happy Mondays, 1998 Robbie Williams. When asked in 1998 for his ideal line-up for the festival, Michael Eavis replied: 'Elvis Presley, Frank Sinatra, the Grateful Dead, the Rolling Stones.' There has also been a conscious widening out from rock music and alternative lifestyles to dance, theatre, circus, multicultural celebration. Integral to the festival project is the swift construction of an alternative community, with infrastructure, inclusive entertainment, safety considerations, self-policing, and so on. Glastonbury balances this ideal of alternative community with practical elements – the introduction in 1979 (the UN Year of the Child) of a Children's Area contributed to a child-friendly, family-oriented atmosphere on-site. Eavis claimed in 1990 that 'Glastonbury now rivals the Edinburgh Fringe', a comment which suggests his view of the cultural importance of the event, but also which sides with the Fringe rather than the Edinburgh Festival proper. It's time to look in more detail at the music and musicians of Glastonbury, both those that play and that *don't* play a role in festival culture, and to consider other forms of entertainment the festival offers.

One of the local musicians who played the first festival at Worthy Farm, the 1970 Pilton Pop, Folk and Blues Festival, remembers thinking of it as 'another grotty little gig under a bit of tarpaulin flapping in the breeze'. For a second, 'Glastonbury was just a gig in a field. We played in a lot of fields that year – all you needed was a generator'. The whole thing was agricultural: the DJs' turntables were in a horse box; when he didn't have the cash to pay Marc Bolan his massive £500 fee, Eavis amicably agreed with Bolan to pay '£100 a month from the milk cheque. He played what I swear was the best set I've ever seen at Worthy Farm.'

The combination of its tendency over the years *not* to book guitar-wielding heavy rock bands as headliners and the Green-tinged and family-oriented nature of the audience, as well as the farm and country setting, means that Glastonbury has often felt more like a folk festival than a rock gig. It's not, of course: it's too loud for a start, as near and not-so-near neighbours in Glastonbury, Street and Wells testify eloquently in their late-night phone calls to Worthy Farm each festival weekend. There is a folk strand, though, from the 1970s onwards – Roger Chapman, Joan Baez, Tom Paxton, the Chieftains, Roy Harper, Billy Bragg, the Waterboys, and even Bob Dylan himself – and found also in varying forms like the roots–world music crossover, or on the Acoustic Stage. Tom Pearce, Old Uncle Tom Cobbleigh and all have made their way from Widdicombe Fair to Glastonbury Fayre. A traditional West Country folk song like 'Widdicombe Fair' illustrates Andrew Blake's point about festival sites that 'folk deals with landscape, and here there are still links to the West Country (including Glastonbury) of Cecil Sharp's heyday [of the English Folk Revival in the early twentieth century], with even Reading on the edge of Wessex, the imaginary heart of

England since its invention by the novelist and poet Thomas Hardy'. I do find Blake's Reading folk–English landscape connection less than convincing, but it should be emphasised that folk music itself of course has been an arena of political engagement, struggle. In the early 1950s the Second English Folk Revival was proclaimed by socialist singers, collectors, organisers and folk writers. The still-extant folk festival at Sidmouth, Devon was launched, as well as the radical folk magazine *Sing*, both examples of a cultural movement deliberately trying to construct a new national tradition of 'radical Englishness'. With the trad jazz developments of around the same time, as well as the burgeoning peace movement that found a more ambitious voice in 1958 with the founding of CND, the links of festival, music and radical politics and alternative national identities were seen long before Glastonbury, before even the 1960s.

But folk music has a serious image problem, doesn't it? Even Mark Chadwick of a kind of folk band like the Levellers thinks so: 'I hate folk music, I really do, it's shit. We've played festivals where we've been booked accidentally and turned up to find ourselves standing in the safest place in the universe: nothing ever happens to these people that is at all bad. They just live in this little world where Betty goes and milks the cows, and the squire shags the fucking maid.' Chadwick, like many on the free festie/DiY side of things, with their preference for in-yer-face action and living, fails to see in the slightest that a folk festival being 'the safest place in the world' might conceivably be its greatest recommendation. Comedian Lenny Henry, born in the 1950s to a Jamaican family in the West Midlands, touches on folk music and identity, too:

> I also remember the black guy in the Spinners, who was astounding. I did a joke about
> him in the last show I did. He was there with his finger stuck in his ear, singing, 'Dance,
> dance, wherever you may be, I am the Lord of the Dance said he.' Every so often they'd let
> him sing the West Indian song. Just once I wanted him to grab the mike and say, 'I shot
> the sheriff . . . ' But, knowing him, he'd have probably gone, 'I'll go no more a-sheriff
> shooting, sheriff shooting, sheriff shooting.' But I remember that guy. There weren't very
> many British black people doing it when I was growing up.

While a few hundred white hippies were making the annual pilgrimage to the stones of Stonehenge to get out of it, while the Vale of Avalon lay quiet for almost the entire decade of the 1970s, in the cities things had moved on. It seems as though, at this time, in this context, the countryside, so white, so straight, was retreating into itself as the wider country, in the cities at least, struggled for a better, equal future. Music

Sidmouth Festival was founded in the 1950s as part of folk music's effort to reclaim a 'radical Englishness'.

crossed with politics at Rock Against Racism gigs and carnivals, at demonstrations and blockades against the organised racists of the National Front and the British National Party. David Widgery described a new anti-racist alliance of urban sub-cultures stopping the NF passing through multicultural Wood Green in London in April 1977: 'Conventional anti-fascist politicos had been augmented by North London tribal gangs, rockabillies, soul girls and tracksuited Rastas checking out the platform oratory and suddenly executing fast sallies into the ranks of flabbergasted Front marchers, who especially hated the racially mixed-up style gangs and the monkey-booted all-women posses.' If there were any folk bands around this new scene they might well break into a Bob Marley song. Rock Against Racism had been founded the year before, in 1976, in response to the following letter published in *NME*, *Sounds* and *Melody Maker*, as well as in *Socialist Worker*:

> When we read about Eric Clapton's Birmingham concert when he urged support for Enoch Powell, we nearly puked. Come on Eric … you've been taking too much of that *Daily Express* stuff and you know you can't handle it. Own up. Half your music is black. You're rock music's biggest colonist. You're a good musician but where would you be without the blues and R&B? You've got to fight the racist position otherwise you degenerate into the sewer with the rats and all the money men who ripped off rock culture with their cheque books and plastic rap. We want to organise a rank and file movement against the racist poison in music. We urge support for Rock Against Racism.
>
> P.S. Who shot the sheriff, Eric? It sure as hell wasn't you!

Clapton's immediate response was extraordinarily unrepentant, especially for a musician whose reputation rested on his blues guitar playing (African-American tradition), and whose most recent hit had been a cover version of Bob Marley's 'I Shot the Sheriff' (reggae then a new-ish indigenous Jamaican music): Enoch Powell, a right-wing MP offering apocalyptic visions and/or desires of race war in Britain, claimed Clapton, 'was the only bloke who was telling the truth, for the good of the country'. God Clapton was not. The first RAR gig was in London in December 1976, riding punk's new wave, featuring the white blues of Carol Grimes and the black reggae of Matumbi. Widgery again:

> It was a wonderfully bizarre night with punks in tens, then hundreds. The art schoolies were outdone by the sheer nerve of fifteen-year-old girls with mauve and green hair, string boleros, leotards and plastic flower wedgies. The kids swanned around as if they

owned the college. Freaks from past history and costume-drama cases from the summer of love queued up quite amiably with maximum dreadlocks and members of the Clash and the Slits. The music was extremely loud, the dancing very rowdy and the stalls sold political and anti-racist literature, food and banners. Something was in the air: not just dope, but a serious music-politics-black-white mix-up.

A few months later a May Day RAR concert in 1977 celebrated this first May Day as an official public holiday in Britain. The London venue is significant, for a space is reclaimed, repositioned, (re?)politicised by a later generation, with some faces from the past. David Widgery himself came out of the 50s/60s milieu: '[The] Roundhouse, melting pot of counter-cultural sixties, was riotously decorated with colossal red and green, purple and gold, and black and white banners with RAR slogans. On stage members of Aswad, the Adverts, the Carol Grimes band, Ari Up and Tessa from The Slits-to-be and Mitch Mitchell of the Jimi Hendrix Experience-that-was ended the evening with a jam.' Again, while it appeared that things were moving so slowly in the countryside as to be almost stationary, in London, at least, the late 1960s were meeting the late 1970s in a multicultural celebration of popular music and politics. It was Culture, it was Two Sevens Clash. While some of the relation between punk and anti-racism has been romanticised, its problems glossed over (the swastika as punk symbol, most obviously), at the same time white punk and black reggae in the late 1970s were moving pop music and subculture in a different direction to the languishing festival scene of the old hippie movement.

On the basis of his experience in pop and politics, including specifically for RAR in the 1970s, I asked Tom Robinson about multiculturalism and festival culture.

Yes, we should ask the question of whether the values which something like Glastonbury embraces or presents are actually manifested at the festival sometimes. More generally, there can be a failure of imagination on the part of white people, who don't always recognise that, when there is a large concentration of white people, that attracts more white people, no matter how inclusive the ideal of the event seems to be. At its best Rock Against Racism could move beyond that. Does Glastonbury, or WOMAD, for instance?

I agree with the question put by Robinson. It's not a case of criticising a particular event as such, it's more the point of identifying the practical rather than rhetorical

Rock Against Racism's fanzine Temporary Hoarding connects music and politics in its first issue.

limits of the counterculture's much-vaunted utopian idealism. If the counterculture proclaims ALL WELCOME, yet significant and identifiable social groups *don't* come to the party, then the welcome, the appeal, becomes an issue. (Such a critique can be applied to RAR too, as recent British Asian writers have done. 'It is worth noting that the early British Bhangra scene was running parallel to these developments, but there was no involvement of Asian bands in RAR,' write Virinder Kalra and others. It is not just the hippie counterculture that can have its rhetoric and idealism undercut.)

On the other hand, maybe Glastonbury could begin to thrive precisely because it missed the whole punk thing. Festivals only in 1979 and then 1981 mean that for Glastonbury it was, as the title of a book on New Romanticism (I think; I never read it) put it, like punk never happened. Because, in spite of Nik Turner of Hawkwind's claim that punk and hippie had much in common, there were those desperate for discontinuity. Robert Garnett finds this, in a piece in a 1999 collection on 'the cultural legacy of punk':

> In the 1979 poster for the Dead Kennedys' 'California Uber Alles', surrounded by a border of cannabis leaf swastikas, is an image of the massed crowds at a Woodstock-style rock festival; over this is the caption, 'Never Trust a Hippie' and the name of the song . . . [There] are few places within which the contradictions of late-capitalist power relations are more palpably evident than at a rock festival. For there was, and is, a Nuremberg rally-type aspect to such spectacles of massed ranks of fans passively consuming the aura of unattainable demi-God rock stars, preaching a would-be liberatory hippie mythology, the whole thing policed by equally massed ranks of security.

Perhaps shocking himself with the strength of the old punk cynicism that survives twenty-odd years on, and maybe remembering that he went to one or two good festivals himself, Robert Garnett continues in the next sentence: 'At the same time, however, such mass events also offer the experience of communality, a temporary refuge from anomie and atomisation that, however illusory, is nevertheless intensely, bodily felt, and, therefore, amounts to momentary glimpse of a utopia.'

As Glastonbury expanded rapidly, perhaps too rapidly, through the 1980s, it did so alongside another festival project, Peter Gabriel's World of Music, Arts and Dance (WOMAD). In spite of on-going funding from Gabriel, WOMAD has been more financially precarious as an organisation than Glastonbury festival (but then few commercial promoters can call on the vast army of volunteers which helps make

Glastonbury possible: 700 stewards work each year for free, or rather for a ticket and a donation to the campaign or organisation they support). WOMAD was founded in 1980, and organised its first festival in Britain in 1982. Since then it has put on weekend festivals and concerts by the sea, in the countryside, in urban areas. More recently, one of the interesting and most ambitious developments of WOMAD has been to present world music festivals around the world (globalising global culture, which is not without its own problems). So where Glastonbury has always been about a sense of place, that very specific location, those actual *fields*, WOMAD has taken festival culture and made it nomadic, moving with its recognised brand name first around the country, then from country to country, then globally, from continent to continent. The two came together for a while in the late 1980s, when Glastonbury invited WOMAD to run its own stage at Worthy Farm, which increased the range and profile of the world music on offer at the festival.

This shows the way in which Glastonbury includes a musical development to renew itself, but also it shows the tactic Glastonbury uses: a stage or marquee is set aside for an identifiable music form or new trend, and if it works or is popular (these aren't always the same thing) the festival will keep it going. Within a few years, the expectation developed that the festival would feature a range of performance arenas, suitable for the likely size of audience attracted. So the *NME* Stage presented promising indie bands for a while, a Classical Stage was tried, the Wango Riley Stage would show up with an old festival vibe, Green Fields and Travellers Fields had their own marquees, the Dance Tent was officially introduced in 1995.

Some music innovations have been more welcome at the festival than others. There was widespread recognition among audiences in the early 1990s that the explosion of dance music was being ignored. The Acid House boom had hit the general public in the late 1980s, with its combination of underground and commercial raves, warehouse parties and gatherings, but Glastonbury took its time to acknowledge the music's popularity. Here the festival was displaying its origins, its preference for *live* music played by real musicians, whether guitar or sitar, the drum kit rather than the drum machine. In fact dance music wasn't let into Glastonbury by the organisers, it was smuggled in by DJs and techno-freaks, and only after a few years was it recognised and formally accommodated.

KG of Sugar Lump sound system from south London offers one originary story:

> Glastonbury we've done every year since the early '80s [sic: '90s]. We found a loophole
> in the law. As a sound system, you had to follow their curfew and turn off at one o'clock.
> But if you were a market stall holder, you could have a 24-hour licence to sell and you
> could have a sound system that was relative in size to your market stall. So for a few
> years we were selling coffee and flowers. We'd build an entrance in our pitch, with
> a tunnel to a spare bit of ground, put up a sound system and party for 24 hours.
> Nobody complained, because it got a lot of customers for the other stalls . . .
>
> [In 1992] they actually gave us land – a huge area in the *NME* field big enough to put a
> marquee on. We spent a week building a city. We bought Pink Floyd's stage covers, a huge

marquee, hired a sound system, a 16K turbo rig, and it went on for a week, partying day and night. People just stayed – there were 3000 people there constantly. It was really well organised. It was the first real house party at Glastonbury . . . We were banned from then onwards because Michael Eavis couldn't control it . . . We just made the loophole bigger and bigger until it was one of their main attractions. People remember Glastonbury 1992 for that, because there were just such a brilliant atmosphere.

At Glastonbury in 1994, among the striking features were the unauthorised sound systems that kicked in after dark. These moved *Melody Maker's* Sarah Champion to gush:

> Glastonbury's ban on raves was circumvented by almost every stall on site transforming itself into a venue. . . . Until daylight, a nutty array of festi-goers danced to acid house – fat, thin, black, white, green, crusties, suburban ravers, travellers, gangstas and trip-heads celebrating together – a true gathering of the tribes. The true goal? Pagan hedonism! Now, *this* is religion! . . . After one hell of a night, the sun rises – a spiritual experience way beyond getting drunk and watching your favourite group. F*** THE BANDS! Mass, commercial stadium stages where the herds gawp at rock stars in the distance SUCK. The spirituality of dance culture holds the true, the original spirit of Glastonbury. Having failed in their desperate bids to quell rave and shut down sounds, the Glastonbury establishment relented. From Orbital headlining the bill to 'clubs' on every corner, it reflected the *real* underground of the nineties.

The absolutely packed Dance Tent at the festival in recent years is testimony to the continuing popularity of the post-rave scene. I wondered as I moved around the festival site in 1999 about the shift in interest and popularity from the main stages to the Dance Tent, which, as Michael Eavis explained to me, was the biggest tent in the entire country. The busiest stall I saw by the Dance Tent was selling Glastonbury Spring Water, surrounded by people seriously out of their heads. I wandered round the field with fragments of a Pulp song wandering round my head. Cyberian (OK – actually, American) writer Douglas Rushkoff compares transatlantic versions of dance culture: 'While the English rave has a quality of medievalism, tribal energy, and Old World paganism, the American cyber disco is the most modern mutation of bliss induction, and uses whatever means necessary to bring people into fractal pattern.' For Rushkoff, presumably, the fact that Glastonbury has eventually embraced dance culture so enthusiastically would be evidence of ancient paganism, tribal culture, an atavistic desire for an authentic experience of nature, mediated through, er, fractal pattern. (Question from one of my earlier books: Technoshamanism or technosham?) This is overblown, of course, but we're back in the land/soundscape of legendary free party sound system Spiral Tribe, for whom 'techno is folk music'. Meanwhile, in a comment pertinent to the various atavisms of Glastonbury, Rupa Huq reminds us of some of the wider issues around easy cultural claims of tribalism, whether Third World or Olde England:

> The imagery invoked by many of rave as hypnotic, tribal, even primal carries dangerous suppositions of western supremacy over a caricatured valorisation of savages in grass skirts banging tom-tom drums, and is deeply offensive to those of contemporary tribal communities. Paradoxically the campaign [against the Criminal Justice Act's anti-rave clauses in 1994] at times comes close to treading a little Englander, parochial path, yearning for an idealised imagined past that never was.

One of the points of this book is to trace continuities and correspondences with other, earlier festival and countercultural moments. The newest alternative lifestyle and fashion of dance culture has antecedents in the trad jazz scene of the 1950s and very early 1960s in Britain. In a manner which I for one find difficult to envisage now, let alone understand, George Melly describes the fashion craze around trad jazz clarinettist Mr Acker Bilk at his peak in 1960. 'His more extreme followers wore, not only the bowler, but army boots, potato sacks, old fur coats cut down to look like stone-age waistcoats. This outfit became known as 'Rave Gear' . . . *'Rave Gear'* was rare in clubs, and *only came into its own at the festivals* or at the gargantuan all-night raves which were held under the echoing dome of the Albert Hall or among the icy wastes of the Alexandra Place. Another mark of the raver was the CND symbol [emphasis added].'

How have musicians themselves found the experience of playing festivals? Speaking of what is often mythologised as the halcyon days of festival culture, the 1960s in America, Roger McGuinn of the Byrds is perhaps surprisingly downbeat:

> I don't like 'em, man. I liked Monterey. That was real. There was a good feeling there. Lately it's been a commercial venture. The promoter loses money and the facilities are bad. There's no dressing room or it's in a trailer. It's hard to find the stage, even after

you're inside the fence. There's no time to tune up and sometimes not even electricity, and if there is, it might rain and you'll get shocked. But it's a gig. You take it for the exposure or because you have an empty weekend or the money is good. But you don't take 'em because you dig doing them. I don't know any performers who like 'em.

The British singer Joe Cocker, who first came to national prominence at a late 1960s Windsor Jazz and Blues Festival, repeated that level of performance on the international stage with his famous Woodstock appearance in 1969. You would think these festival successes would have endeared such events to Cocker, but he admitted in 1970 that 'the huge crowds which attend these festivals now frighten me . . . At Woodstock it was very difficult to pick up on the audience because it was so vast that you lost contact. I was screaming in my heart on that stage because you just cannot reach people.' Another Sheffield J. Cocker, Jarvis of Pulp, was interviewed by Ben Thompson about his band's 1995 triumph at Glastonbury:

> It must be strange, though, to have had fifty thousand people eating out of his hand at this year's Glastonbury, when so much of the point of Pulp seems to be *not* being accepted. 'But I never wanted to be different,' Jarvis insists. 'I wanted to be the same . . . I suppose that's why I now get a kick out of communicating on a mass level.'

Being the same is a relative experience for Jarvis Cocker (the last song of Pulp's Glastonbury set was 'Common People'), as he explained to the Glastonbury audience: 'We're just like you, we're sleeping in tents too. Of course, ours are gold lamé.'

Performers at the original Glastonbury festival of the early twentieth century, organised by Rutland Boughton, were enthused by the setting, the space of the place. One wrote to Boughton, 'Glastonbury seems like a delightful dream . . . it was one of the happiest times of my life'. Another, 'I've set my heart on entering the promised land. I feel certain now that with resolution it can be created.' The oneiric, spiritual, otherworldly metaphors give a sense of the contribution which the surrounding landscape and legend of Glastonbury could make to music and performance. I asked musicians who have played at Eavis's Glastonbury festival for their thoughts on performing at festivals. Nik Turner used to rehearse with Hawkwind in the barn at Worthy Farm in the run-up to the 1971 Glastonbury Fayre. He told me:

> If there was a free festival we were up for it. It was all about accessibility. Even when the music changed and there was the punk scene, for all its anti-hippie hype, the ethos was very similar: do it yourself, anyone can play it. Loads of guitarists tell me the first song they ever learned to play was Hawkwind's 'Masters of the Universe'. The 'I hate hippies' thing was a front – Johnny Rotten had been a fan of Hawkwind, he'd even worked as a Hawkwind roadie. Didn't you know that? I thought you said you knew about punk! And special festivals? Well, Stonehenge has to be the one, doesn't it, more than any other. How can it not be? I remember I designed this fertility ritual for the 1984 solstice at the stones, the last Stonehenge Free, as it happens (so far anyway). It was an all-night thing, the death of the sun-king in the evening and the rebirth of the new with the solstice sunrise. I got to be beaten by vestal virgins with leafy oak branches. Great fun, very Hawkwind. The spirituality of Glastonbury – you know, the zodiac, Joseph of Arimathea, the once and future king, Michael's quite into all that – does make a difference there, I think.

For Tom Robinson, performing at Glastonbury is different in that the crowd at Glastonbury, and the festival's reputation, function as what he calls 'a musical leveller':

> If you're overhyped and crap live it'll show. I've played many festivals in twenty-five years in the business, and at Glastonbury the only thing you have to be is *good*! Playing on the big stage at Glastonbury demands an emotional honesty – if you're really a cartoon outfit it'll show, believe me. How does Glastonbury achieve that? The two times in recent years I've played there the quality of performance has been great, because of the feeling coming from the audience. Glastonbury involves commitment just to be there – queuing to get in, carrying your gear for miles, sleeping a bit rough – so it's a committed audience, and musicians sense that. I also wonder whether dope plays a big part: the older I get, the less

time I have for a drunk crowd, and would rather have a stoned one!
I like the variety of audience too: Glastonbury pulls in the potential
Glyndebourne-ites, smoking dope in the Range Rover.

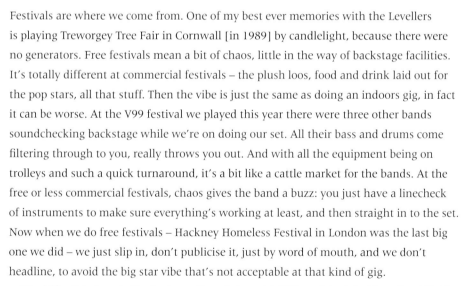

Glastonbury can make reputations, as well as break them, of course
– Pulp in 1995, for instance. Also it can signal, by the simple of act of
booking them, that a band or musician has arrived on the scene,
that a reputation been resurrected, that veteran status has been
achieved. The 'golden oldie' tradition illustrates this. Glastonbury
audiences have come to expect some elder statesperson of the music
industry to play, sometimes re-cooled for contemporary ironists:
Tom Jones, Johnny Cash, Tony Bennett, Al Green, even Rolf Harris
with the iconic didj. (Similarly, some musicians are not considered
worthy of that imprimatur: Michael Eavis tuned down George
Harrison in 1998, for example.)

In another connection of pop and festival, Jeremy Cunningham
of the Levellers told me:

> Festivals are where we come from. One of my best ever memories with the Levellers
> is playing Treworgey Tree Fair in Cornwall [in 1989] by candlelight, because there were
> no generators. Free festivals mean a bit of chaos, little in the way of backstage facilities.
> It's totally different at commercial festivals – the plush loos, food and drink laid out for
> the pop stars, all that stuff. Then the vibe is just the same as doing an indoors gig, in fact
> it can be worse. At the V99 festival we played this year there were three other bands
> soundchecking backstage while we're on doing our set. All their bass and drums come
> filtering through to you, really throws you out. And with all the equipment being on
> trolleys and such a quick turnaround, it's a bit like a cattle market for the bands. At the
> free or less commercial festivals, chaos gives the band a buzz: you just have a linecheck
> of instruments to make sure everything's working at least, and then straight in to the set.
> Now when we do free festivals – Hackney Homeless Festival in London was the last big
> one we did – we just slip in, don't publicise it, just by word of mouth, and we don't
> headline, to avoid the big star vibe that's not acceptable at that kind of gig.
>
> It's difficult to knock Glastonbury, though I used to! When it had the Travellers' Fields
> on-site you could get away from the main drag, and it was good for all the straight people
> to see New Travellers, often that was the only direct contact they'd have with travellers.

The first time we played there, I think, we were on the Wango Riley Stage at four o'clock in the morning, with the sun just coming up. Fucking magic! And the Glastonbury spiritual vibe – even if you're not really into all that stuff you can still get a sense of it.

Have rave and dance music changed the scene? The Levellers did embrace techno for a while – we had techno supporting us, and a sort of ravey light show. John, our fiddle player, uses lots of techno and sound effects. Now I think what we're doing is a reaction against all that, though.

The Levellers' singer, Mark Chadwick, puts part of their success down to the fact that the band tried to perform professionally at free and less commercial festivals: 'We used to make sure we weren't too out of it when we played. A lot of festival bands would windle on for ages, but we used to play songs all shorter than four minutes. We used to say, What time are we on? Oh, you're on after the Ozrics. Well, what day is that?'

On the other hand, at their best, music festivals aren't really about music, are they? Its centrality is undercut by the sheer range and wealth of other entertainment on offer – after all, who goes to Glastonbury with the sole or primary reason of seeing a single headlining band? Whoever that band were, you could see them in Bristol or Birmingham or London with a better sound, better view, *much* better toilet facilities (even in the dingiest rock fleapit theatre), more comfortable bed afterwards. At Glastonbury, theatre, cabaret, circus, street performance, comedy, story-telling are all available, with dedicated spaces such as fields or tents. They are frequently presented with some kind of alternative, or eco, or Avalonian-style material, too. Arabella Churchill organised the first theatre area for the 1979 Glastonbury Fayre, for instance, which included Footsbarn Theatre Company telling the story of King Arthur. According to Michael Clarke, it was the free festival movement that really widened out the cultural ambition of festival culture (though the ambition was there at Woodstock in 1969, called the Music *and Art* Fair):

> Music at a free festival rapidly became only one of a variety of activities which, apart from participation in running the site, and preparing and distributing food, may include arts and crafts of various sorts, music and forms of theatre, folk dancing, fireworks and various manifestations of commitment to ecological awareness and to the occult. As a cultural activity then, free festivals have moved from total dependence on music to a mingling of counter-cultural interests.

ABOVE: Performance and theatre are increasingly prominent at Glastonbury.
RIGHT: Dubhenge combines icons of festival culture: camper vans and Stonehenge.

Performance art commissioned for the festival covers a wide range of activities, such as the 1997 massive eco-maze Carmageddon, built out of cars, that doubled in the evening as the backdrop to a theatrical battle by barbarian theatre group Kiss My Axe. Ritual ceremonies involving dragons or Wicca Men, elemental fire and rebirth are pretty common, the kinds of events that tap into the summer solstice, into festival-goers' general sympathy for things neo-pagan. Then there are the street performers distributing weirdness around the crowds – whether headless wanderers that make you double-take, or casual aliens. Members of the Natural Theatre Company have wandered through the site almost since the beginnings of the festival: if police in uniform start kissing each other you can almost guarantee that you are seeing one of their better-known acts. NTC founder member Ralph Oswick offers a couple of rules for the company's Glastonbury performances: 'We have always tried to stand out by looking smart, conventional or "straight" . . . anyone who shows an aptitude for unicycling or juggling is immediately invited to leave.'

The rise of alternative comedy through the 1980s quickly found a space for itself at

Glastonbury. One year found hippie Neil from *The Young Ones* sitting meditating in a tipi circle in the Green Fields. When comedian Dennis Pennis introduced 1997 headliners the Prodigy as 'the world's leading lookalike band, the Australian Prodigy', who was the joke on? Comedian Bill Bailey observes that the audiences in the Comedy Tent at Glastonbury know just as well as any other audience whether acts are good or not, but, you know, it takes them a bit longer to express their judgement: 'So if you were bad, whoever's on three acts after you will get it.' I will kindly note that Glastonbury jokes sound funnier in the Comedy Tent at the festival than they do written down. For instance, 'I parked my car at Glastonbury and when I came back it was gone. I'd parked it on a double yellow ley line.'

Glastonbury 1999

Now Hole are on the Pyramid Stage, er, Courtney Love wearing pink angel's wings, grungy punk, there's a stage invasion by all the young people desperate, she lets lots of them get up and all the security, bouncers are trying to stop them, and after a while there's loads of youth up there, and it's getting a bit out of order, and she says, 'Right you've got to stop now.' She says, 'I love you Brits, you're so good at rioting, you taught me everything I know.' This after the Carnival Against Capitalism last weekend in London, where Mercedes and McDonald's got trashed. A posh Merc was smashed in the showroom by someone dancing on its roof: Party & Protest brought to life. The burger joint was daubed with EAT SHIT. Now the Festival of Alternative Capitalism this weekend in Somerset, field after field full of cars, including mine, and far too many burger–donut stalls making it look like Blackpool on a good day. Welcome to the city centre.

Now Mary Coghlan's on in the Acoustic Stage, and she's just introduced an old hit by Nancy Sinatra, played by a jazz, one two three, trio, piano, guitar, double bass. 'Uh,' she says, 'Some of you might remember this one, if you're old enough, depending how old you are,' and then she talks about the parents being here, she says to some of them, 'Hey you've even brought your grandchildren.' For an encore she does a slow folky blues song, that she first heard in Ireland when she was thirteen, that made her run away to a festival so she could hear it sung again. She remembers his kiss, and the warmth of his embrace, and the word kisssss is so long, it's a perfect piece of music, perfect early evening sun going down on the festival, kids running around, mums and dads holding hands, smiling women remembering Coghlan's 'kiss', the warmth of her voice's embrace.

The field of the Acoustic Stage is another one of those areas with a different feel to it than the two main rock stages, the big ones. This one is up on a bank, looking down into the valley, the sun setting over there, there's the Common Ground café, 24-hour café, on one side, then a friendly big beer tent on the other, and in the middle there's the Acoustic Stage, a blue big top really, with a series of curved pointed roofs on it – pvc medieval – and sitting outside in the glorious sun, gently going down the valley, there's a nice sprinkling of people, with lots and lots of children round, running around chasing each other with pushchairs, tiny babies being changed and crying a bit because they're probably wondering what's happening to their routine, and the, em, yeah, lots of mums and dads around, and what look like grandparents who haven't got their kids with them, they keep looking around a bit like I do, smiling at the little ones and their mums or dads. I mean, OK, I'm here to research the festival for this book, but that's no reason to come on your own: I miss my wife, my little daughters, they'd love this bit here, you shouldn't come to Glastonbury on your own, that's sad. And the hot air balloons are out, coursing slowly over the sky, up over the valley, coming over for their fix of Glastonbury Festival, and the daytime moon as well, three-quarter moon, a minute ago I saw an orange hot air balloon and then behind that I saw the moon, and, yeah, now it feels like everyone's here. I'm gonna sit here for a few hours, this is good.

By 1977, alongside its established concerns such as the health of festival-goers and legal issues to do with organising events, the government-funded Festival Welfare Services was examining the provision for children at festivals in more detail. This was an indication of the counterculture growing up (getting older, anyway), its next generation beginning to voice its needs. Arabella Churchill realised this in her work on the 1979 Glastonbury Fayre, as Lynne Elstob and Anne Howes describe in their photo-book account of things, *The Glastonbury Festivals*: 'She established the Children's Area, with its adventure playground, art workshops, inflatables, children's theatre, paddling pools, sandpits, clowns and puppets.' Almost the archetypal rich hippie dropout – her grandfather was the wartime Prime Minister Winston Churchill – Churchill has been involved with the festival since 1971. 'The children's area [of 1979] resulted in my running a charity called Children's World which takes drama, puppetry and creative play around Somerset and Avon schools and special schools and provides integration opportunities for "able" and "special needs" children to work and play together,' she explained in 1995. Greens too, though their election manifestos generally included pledges to reduce numbers of children per family, wanted festival culture to embrace children. The 1983 Green Gathering was the last to be held before the event's transformation the following year into the first Green Field at the festival proper. Extending some of the 1979 Glastonbury Fayre ethos, as well as the community focus of the East Anglian fairs, it was intended to be 'a child-centred event', as Richie Cotterill, one of the organisers, remembers:

> We tried to instil this consciousness, and to involve the children as much as possible in the happenings. The children's area was central to the site, respected as their domain, a place where adults could go to share the joys and revelations of interaction with children on their terms. It was alive with activities . . . What I feel was most difficult was for the normally sacred areas of adult workshops and speakers to lay aside their own self-importance and to involve the young.

(Though there used to be an Ex-Services CND stall, and though Michael Eavis himself is of pensionable age, I'm uncertain of any plans for an Elders' Area at the festival. This may be because people do not go to festivals to feel their age – that happens on the way home – but to feel younger. Lawrence Whistler wrote in *The English Festival* that 'the presence of children is the best excuse for the keeping of any festival'. At Glastonbury a couple of months after the 1999 event, Worthy Farm fields were being used for a Scout Jamboree.) Stephen Abrahall of Mid-Somerset CND, a local branch still funded by the festival today, used to take his children out of the local school and up to the festival each June. 'I'm convinced it was a significant contribution to their education,' he says. In the school playground his kids were called hippies but now, says Abrahall, many of their old school friends admit to secretly being envious at the time, and may envy still his children's memories. This was in the 1980s, when local feeling ran particularly high on both sides, those supporting and those opposing the then CND event. In fact, at a school meeting to discuss fundraising, Abrahall suggested that the Parent Teacher Association provide volunteers for car park stewarding for the festival, which he knew would raise more money than the traditional jumble sale or sponsored walk. 'The response was outrage. It was as though I'd suggested setting up a needle-exchange scheme in the school playground!' he recalls. The school did not do it – now, of course, there is a waiting list of local organisations wishing to be involved.

In *Festival!*, a book mostly covering the 1960s American scene, Jerry Hopkins wrote of Woodstock that 'It is interesting but not surprising to note that few of these [journalistic accounts] gave more than passing mention to the music of the Woodstock Music and Art Fair, for this was a pop music festival whose musicians were eclipsed by the celebrants.' *Time* magazine famously hailed Woodstock as 'history's largest happening . . . one of the significant political and social events of the age.' Yet, as Arthur Marwick points out:

> Actually, none of the most 'significant' performers were there – no Beatles, Rolling Stones, Bob Dylan, Simon and Garfunkel, Doors, Led Zeppelin, Aretha Franklin, Stevie Wonder, Marvin Gaye, or Temptations. But then the point was more the people who participated, all 250,000 of them, rather than the stars who perfomed.

The 'contemporary performing arts' signalled in the full title of the Glastonbury festival today includes but does not foreground music, while the crowds themselves, the celebrants in Hopkins's term, along with their field villages of canvas and camp fires and drags, make the event what it is. Michael Eavis acknowledged as much in 1989: 'People come for the festival as a whole, not just for any particular bands that happen to be playing. If this wasn't the case, then the bands could play in a football stadium somewhere and their promoters would make far more profit.' (As often the case with the festival, there is as well a practical, in this case legal, angle to this position. The local council refused a licence for 1989, which the festival's lawyers hoped to bypass by reducing the amount of music. Only events with 'a substantial music content' require a licence by law. The following year, 1990, the festival was retitled with 'contemporary performing arts' to underline its extra-musical identity.)

I asked musicians how important they thought they were to the overall festival experience. In Jeremy Cunningham's view, 'partly the Levellers are successful as a festival band because people come to see their mates – it's not so much us on the stage making the vibe as the crowd all pleased with itself and having a good time. The

In 1990 music features heavily – but circus, theatre and cabaret have as much space in the advertising.

Music in the fields as well as on the stages.

band then is more of a catalyst. There's a strong creative vibe going on at a gathering: so many people have had good experiences at festivals.' With his experience of Rock Against Racism in the 1970s, Tom Robinson concurs: 'Pop and politics consists of preaching to the converted – no National Front skinhead ever came to a RAR gig and was converted to multiculturalism! It worked best at a grassroots level, where the audience coming together was the significant achievement, not the bands that were playing. And festivals like Glastonbury are like that too: the audience is the thing.' Both Cunningham and Robinson are talking here of the kinds of gigs and festivals that offer a variety of acts, that therefore appeal to audiences either catholic or liberal enough in their tastes to find such bills attractive, but the point stands.

Glastonbury 1999

OK now it's night and I'm walking down from the Jazz Stage after having a glass of beer, well a paper carton of beer, in a bar called District Six, and I've been walking for several miles and eventually to my surprise find myself back where I hoped to be, broadly anyway, and in the field, the arena field, that's looking on to the Pyramid Stage which continues to be disappointingly semi-circular, globular, and when I come round the corner past these big hedges and trees, I am just amazed. There are all these thousands of – and it's a beautiful clear night, you can see stars, not many, but stars, the moon – and they're all around: everyone's got fires alight, little single fires, little flare things, like candles and stuff, and they're everywhere, all around, all around, gently sloping up the hill. It's dark, you can just make out the trees in faint silhouette, against the darker horizon, black on black, you can see the forest around and about, and then there's just fires everywhere, flickering candles, hundreds and hundreds of them, it's a fantastic evanescent sight to stumble on to in the dark. Crowd as spectacle, and we're gazing at ourselves. Wonder what band we're waiting for. They won't be as good as us.

Fun da Mental, 1998.

6

A green field far away:
the politics of peace and ecology at the festival

> . . . festival can become a site of political activity. In their different ways the 1971
> concert for Bangladesh organised by George Harrison, the 1985 Live Aid concert
> and subsequent phenomena such as the concert for Nelson Mandela, campaigning
> tours such as Rock Against Racism, the Anglo-Irish Fleadh held annually in North
> London and the gay, lesbian and bisexual celebration, Pride, all have built on the
> notion of a popular festival as a way of proposing, trying to create, a truly vital
> cultural politics, one which has involved thousands of people and their pleasures,
> generating a far greater level of enthusiasm than other political events.
>
> Andrew Blake, *The Land Without Music*

It's intriguing that a place associated with pilgrimage, spirituality, legend, should also be so insistently engaged with the real world, that its festivals, of all its offerings, can have sound political resonance. Both the early and late twentieth-century festivals, those of Rutland Boughton and Michael Eavis, have been politically engaged: for all his bohemianism, Boughton was a long-time member of the Communist Party, wrote socialist pageants and contributed to strike funds (when financially fluid). An ethic of social change from a left perspective is one of Glastonbury festival's claims too, and, perhaps more importantly, one of the features of the event which continue to set it apart from more obviously commercial rock festivals.

In parliamentary political terms, the local Labour Party has been identified with the festival in that local party members have been involved as stewards at the festival. Michael Eavis is also a party member, and indeed has stood (unsuccessfully) as an election candidate for Labour. In 1999 the Labour Party had a stall at the festival

A green field far away

159

(though I didn't see it). The Liberal Democrats have also been touched by the festival, not least in that Michael Eavis's brother is involved in that party. The rise of the Green Party has seen its involvement in the festival, too. As discussed elsewhere, the Greens, as the Ecology Party, were involved in the Green Gatherings at Worthy Farm in the very early 1980s, which would feed into the founding of the Green Fields as a designated feature of the festival in 1984. The Greens have also organised the litter pickers on site, for which they received a financial donation. The Conservative Party? Well, never renowned for their liberated sense of fun and sharing, the main response of local Tories to the festival has been to oppose it at all lengths and over many years. This attitude may be softening: the local council has become more supportive, perhaps because fewer Tories are elected to it. The local MP is David Heathcote-Amory, a Tory who lives in Pilton village itself.

You may be struck by the sheer surprise that, in this apparently True Blue English countryside, a happening such as Glastonbury can ever take place, let alone with great annual frequency over a period of thirty years. Yet that may be both to mistake electoral success as representative and to overlook the traditions of radicalism, of alternative experimentation which rural parts of the country frequently host or produce – the West Country as haven of New Travellers, old hippies, ciderpunks, Dongas, alt.culture, etc. down the green lanes.

The hot political campaigns of the times filter down to the festival, which expresses its sympathy by sharing its space, as, for instance, with the noticeable number of miners' helmets on site in 1984 at the height of the miners' strike, or the march around the site by protesters against the still extraordinary anti-rave clauses of the Criminal Justice and Public Order Act 1994. It is in the extra-parliamentary arena that the Glastonbury political ethos is most keenly felt, though. The politics of the festival are a central issue in its identity because they contribute to its continuing ethic, its idealistic sheen, of course. More problematically, as the event has become larger, more commercialised, altogether more *expensive*, particularly through the 1990s, the notion that the festival maintains some kind of radical edge must be looked at.

'The CND Festival'

The main political focus for funds at Glastonbury started as the peace movement, and later embraced environmental campaigning more widely. In this context, the long-term relationships have been with the Campaign for Nuclear Disarmament (1981–90), Greenpeace (1992 onwards), and Oxfam (because of its campaigning against the arms trade), as well as the establishment of the Green Fields as a regular and expanding eco-feature of the festival (from 1984 onwards). The radical peace movement and the rise of the Greens in Britain are interwoven at Glastonbury. The festival has offered these campaigns and groups space on-site to publicise and disseminate their ideas, and it has ploughed large sums of money from the festival profits into them, as well as other causes. For Michael Eavis, 'It's in the weeks running up to the festival, when I wake up at 4.30 in the morning before the milking, and I'm lying there scared, that I think about Greenpeace and the other campaigns we're doing, and that helps me justify the effort and the worry.' The idea of having a good time for a good cause – the audience, anyway – a politics of pleasure if you like, has frequently been criticised for lacking a class or economic basis. Yet, as we have seen, having fun is invariably a highly regulated experience, legislation seemingly at its strongest when the fun involves youth, a crowd, the countryside, loud music and the promise of narcotic. Add an oppositional politics to that and you have a potent brew.

June 1981 saw the first Glastonbury CND festival, the first time CND was involved. The formation of Mid-Somerset CND early in 1981 had sparked greater interest locally. I have seen figures ranging from 12,000 to 18,000 people attending, with £20,000 raised for CND. The following summer, in spite of awful weather, the numbers doubled. Like alternative comedy, perhaps, or the New Traveller movement up to 1985, Glastonbury would begin to be recognised as one of those cultural phenomena working, and significantly thriving, against the dominant individualist, right-wing, pro-nuclear ideology of Thatcherism.

In retrospect, what seems extraordinary about the connection between Glastonbury Festival and CND in 1981 is that it happened at all. At first glance it is a most unlikely alliance: a campaign organisation with an international profile, built on a sense of moral authority, lends its name, its reputation, and not least its organisational facilities in London to a West Country farmer whose track record in putting on festivals is patchy at best. Recall that in 1981 the festival had only ever taken place three times before, spread over the previous decade (1970, 1971 and 1979), once as a local fair, once as a free event, and, most recently, losing sums of money for the organisers. This would hardly appear to be most promising way of raising funds for a campaign which had itself been through the doldrums for much of the seventies. But CND was up for a revival in the 1980s, thanks to a cluster of MAD (Mutually Assured Destruction – with acronyms like that, no wonder everyone was paranoid) personalities and policies: Thatcher and Reagan, US-controlled Cruise missiles being sited on European air bases in Germany, Holland and Britain, and the peace protest against the Falklands War in 1982.

As well as national demonstrations and carnivals and the (apparent) support of some politicians on the parliamentary left, there were more interesting symptoms of resistance against nuclear weapons all over the country. Best known of course is the grassroots activism of peace campers at Greenham Common and many other air bases (in November 1983 24-hour vigils began at all 102 US bases in Britain), and still least known is the decentralized cultural pacifism of the spectacularly successful anarcho-punk scene. Glastonbury festival became another highly visible, and a profitable, focus of opposition to nuclear weaponry – and it's significant that all three examples cited (camps, anarchopunk, and festival) are all cultural manifestations of protest, *and* are regional, frequently rural ones.

Bruce Garrard, the Glastonbury-based peace and then Green campaigner and writer, has lived in a bender, on the road, at Rainbow Village peace camp in 1984–85, and was a site co-ordinator for the first Green Field at Glastonbury in 1984. He was at the first festival at Pilton in September 1970, and has gravitated around Glastonbury ever since. Garrard wrote an article about the peace movement for Salisbury CND in 1981, which illustrates that the festival's connections with the peace movement were symptoms of a changing sensibility on the part of newer activists in the 1980s (who were perhaps not always aware of the similar debates among older activists from the 1960s and 1970s):

It is in the social sphere that CND can be most active in bringing people together – for musical events, parties, even sports and games. The importance of such things is not just 'fund raising'. Bringing people together, particularly different types of people, to enjoy themselves, is working for peace . . . If the logic of this is that we open shops, cafés, perhaps even social clubs, then so much the better. Let us find the means to do it. And if

this is turn leads people to find ways of self-expression, whether in decorating, or making things to sell or to eat, or singing, dancing, or making music, then so much the better again.

In a way, CND made Glastonbury. Both CND's national office's organisational skills and the regional structure alike came into play to provide a professional administrative backbone to the festival. For Stephen Abrahall of Mid-Somerset CND, it is significant that it was only when CND became involved that the festival made a profit – 'It was a magnificent way to celebrate life and support the cause,' he told me. CND gave the festival a national and even international profile, and allowed it to take advantage of the campaign's own lengthy, if often overlooked, tradition of festival culture. Tony Myers of national CND, whose personal involvement in both the festival and the campaign goes back to the early 1980s, sees the relationship as mutually beneficial.

> The festival was a high-visibility event for us, and CND was the fashionable thing at that time, the early 1980s. So we both gained out of the connection, it was good for both sides. CND would employ a worker specifically on ticket sales from the national office, and we would be the gate crew too, selling tickets and putting on wristbands there. I remember sitting in a cabin at the festival gate with huge piles of money all around, Monopoly-style. And it was all really good fun. On the other hand there were dissenting voices within the organisation, there was an element seeing all the press coverage about hippies and drugs, and seriously wondering whether CND was benefiting from being connected with that kind of thing. Michael [Eavis] was aware of this – he'd sometimes be a guest at CND National Council, when these reservations would be expressed.

In spite of such disquiet on the part of some CND-ers, CND's willingness to embrace the possibilities of Glastonbury, its ease of recognising the potential of Eavis's offer, were rooted in the campaign's own lengthy tradition of festival/alternative community as a means of protest, education, a vision of alternative. From its beginnings in the Aldermaston Nuclear Weapons Research Centre marches from 1958 on, we can see in CND what we now recognise as a youth or lifestyle protest movement. (I'm not intending to be ageist in overlooking the high-profile contributions of more senior campaigners such as octogenarian philosopher Bertrand Russell or writers J.B. Priestley, Hugh Macdiarmid and Herbert Read here – but am reading the campaign's formative years in light of later developments around culture and festival, to help explain the decision of CND embracing Glastonbury in 1981.) It is not a coincidence that some of the first seeds of alternative youth culture in the context of festival were themselves beginning to germinate, even sprout during the late 1950s. It is easy to lose sight of that decade, the 1950s, either caricaturing it as one of austerity or conformity, or being blinded by the psychedelia that came after it. Multiracial British reggae band UB40 played the festival in 1983. The father of band-member brothers Ali and Robin is Ian Campbell, who himself has a music and politics background. For folk singer and activist Ian:

> It is significant that 1958, the year that saw the climactic boom in jazz popularity, also produced the first Aldermaston march. The jazz revival and the rise of CND were more than coincidental; they were almost two sides of the same coin . . . At one of the Easter rallies of the early 1960s . . . every hundred yards or so there was a group of musicians – some of them rare and wonderful combinations, such as a bagpipe-tuba duo or a children's kazoo and percussion band – but predominantly they were jazz combos, and I lost count of the versions I heard of 'Down by the Riverside' and 'When the Saints Go Marching In'.

Pinpointing its prescience, David Widgery described that first march as 'a student movement before its time, a mobile sit-in or marching pop festival'. The second national CND march took place during Easter 1959, this time from Aldermaston to London rather than the other way round. 3,000 marchers covered the fifty-odd miles over several days, and were joined for the last part in London, from the Albert Hall to Trafalgar Square, by 12,000 others in a national demonstration on Easter Monday. CND historians John Minnion and Philip Bolsover describe how the protest has all the paraphernalia of a moving festival, including 'jazz bands and guitars, songs and slogans, banners, placards and pamphlets . . . luggage vans, banner wagons, litter collectors and Elsan toilet teams; stewards, dispatch riders, first aid teams'. Looking forward a few years, Ian Campbell notes a shift in musical taste if a consistency of political campaigning:

> Just as in the fifties the rise of CND coincided with the jazz boom, so in the sixties the great flowering of the peace movement went hand in hand with the folksong revival. . . . As the folksong movement burgeoned and clubs opened all over the land they more than filled the place left by the shrinking jazz movement. The folk clubs became the places

where duffle-coat lapels flaunted CND badges and anti-war songs were assured a sympathetic reception.

Mick Farren, self-styled White Panther (or 'one-man tribe', as he was less sympathetically described), rock journalist and musician, organiser of Phun City Free Festival in 1970, wrote in 1972 his touchingly juvenile, mishmash self-heroic paean to the 'alternative society' of the hippies in Britain, *Watch Out, Kids*. Here Farren traces the links between the early CND movement and those who would become the hippies of a few years later:

> CND, although predominantly a youth organisation, seemed divorced from the instinctive revolt of the rock-and-roll teenage rebels. The fact that CND was based on the linear concepts of a previous generation, and that it drew its music from Dixieland, gospel songs and leftist folk songs, seemed a denial of what the young had established for themselves. Ban-the-Bomb marches had a usefulness, however, in terms of the interchange of information between traditional pacifists, left-wingers and young potential freaks. The later sitdowns and civil disobedience campaigns also brought many middle-class kids into first hand contact with police repression. It was also around the CND environment that a number of us first came into contact with the reality of smoking dope.

CND, then, held an important if implicit role in the development of festival culture, which began to become more explicit as festival culture hit an early high point in the late 1960s. The campaign signalled its awareness of what the late 1960s recognised as 'play power', and the 1990s calls 'party & protest', and developed new forms of action accordingly. Minnion and Bolsover describe the traditional Easter march alongside the perhaps newer emphasis on rock festival, and guess which is more popular:

> The Easter march from Crawley (Sussex) to London in 1970 attracted a comparatively small number of people, but a 'Festival of Life', in Victoria Park, Hackney, the following day was a great success, with 20,000 people there. The festival was initiated by a small group of campaigners anxious to move way from 'Trafalgar Square-ism', and it showed a welcome tolerance of diverse approaches in the re-awakening peace movement. It began to build on the anti-war mood of recent rock music festivals, particularly the big events at the Isle of Wight and Woodstock, in America (rock bands were now returning from the US with CND symbols painted on their instruments). The theme of the festival, peace and the abolition of nuclear weapons, came across in a variety of ways. There were five

stages accommodating rock bands and jazz bands, folk music, poets . . . and variety turns. In the crowds, street theatre groups organised by Joan Littlewood and others, performed. On one stage, John Peel conducted a telephone interview with John Lennon.

Liverpool poet Adrian Henri performed with the band The Liverpool Scene at the Hackney festival. (According to John Peel, The Liverpool Scene, like Hawkwind, were unavoidable at festivals.) For Henri, memories of this utopian gathering to celebrate peace and life are dominated by a pitched battle between Hell's Angels and skinheads reluctant to appreciate his northern music and humour. Nonetheless, CND's 1970 Festival of Life featured multiple stages, rock bands and street theatre, DJs and different youth subcultures, variety acts and political campaigning, all in the idealised alternative space of festival itself.

In this light, it becomes altogether less surprising that a decade later CND looked with enthusiasm on an offer from a Somerset farmer. From this perspective, Glastonbury can be seen as the next step in CND's long and successful tradition of bringing together festival and activism, from its very earliest days. Stephen Abrahall reminded me that 'there was a time when Glastonbury festival was as important an event in the peace campaigner's diary as was going on the demonstrations, and the ability to make both events exciting was a necessity to sustain what was not going to be a short campaign. Certainly for fundraising purposes, at a local, regional and national level, the festival beat an awful lot of jumble sales!'

The impetus behind CND's connection with Glastonbury lies in the formation of a local branch of the campaign in early 1981. The arrival of Cruise missiles in Europe was the major impetus behind CND's revival during the 1980s, yet campaigning against Cruise was not the primary reason for the founding of Mid-Somerset CND. As so frequently with Glastonbury, the trajectory is from local to global. Mid-Somerset CND was formed following a packed public meeting called in response to a planning application with Mendip District Council to convert disused railway tunnels under the local hills into nuclear fallout shelters. Within the space of a few hectic months there was a regional branch of CND, a festival being organised at Pilton again after the break in 1980, and the input of the organisation nationally to sell tickets and help with publicity. Abrahall recalls that, for that first CND festival in 1981, 'We had three days to organise and staff the solitary information tent: now it takes nearly six months to gather and glean info from hundreds of sources,' with up to half a dozen information points across the site. Abrahall explained to me both the activity and the strategy of the information service:

> There might be some confusion (and there still is!) about what Mid-Somerset CND offered at the festival. Basically it is a Festival Information Service, not a CND Information Service. We tack on as much campaigning as we can, according to the climate. When no self-respecting 'leftie' would leave home without his or her CND badge on, we sold them in thousands, along with the stickers for the Morris Minor or the 2CV. When Greenham Common and the women's movement was the flavour, we helped staff the women's tents and gave them other support. When the miners were big, we made much of the links with nuclear power. When it became clear that it was not so much specific weapons that were the problem, but the thinking behind them, we pushed the arms trade and the links with poverty – which is why I mentioned that it was my suggestion that got Oxfam involved.

Trying to combine recruitment with entertainment can be a 'little tricky', as Abrahall told me. One illustration of the sometimes tenuous relation between the two is seen during one of the early CND years. (Once again *no one* remembers exact dates, festivals blur, for predictable reasons.) The CND magazine *Sanity* was on sale on-site, and it included the full festival line-up. There was no official programme at that time, so of course the magazine sold in its thousands, convincing CND that the message really was getting across to a highly receptive, captive audience. The following year, *Sanity* was supplied by the thousand – but there was an official programme now, and it hardly sold at all. For Abrahall, this anecdote illustrates the difficulty of balancing politics and pleasure at festival. There is as well a tradition of peace campaigners addressing the audience from the main stage. In the past these have included the historian and campaigner E.P. Thompson, CND chair Bruce Kent and women from Greenham Common. Advice to speakers was simple: don't outstay your welcome. More recently, music has leavened even such brief overt political discourse: in 1998, a duo sang about the Ploughshares civil disobedience campaign against British fighter jets being sold to the Indonesian government to be used for internal repression, while in 1999 the singer Tom Robinson spoke about CND's continuing relevance in anti-arms campaigning around the world.

Michael Eavis recognises that '1981 was our breakthrough: 24,000 people turned up, delivering a £20,000 profit, which contributed to the million pounds raised for

CND through the eighties.' This was the breakthrough year because of the national profile and marketing that CND provided, because of the peace movement's currency via the threatened arrival of Cruise missiles. It was also because of the apparent contradiction that mass festival culture, as indicated by other events at open spaces (ranging from Stonehenge to Reading), was thriving in this individualistic Thatcherite decade. And the fact that it was the first year Eavis himself had taken more full control of organising the festival, following the commercially disastrous 1979 event that was organised by a committee, may be more important than all these other reasons. (Arabella Churchill, involved in the festival since 1971, calls Eavis an 'amiable and beneficial autocrat'.)

Today, national CND still always has a stall in a prominent position on site, though, as in society generally, its overall profile is much lower than in either of its boom times (apologies for the metaphor) of the 1950s and 1980s. CND membership numbers over the time of the festival illustrate this:

1979	*4287 members*
1984	*100,000 members*
1989	*62,000 members*
1998	*38,000 members*

From the heady 1980s days of Glastonbury being generally known as 'the CND festival', peace groups are most visibly active on site today running the property lock-up facilities. This certainly seems to me something of a come-down, yet CND-ers disagree, or are, I suspect, too polite, diplomatic or grateful for past involvement to say so. For the key local players, Mid-Somerset CND, the timing of the move from CND to wider green issues and campaign groups, was 'excellent'. As Abrahall wrote in 1995:

> When, in 1992, Greenpeace became the main beneficiary of the Festival, we were not all that glum. Their very first campaign had been against nuclear testing and many of their activities since then have been anti-nuclear, often alongside CND. In the public mind, not supporting Greenpeace is often seen as being in favour of clubbing baby seals, so the switch has meant greater local acceptance of the festival.

For CND in London, according to Tony Myers, there was 'real disappointment' about being dropped in favour of Greenpeace. With hindsight Myers can explain:

In some ways, Michael [Eavis] felt we weren't doing enough any more. He had wanted national CND to have a higher profile, to make more of the 100,000-strong captive audience. Workshops, links with the Green Fields – we didn't follow those through to their full potential. We were very stretched at the time, and it was as much as we could do to staff a large marquee each year. You have to bear in mind that we, CND, were getting smaller as the festival was getting bigger. And commitment to the festival for CND staff members as well as volunteers always counted on top of all the things you did as part of your job anyway. Couple that with serious internal tensions at the time within CND to do with the Gulf War, as well as the more mundane fact that people left and new people came in without a history of commitment to the festival, and you see how things just moved apart.

Included in the pack of briefing papers CND in London produces in order that branches can deal with things like press and student queries is 'A Brief History of CND'. Stephen Abrahall drew my attention to the fact that, 'considering the importance of the festival to CND's funds, it is strange that no mention of the [Glastonbury] festival is in there, anywhere'.

Glastonbury 1999

Space at Glastonbury is organised schizophrenically (or is it just organised? No – it is divided, demarcated, and it may be that the division strengthens the festival, its appeal, its mostly charming splitness). In spite of Andrew Kerr's assertion in 1971 that 'Glastonbury is too beautiful for just another rock festival', it is that – or at least two-thirds or three-quarters is that. The rest is Green, crafts, organic, travellers. Talking about this with one of the press tent people (when anyone's there) who said REM, etc., pay for the Green Fields, Kidz Areas etc., all those nice things around the edge wouldn't be possible without the beer cans and hot dogs in the stadium rock valley floor. There are one or two smaller areas on site of what seem to be darker, dirtier, slightly more edgy communities. E.g. near the old railway line on the way to the Green Fields is what you might if being kind call a wooded glade. It's dark, very dusty – and smelly, since a number of the more primitive loos have been sited here. There are a few rough benders, a rusty car, one or two nice old hippie trucks, converted FG trucks. What is it about the people in here that makes most of the other festival-goers pass through rather than pause? Mostly young men, serious about something, probably about getting out of it, and they are deliberately refusing the glorious sunshine. They are distrusted because they've come to this open-air feelgood event (logo: dancing people, fun people) and kind of closed it off, gone semi-subterranean.

Yeah, why is it called the Pyramid Stage, it's got TV screens on each side of it, huge big things that are saying WELCOME TO GLASTONBURY '99, it's just the kind of bog-standard outdoors stage now, which is disappointing, like I said. On either side of it, about one or two hundred yards away, are these big wooden frames, made out of what look like telegraph poles, with hanging baskets crammed with flowers dangling down, a nice organic touch among all the computer screens, decks of lighting and PA stacks and stuff like that. They're superfluous too, which I like: splash of colour and decoration of nature around the site, not just in the Green Fields.

Sacred Ground/Avalon Field. These are what define Glasto's difference from other commercial rock festivals. People here state and reiterate the significance of these pieces of space – of land, of mind. (Note that the Avalon Field is next to the Kidz Area. 'You're never too old for a happy childhood'.) These areas contribute both to Glasto's perception of green-ness and raise the profile in festival-goers' minds of the issues. Avalon Field: 'Cross the bridge and it's different,' said someone. Its name obviously taps in to the Glasto/medieval myth, and the ethos there does too. Talking to stallholders, there was a – I just fucking can't believe I'm writing this – a gentle capitalism. (I've been here too long, time to get out . . .) Or maybe that was just when I was buying things from them, some stained glass, a garden decoration.

Sitting in the Sacred Ground. A couple of people over there are playing with, er, a frisbee, there are some drummers with the djembes, clapping, singing a bit, two or three drummers by the stones, there's a guy rather precariously dancing on top of a thin stone in the circle, that looks not much bigger than, well, he hasn't got much more room to dance than to stand, he could come off at any moment, and he's framed in the background by a lovely oak tree, and, in fact, the trees are a real nice feature, they just kind of go round and round and they block off parts of the site, and then open it up with a view. I can see down towards a wooden, a little fort thing, at the bottom of the Sacred Ground, there are flags and streamers, there are big poles sticking up out of the ground twenty, thirty feet, it's like a fair, it's like Rougham Fair or a Sun Fair, something like that. There's a big totem pole over there which looks like it's been around for a while, I looked at some of the things carved on it, it's maybe thirty–forty foot high, I looked at some of the carvings and they were faces, and symbols, ancient mishmash, and then at the top there was an A in a ring about a foot and a half wide, so there you know you're going from a sort of, er, what are you doing there, you're mixing a native American culture with a sort of Celtic imagery and then contemporary sort of anarcho-subversive things, and it's all there, you know, just in a totem pole. And Glastonbury's full of these, these sort of mergings, some of them contradictory, some misunderstandings, fantasies, wilful fictions.

Another very easy, simple one at the back, there's the, em, totem pole and the stone circle – everyone's clapping the two drummers now, yeah, that's nice – there's the totem pole – the guy who's dancing on top of the stone is whistling loud, saying more more more – there's the totem pole, there's the stone circle, there's the wicker man, and then behind that there's a big white fence with a sort of no-man's-land, really, and then behind that there's a big wood solid fence. And then just along from those, which are obviously intended to keep people out, they're twelve–fifteen feet high, just beyond those there's

a watch tower, literally a fucking watch tower, with one or two guys, two security guards, watching along the wall and fence, making sure no one gets in. That's pretty elaborate security, and it's also, you know, I know it's about drawing up boundaries and limitations, it's also quite, er, well, it's more than ironic, it's problematically ironic that, I think. We've got sacred space, fields, freedom, and it's closed in with doubled fences and security guards. What are they doing, really? Are they watching what's going on outside or are they watching us inside, us being free inside the fences? This is a different sort of exclusion zone to the one the police usually put up around Stonehenge round about now, but how different?

Eco-politics

The sky is not the limit; the earth is.

Theodore Roszak, *The Making of a Counter Culture*

Conservationism has been a dominant strategy in environmental campaigning for a lengthy period of time: Victorian groups from the Society for the Protection of Birds to the National Trust, to post-World War Two groups such as the Nature Conservancy or the Noise Abatement Society. In her book, *Fantasy, the Bomb and the Greening of Britain*, Meredith Veldman identifies a specific date when one form of concern for the environment began to wane and another more fully to develop. 'During the decade after 1965 conservationism continued to prosper, boosted by newer, more holistic, more radical forms of environmental concern, the beginnings of *eco-activism,*' she writes. While this sketch ignores the contribution of previous generations of direct activists to the green movement – urban-based socialist cycling and walking clubs, for instance – it nonetheless illustrates a burgeoning interest in environmental issues as part of the countercultural project. Nineteen sixty-five also saw the beginnings of a switch from CND's position of authority in peace campaigns to the Vietnam War as a focus of a partly new generation of activists. Is the date a coincidence of single issues? No: Veldman explains that 'the Vietnam conflict demonstrated in unforgettable ways the destructive potential of modern science; not surprisingly, eco-activism emerged at the same time as the protests against the Vietnam War.'

In festival culture, or that part of it associated with the counterculture rather than

Images of the Glastonbury Green Gathering, June 1982.

with commercial pop music at least, there has generally been a very keen interest in issues Green. Sometimes this has been more rhetorical than practical – Stonehenge Free being about nature, the sun, reclaiming the land for an alternative community, but who cleared up all the crap, unrecycled glass and rubbish, the burned-out cars afterwards? I remember a young Earth First! activist who had been at Castlemorton Common free megarave in 1992 (a semi-legendary event today) telling me, shocked, 'All we did was leave shit and broken glass all over that beautiful piece of country-side.' Festival culture of course provides many more positive examples of a practical vision of alternative Green values and lifestyles, and the Green Fields at Glastonbury offer one instance of this, a particularly important one, perhaps, because of the sheer numbers and broadly sympathetic attitude of the festival-goers who make their way up there. With hindsight, the seeds of the Green Fields were planted at the 1971 Glastonbury Fayre. Organiser Andrew Kerr explained of his free festival in the idiom of the time: 'If the festival has a specific intention it is to create an increase in the power of the Universe, a heightening of consciousness and a recognition of our place in the function of this our tired and molested planet.'

The Green Collective grew out of the group formed to organise the Ecology Party Summer Gatherings which took place around Glastonbury, in particular at the festival site at Worthy Farm and at Lambert's Hill Farm in later summer between 1980 and 1983. The space, the green land of the festival, thus began to be used outwith solstice time for other gatherings, introducing other political issues and campaigns. From 1980 to 1982 Summer Gatherings by Green activists were held at Worthy Farm, which saw numbers attending grow from 500 to 5000 in that short period. Entertainment, workshops, experiments in low-impact living, sweat lodges: Glastonbury was beginning to be politicised, as David Taylor wrote in 1984.

> Green CND had been born at the '81 Gathering,
> but 1982 was the first year in which we saw a large

involvement of feminists, with Women For Life On Earth organising a women-only marquee and workshops. It was in 1983 that we first agreed on one overall theme for the whole Gathering. It was to be a child-centred Gathering, and we tried to plan the entertainments and workshops accordingly.

In 1983 the Green Gathering – by this year removed to Lambert's Hill Farm near Shepton Mallet in order to lessen any perceived link with the Glastonbury festival – provided a broadly sympathetic welcoming space to the Peace Convoy of New Travellers. According to Collective members writing a few months after the event, the Lambert's Hill Green Gathering 'was virtually besieged by the largest police operation ever seen at a Green event in this country. Large numbers of people – many of whom had never had much dealings with the police beyond asking a bobby for the time – found themselves being stopped, searched and treated in an intimidating fashion.' While ostensibly looking for drugs, prescription medicines were confiscated, and the Collective's treasurer had to 'run the gauntlet several times a day on his way to and from the bank.' A naked protest march by some Greens ensued. The bad publicity from the Gathering worried the Festival organisers, and, according to David Taylor, 'farmer Michael Eavis has asked us not to put on Glastonbury Green Gathering in 1984. He has, however, put aside space for a "Green Field" within the 1984 festival, and the link with Glastonbury will continue.' Bruce Garrard told me that the local authorities put pressure on to end the Green Gatherings, as well as the parties that had gone on in the barn up at Worthy Farm. In return, the festival would be supported in 1984.

It is hard to imagine now Glastonbury festival without the Green Fields, since they are integral, even fundamental, to its alternative identity, energy and attraction. The first Green Field was planned as a quietly ambitious affair, and when the Green Collective turned up at Worthy Farm, to their allocated site of Norman's Close, Garrard remembers:

We sat in a circle and did a visualisation of what we wanted to create in the Green Field – and then we *did* it. We had a Tipi Circle in the middle, with open space inside it (that nearly got filled with nylon nightmares, but we did save the space in the end). We created a different atmosphere to the rest of the festival site – and that was one of our aims and, more importantly, one of our achievements. It's true to say that Michael took time to realise the significance of the Green Fields – and, in fact, there were some tensions between us and the established festival. I remember arriving to comments from heavy-duty and macho scaffolders and stage crew about 'these hippies'. Jokes like, 'Let's build a tower so we can view the mating habits of all the Greens.' We then set ourselves apart a bit from that aspect of the festival, in particular setting up our own site kitchen away from the main one everyone else used. There was a tremendous energy generated from that Green Field – and look what it's led to in the fifteen years since.

In spite of Garrard talking above of the slowness of the festival accepting the success of the first Green Field, it was reported in 1985 that:

The advance publicity for this year's CND festival calls the Green Field 'one of the greatest successes of last year's festival'. The budget has been doubled as compared to last year, on top of which exhibitions from Greenpeace and the National Centre for Alternative Technology have been booked independently. Last year we weren't even mentioned on the leaflets, so we must have achieved something!

By 1990, the Green Field had actually become Green Fields, an ambitious and large-scale feature of the festival which threatened to take attention away from the music at the main stages. Festival publicity advertised 'Extended Green Field covering 60 acres', and the eco message could even stop the music. For instance, attempts were made to recycle rubbish on-site, the idea being for performances to stop at 4 p.m. each day for twenty minutes with the hope that everyone would clear up rubbish around them, encouraged by litter collectors amusingly/ sinisterly called the Green Police. (The Rolling Stones had tried a bin bag self-help eco-strategy at one of their free concerts in Hyde Park, in 1972. For every full bag of rubbish he or she collected, a concert-goer would be given a free Stones album. For anyone post-punk there's probably a joke

there somewhere.) An article in *Glastonbury Green Magazine*, specially published for celebrations, rituals and actions around Glastonbury for Earth Day 1990, explains:

> The emphasis in 1990 has moved a step further away from the main stage and the
> superstars, more towards theatre, circus, crafts, spontaneous events . . . and the Greens . . .
> The Greens now have their own Press Officer, Steve Henwood, who says that this year's
> festival is 'your best opportunity yet to get to the heart of the Green Movement that
> so many are trumpeting but so few understand. It's an opportunity to meet, learn from,
> share with, the greatest ever concentration of Green organisations, businesses, charities,
> researchers, writers, practitioners, artists and craftspeople in one place for one weekend.'

The Green political project to combine macro and micro understanding and practice, the local–global dialogue, can be seen at the 1990 festival, 'making it a condition for traders to use paper cups instead of plastic, and all-aluminium beer-cans without the ring pulls that are so dangerous to cattle'. From global Earth Day to local beer-can ring pulls, the festival was becoming more and more Green. Even if the pasture that the cows graze on continues each year to be covered in *massive*, massive, amounts of litter. Even if the effect of the festival is to make official organic status for Worthy Farm's dairy products unachievable, according to Eavis, 'because we have to buy in so much non-organic fodder for the cows after the festival while the land recovers'. Even if there is field after field packed with parked cars, traffic jams for miles, stink of exhaust fumes and asthmatic particulates pumping out of diesel engines. Even if the music volume booms through your body and then carries on for miles and miles so people who don't even like pop music have to put up with it in villages and towns miles away from Worthy Farm. One more contradiction for the festival.

By the 1990s, a new series of gatherings, the Big Green Gatherings, came to be held on the Downs in Wiltshire most summers. These have been helped by the loan of materials from Glastonbury festival. We've travelled full circle. Two new stone circles have been built, in fact, in Wiltshire (at the Big Green Gathering) and in Somerset (at Worthy Farm) – stone circles designed on computer, actually. According to a *Festival Eye* review of the 1996 Gathering:

> If you have ever spent time in the Green Fields at Glastonbury then you will have some idea of what to expect as far as attractions go, but it's much less intense than the Pilton festival . . . The event hosts a huge range of workshops on many different subjects within the fields of green politics, environmentalism, alternative technology, health, mysticism, and the paranormal . . . The Rinkydink bicycle-powered sound system toured the site throughout the festival . . . Power for all stages and attractions was from renewable sources, namely pedal, wind and sun!

Even the police communications set-up at the BGG in 1998 was solar-powered (perhaps this was to make up for the by now familiar over-policing in previous years: in 1996, in an echo of the 1983 Green Gathering – don't the police *ever* learn? – some turning up for the gathering were welcomed with an unrefuseable invitation to be strip-searched for drugs).

The range of offerings from Greenpeace at Glastonbury is indeed more inventive and ambitious than anything CND used to organise. In 1999, for instance, Greenpeace focused on genetically modified crops. Working with the Soil Association and the Henry Doubleday Research Association, as well as with the development charity Action Aid, Greenpeace connected Grow Your Own organic food advice (from allotments to window-boxes) with the 'campaign against the patenting of life in the developing world' to illustrate contemporary global–local links. A Greenpeace flyer continues:

> If all that is food for thought then get yourselves down to Café Tango, our 100% organic café. The tastiest food on site and definitely a GM free zone . . . Adjacent to Café Tango

you'll find the other hot spot of the festival, the Greenpeace venue where you are guaranteed wall-to-wall entertainment . . . If all that gets you in a lather then be sure to drop in to the hot showers where up to 6000 gallons of solar-heated water await you. After which you can lounge in the juice bar or get involved in the daily fitness programme. More adventures and interaction are promised at the Greenpeace communications centre, an arts-lab, where film, video, internet and performance will combine.

Sounds a bit restless, doesn't it, not really what E.M. Forster called 'the peace of the country'?

Michael Eavis discussed the shift from CND through the Green Fields to Greenpeace in the official 1995 booklet, *Glastonbury: The First Twenty Five Years*: 'When we were making large donations to CND, Jean and I wanted to get people to think about the futility of spending £12,000 million on Trident to fight an enemy we'd never even been to war with. The time came when we began to understand that, although the Bomb was the ultimate act of pollution, it was part of countless such acts, a little less gigantic, a little slower, yet none the less fatal to our planet'. In *Fantasy, the Bomb, and the Greening of Britain*, Meredith Veldman writes of the medieval fantasies of C.S. Lewis and J.R.R. Tolkien:

> Several common themes linked fantasy literature, CND, and the early Greens. The vision
> of the past as a guide for the future surfaced again and again. Narnia and Middle Earth
> rest on idealized versions of medieval and Old English society . . . For eco-activists, the
> past became a repository of simple technologies, farming and healing methods, and
> guidelines for the optimum size of political and economic structures. [This] backward
> orientation also indicated a rejection of the modern, degraded world status of Britain.
> Within CND, especially, but evident among all the players of the romantic drama, was
> a view of the past as a time of British – or, more often, *English* – glory and as a source
> of British strengths that must be revived in order to make a better world.

There has been a strong strand of medievalism in Green thought – in counterculture generally, in festival culture in particular. The 1971 Glastonbury Fayre was envisaged by Andrew Kerr to be 'in the medieval tradition with music, dance, poetry, theatre, lights and the opportunity for spontaneous entertainment'. In East Anglia around the same time, you could get free or reduced entry to some of the fairs by coming in medieval costume, while the inspiration of the East Anglian fairs came in part from 1960s medieval-style events in, of all places, California. Jerry Hopkins writes in *Festival!*:

> The Renaissance Pleasure Faire had been held in Los Angeles for several years as a fund-raising function of Pacifica's FM radio station there, KPFK. Everyone got all dressed up in medieval clothing (which seemed to be the clothing style of 1966 anyway) and craftsmen set up booths. There were games and pony rides and Punch and Judy shows and dramas and minstrels and troubadours and lots of food and drink . . . [They took] this format (mood) and stage[d] what was to become, in June 1967, the world's first pop music festival, the Fantasy Faire and Magic Mountain Music Festival, held on the top of Mt. Tamalpais, not far from the redwoods forests slightly northwest of San Francisco.

The first alternative-style shop in Glastonbury opened in 1975. It's called Gothic Image, a clear echo of the nineteenth-century Gothic Revival, which featured the Pre-Raphaelite Brotherhood, the Arts and Crafts movement and Arthurian imagery in Tennyson and William Morris. One of the East Anglian fairs organisers, Keith Payne, wrote of the fairs:

BELOW: Alternative press in East Anglia reports on a medieval-style Faire at Barsham.

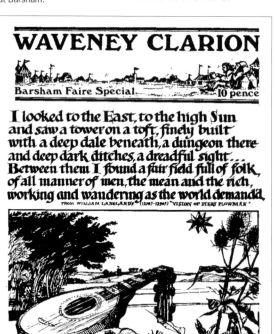

So seeds were planted in East Anglia, and some of the seeds blew far away, to Devon, Cornwall and Wales. As these other fairs developed, so the finer aspects of Barsham [Fair] – the medieval, acoustic and cheapness – became slowly diluted and the heavy metal and more commercial aspect of craft trading arrived.

At Glastonbury, once you've walked three miles and pitched your tent ('Think developing world!' is the advice of the Festival Information Service to weary newcomers), it's easy to ignore or lose the atavism amidst all the stages, mega-PA systems, light riggings, temporary bank machines, CD stalls, mobile phones. Yet, as Dion Fortune wrote in *Avalon in the Heart* in the 1930s, 'Glastonbury is not only deep-rooted in the past, but the past lives on at Glastonbury. All about us it stirs and breathes, quiet, but living and watching.' The swiftly stinking toilets at festival may be one reminder of days gone by (which explains the story of the Manic Street Preachers bringing their own portaloo in 1999). The Acoustic Stage sounds like it ought to be another, but the music, by necessity for the size of the crowds there, is all mic'd up. But the links with CND, and with eco-groups such as the Green Collective and Greenpeace, are evidence of a longer-lasting effort to present or explore different ideas and solutions, possibly counter-modern ones, by re-examining alternative traditions from real and mythic pasts alike. This merging of past and politics is one of the festival's lasting achievements.

GOTHIC IMAGE

Gothic Image Limited, 7 High Street, Glastonbury, Somerset BA6 9DP
Telephone 0458 831453   Fax 0458 831666

Glastonbury plc?

Monterey – my God it was Groovy! Woodstock – thank God it was groovy. All the
others have been promotions. There are festivals and there are promotions.
There's a difference.

Dick Davis, manager of Buffalo Springfield, 1970

Glastonbury has become one of the most important, certainly at least the largest,
annual events in Britain's alternative calendar. More than a music festival – although
it is one of the great music festivals – it has turned into a huge gathering for members
of the varieties of tribes (the hippies, punks, ravers, eco-warriors) that make up
Britain's extraordinary and colourful alternative culture. The festival has become both
a fixed point in the alternative calendar and the shared experience of generations.
Parents take their children, the youth head down there just like their elders had in
their day, or, just as likely, mums and dads go to get away from their teenage kids.
Michael Eavis has called the festival 'utopian'. But to identify carnival, and its perhaps
more rural manifestation, festival, as utopian is complex. (For sure, utopia is complex
itself: Thomas More, who coined the word and its fictive space nearly 500 years ago,
inscribed ambivalence into it, making it both a good place, *eu-topia*, that is no place,
ou-topia.)

But Glastonbury seems to conform to a familiar trajectory of just about anything to
do with the counterculture of the 1960s, a 'narrative of decline' some of the features of
which are identified by Andrew Ross:

There already exists a dominant media narrative about 'the sixties' that involves New
Age and that recounts the falling off of radicalism, and the absorption, recuperation,

commodification or Yuppification of countercultural politics. It is a narrative about . . . how a liberatory revolution in individual rights became a privatized cult of self-interest . . . how the bohemian rejection of materialism became an acceptance of corporate transmaterialism . . . how the collectivist experiments in cooperative community living became experiments in small-scale entrepreneurship; . . . and how the semiotic gestures of disaffiliation from a dominant culture became incorporated in the business of marketing lifestyles.

One of the ways Ross deals with this narrative of attenuated radicalism is by questioning the entire premise of 'resistance' in especially youth culture in the first place, as an over-fetishised feature of cultural studies in general. But this worries me when I see the simple gaps in the telling of radical cultural history which clearly *are* engaging, however problematically with clear political issues, even in the dread, maybe oxymoronic area of lifestyle politics. Besides, in his massive eponymous history of the sixties, Arthur Marwick argues that commodification was there all along, was indeed central to the cultural revolution of the time: 'Most of the movements, subcultures, and new institutions which are at the heart of sixties change were thoroughly imbued with the entrepreneurial, profit-making ethic. I am thinking here of boutiques, experimental theatres, art galleries, discotheques, nightclubs, "light shows", "head shops", photographic and model agencies, underground films, pornographic magazines.' The much-heralded New Age, the Age of Aquarius, is most clearly seen by Harry Shapiro in the music industry scramble to commodify the new sounds of American rock in the 1960s:

> The record companies, too, were hailing a new age – of increased profits. Jac Holtzman, head of Elektra, told an industry conference at the time: 'To comprehend the music of tomorrow, expand your musical vistas, sensitize yourself, because the vibrations of contemporary existence cannot be had secondhand'. The dark blue suit gave way to the Afghan coat, hair cascaded over ears, dope wafted from nostrils and "man" fell from every corporate lip. Apart from that nothing much had changed.

With these rather negative readings of the counterculture and its legacy, it seems that George Melly was accurate when he commented that, in those days, 'you had to dig pretty deep to stay underground'.

Debates such as this resonate across the decades, partly because pop music (at its 'serious', or 'political', or 'self-important' boundaries) is frequently a discourse of authenticity, in which bands and fans alike have or demand street-cred, are 4REAL, tell it how it is. 'But if it spreads, it thins,' writes John Dean of bohemian counter-culture, pinpointing 'American crowd-culture, festival entertainment' as part of the thinning of opposition even in the 1960s themselves. In 1994 in the United States there was Woodstock 2, the new counterculture's festival sponsored by a soft drinks company (unnamed, no plug) – to what extent has Glastonbury itself 'sold out' or maintained its original ideals? Has it commercialised or is the issue really one of professionalising? Stephen Abrahall of Mid-Somerset CND takes me to task for even posing such questions (come on, that's my job!):

> Your portrayal of the festival as having somehow lost its radicalism, or even worse that its idealism is a 'sheen', is just not so. The causes that it supports are just as important as the event itself, and that is what makes it different. Most, if not all, of the 'commodification' has been done at the behest of the local council, and increasing levels of crowd safety and communications have been regulations imposed by the licence [which the council grants]. There don't seem to be too many who complain at the provision of decent facilities, save perhaps clever journalists who are still trying to slate the event.

I wrote in *Senseless Acts of Beauty* of how the nineties has rewritten the sixties, 'minus the politics'; how far is the idealism of the counterculture revived annually at Glastonbury or lost among the credit card bookings and technology? Has festival culture more generally had its day, the hazy, slow, drawn-out experience of the social gathering being replaced by the hedonistic, me-centred five- or ten-hour party scene? A common pilgrimage being overtaken by what Bowie called 'a crash course for the ravers'? Or is it possible that Glastonbury succeeds where others fail, in managing to meet the dancing demands of both 50 year-old naked hippie and lycra-clad young thing? Does Glastonbury offer a model of alternative living, a temporary illustration of possibility, or does it confirm majority culture by entirely and even facilely replicating the structures of finance and exchange – in the very obvious charge that there is a large charge (weekend ticket prices exceed the amount of money unemployed people get for a fortnight's benefit), that the gate pressure functions as a tactic of social exclusion, for instance?

The commodification of the counterculture.

Glastonbury 1999

In fact (overlooking the necessary, if it is, exclusionary fact of up to £100 per ticket)
there's something for everyone here: eco-consciousness, acoustic music, rock megagig,
drugs, spirituality. Glastonbury is one of those open spaces in part characterised by
its capacity to be whatever you want it to be, within reason (rarely challenging that
safety). This is a fairly banal observation after three days here. But is it the observation
that's banal, or actually somehow the festival itself? I mean in the sense that what is
here is everything you'd expect to be here. There's a predictability that may be that of
counterculture, of the fairly limited nature of its imagination. But while Glastonbury
and its longevity may be a sign of the scale, the energy of traditional aspects of
counterculture – in the Green Fields and Sacred Ground, at least – in other ways
the lack of surprise should be considered more critically. This may be a point about
counterculture, not of festival per se. Like the old fading stuff on festivals that the
second-hand book dealer near Pottergate in Norwich dug out for me (stuff he thought
no one would ever want) said, 'There's only so many times you can watch a wicker
man burning before you start looking for something else to do with your life.' The
surroundings, the proceedings are so familiar here, I suppose comfortably so . . .
my personal symptom of that cosy banality is that I keep feeling churlish, writing
anything that sounds critical – I'll have to carve out a space of critical distance.

'Having given birth to and fostering [sic] the growth of the UK's open air festival
culture, the alternative festival scene is under severe pressure, with big event
promoters now cashing in and throttling the creation.' This is a complaint voiced
in 1996 in *SQUALL*, one of the leading underground magazines of the DiY decade. It
is historically inaccurate, of course, as we have seen: massive commercialisation was
evident even from some of the earliest and largest so-called 'alternative' festivals,
whether Woodstock (1969) or the Isle of Wight (1970), or even the free Glastonbury
Fayre (1971). And there has always been tension between commercial and free
festivals – Woodstock and the Isle of Wight were riven by these tensions, to the extent
that they started as major commercial events and ended as even more major free festivals. Yet *SQUALL* has a point about the ways in which one of the counterculture's
most significant and longstanding socio-cultural contributions, festival culture itself,
has been recognised and commodified. (Of course, it may well be that the reason

festival culture has lasted and often thrived is because it has been commercialised.) *SQUALL* had complained in 1995 that:

> With no festivals, a whole economic support system is swept away. An economy of exchanging wares, selling tat, swapping favours, trading vehicles and doing odd paid jobs associated with running a festival. The festival circuit represented a fast growing alternative economy, supporting a culture of late night cafés and bars, theatre, music, dance, story-telling, rants, raving beat-heads and talking in tongues. A culture where people with crafts and performance skills could both learn and ply their trade, and a place where such talents were rewarded and encouraged in recognition of their necessity.

While decrying what it sees as the demise of festival culture by rampant commercialisation, *SQUALL* could express a characteristically generous line on the commercialisation of Glastonbury itself. 'Many festival-goers say Glastonbury festival becomes more commercial each year. However, whilst there is much by way of evidence for their observations, Glastonbury still retains a relatively high element of alternative culture and will be sorely missed as a meeting point this summer [1996].'

Glastonbury Fayre 1971 was offered as a free event in direct response to the negative experiences at the Isle of Wight, the gross commercialism (even though it was declared free halfway through), which Andrew Kerr had had the previous year. Has, though, Glastonbury merely turned into what it started out against, become what it was critical of? The radical tradition is traceable, as I've been doing through this book, as Bruce Garrard does in microcosm here:

> Do you remember the Isle of Wight festival in 1970 . . . the great big commercial mega-festival became free, the gates were opened and fences were taken down and the festival became free for the people[?] Out of that spirit came the Glastonbury festival in 1971 and the Stonehenge festivals and then, by degrees, the Green Gatherings, the Convoy, the second wave of CND, the peace camps, and all kinds of other trips which people got together in groups or large numbers on their small-holdings, in Ireland, in the squatters' movement, on the road . . .

While Garrard begins with the Isle of Wight in 1970, I have traced a characteristic festival culture back to the 1950s, to the founding of CND, trad jazz and skiffle at early jazz festivals, all-night raves, Aldermaston marches, direct-action politics. Embrace also the strands of influence of political pageants and the early twentieth-century Glastonbury festivals of Rutland Boughton, and the line goes further back. This is something not to be lost. I can't say that strongly enough. *We must cherish, celebrate and learn from our own radical histories.* We must, because we can, surprise ourselves with past ambitions and projects, musical, social, political, idealistic. It's not just self-education, it's surprise and the energy that comes from that. It's caring for what we have done, recognising its importance, maybe its power. And part of the point of this book has been to illustrate ways in which festival culture has played a significant role in those radical histories, a role which has often been neglected or underplayed.

Stencilled news-sheet given out by 'one-man tribe' Mick Farren before the fences came down at the Isle of Wight, 1970.

The 1971 Glastonbury Fayre was the only formally organised free festival at Worthy Farm – but how far does *free* equate to *non-commercial*? The Glastonbury free festival was such a success precisely because of the business acumen that lay behind it, a point Michael Clarke makes.

> It was not appreciated at the time by the participants that a substantial degree of material and commercial organization went into this success. Film rights were sold and a record of the music sold 16,000 copies by 1973. In addition funds were raised by those involved in the fayre by way of donations. Glastonbury may have generated much goodwill and enthusiasm, but it also drew on a good deal of goodwill for the idea of a free festival in its organization and backing.

(It should be remembered too that when many of the same people tried to repeat the success of 1971, as committee members organising the 1979 *paying* Glastonbury Fayre, they made a significant loss.) Even the organisation of the record company that released the triple album of the 1971 Fayre was intended to be idealistic, alternative: long-haired capitalism. One of the counterculture's many self-help manuals was called *Makin' It: A Guide to Some Working Alternatives*, by Nigel T. Turner. Turner chronicles two or three forays into what was even then, in those last pre-punk days, called the 'indie' record scene, including Revelation Enterprises, which is described as 'an attempt to be a real alternative in the gramophone record business – not only in the material they are putting out and the way this is packaged, but much more importantly, on the business side. The company directly evolved out of the Glastonbury Fayre, an event staged in June 1971.' The original press release for Revelation explains the company's rationale:

> The Fayre was a totally free event; there was no admission charge, lots of food, and
> four days of almost continual music. Thirty-eight bands actually played during that
> period. The Fayre might be described as an attempt to awaken a more acute sensitivity
> to the needs of the earth and the minds and hearts of the thirteen thousand people
> who attended. On one level, it was an ecological experiment and on the other hand
> it was simply a joyous gathering of all kinds of people. It was a success by everyone's
> standards. The people who now form Revelation Enterprises were each in some way
> or other involved in organising that event and when it was realised that there were
> going to be a number of debts as a result of the free nature of the Fayre, they began
> to look for ways to pay these debts and make resources available for a nucleus that would
> in future operate with the same kind of ideology.

Unlike the experience of Richard Branson, who had launched his own record company, Virgin, round the same time, with an instrumental concept album by an unknown teenage guitarist who played most of the other instruments on the album too, this company did not become an international success. On the other hand, such success would have been seen as anathema (at least rhetorically): 'We do not intend to build a large corporation with our resources. Smallness and care are our criteria: we know that we can still be effective despite the increasing belief that massive business organisations are good at what they do and have a reason for being. We know, through our corporate experience, that this is untrue. Things will only change if we help them.' (A few years later some of the Revelation people set up one of punk's key independent labels, Stiff Records, releasing records by Ian Dury, Elvis Costello and the Damned.)

Glastonbury festival may frequently valorise (even mythologise) its (with hindsight) extremely brief free flourish, but note that most years the tradition remains for the gates to be thrown open on Sunday afternoon, for all-comers to get their hit, not just those with £80–90 to spare. This is both a gesture to the locality – since most of those coming in for a free lazy Sunday afternoon are from the West Country – and a nod to the past (not only of Glastonbury 1971, but perhaps also of Isle of Wight 1970, Woodstock 1969), a gesture aimed at diluting the consumerist overload.

In some ways Glastonbury does conform to that model of Andrew Ross's. Yet commodification is not the end of the story. It is necessary to keep in mind the festival's fundamental formation as a *fund-raising enterprise*. In terms of fund-raising, there is a lengthy tradition of music festivals organised for charity purposes: the Birmingham Festival (1768–1912), the Norwich Festival (founded 1770), the Leeds Festival (founded 1858) – all of these had their origins in raising funds for local medical charities and hospitals. The bottom line with Glastonbury is that it raises money for worthy (though increasingly less radical) campaigns and projects. Michael Eavis claims £1 million was raised for CND through the 1980s, that is, through the dark years of Thatcherism: £1 million was to support one of the most clearly oppositional, high-profile, international campaigns at a time of apparent parliamentary retrenchment and in-fighting, even deterioration, on the organised left. CND's range of actions, whether huge public demonstrations, support for peace camps, or its network of regional branches – these were made a little easier, more likely actually to happen, by the hard cash donated by Glastonbury festival. Since then the main campaigns funded have been less provocative (if you see CND as provocative), more humanitarian than politically oriented. The main recipients in 1999 were Greenpeace

Revelation staff packing the Glastonbury Fayre Album.

(campaigning against genetically modified crops), Oxfam (funding emergency aid and development around the world), and WaterAid (providing water and sanitation to poor communities in Africa and Asia). Balancing such global activities, the festival also funded a new community hall for Pilton, the nearest, and most long-suffering, village to the festival.

Sometimes the festival turns money down: I am told that in 1999 festival organisers refused a multinational confectionery company's bid to promote some of its products at the festival. The £30,000 offer for the right to hand out free chocolate bars to festival-goers was turned down because organisers were unwilling to be associated with a company they understood to be promoting baby milk powder in the developing world. A leaflet in the student information pack sent out to enquirers from the festival office explains that 'the opportunity to be more overtly commercial has always been resisted. None of the stages are branded or sponsored, and the decision to exclude alcohol or tobacco companies, armaments companies or those with a history of unethical trading significantly reduces the number of companies willing to spend serious money linking their company or brand name to the festival.' (But commercial sponsorship is clearly evident, as a glance at, for instance, the *NME* Stage, the *Select* Glastonbury daily newspaper, BT festival phone cards, Orange mobile phone support, the free *Guardian* mini-guide, etc., etc., confirms.)

Information about the breakdown of festival finances is openly available, on the official website, in press releases and student packs. (Glasnostbury, as someone said a few years ago.) For the 1999 event, out of a budget of approximately £7 million, here are the main expenses:

300 bands, plus stages and PAs	£2,000,000
policing, security, fencing	£1,500,000
water, welfare, power supplies	£1,300,000
administration, legal fees, rent/rates	£700,000
theatre, circus, cabaret, comedy	£450,000
donations to campaigns and causes	£600,000

Over twice as much money is spent on policing as is raised for good causes, which has led to accusations from some activists that the festival is a glorified and, worse, surreptitious 'police benefit gig'. Less than 10 per cent of the overall budget is passed on to good causes, which struck me as rather low. When I asked about what might be acceptable ratios of fund-raising in relation to overall running costs, the Charity Commission explained to me the general point (*not* a comment on Glastonbury in any way) that events such as music benefits do not just raise money but also provide a service included in the admission price – the performances, facilities and so on – which clearly impacts on overall budgets. Michael Eavis told me that 'the show doesn't make me a millionaire – we make more money out of the cows than the festival! Selling 78,000 tickets is the break-even point, so it's a very tight budget all round.' At the press conference at the 1999 festival he explained in more detail:

> We give away about £700,000 a year, you see. We haven't got a pot of gold to cover
> if things go wrong – with savings you pay so much tax, about 40 per cent I think,
> so you just lose it for stacking it up for a rainy day (*smiles*), so we give it all away, and
> there's no tax to pay. We just hope and pray every year that we at least cover our costs.
> I was really worried about a month ago about ticket sales, I didn't think we were going
> to break even. We didn't sell out until this weekend. The weather forecast was good
> last weekend, and people didn't really buy in large numbers until about ten days ago.
> I think people were put off by the last couple of years of mud. Anyone here from *NME*?
> Yeah? Ah! Those stories you printed last year – anything to answer for? (*Laughter from
> all press except* NME*'s young reporter.*) They weren't very flattering. It didn't help any.
> We get a good clear warm year, we'll probably get some good reviews in the music press.
> (*To* NME *boy.*) What do you think of that? Yeah? We should do. Well, are you going to
> write them? (*Laughter.*)

(I felt a little like the *NME* boy during a telephone interview I conducted with Eavis. 'What's this for then, George? Oh, it's for a book, is it? Who's publishing that, then? Is that a commercial thing, you on a percentage? You're making money out of the festival, what are you doing with the money?' I reassured him with confidence that my book, like his festival, would not make me a millionaire.)

For thirty years, on and off, Worthy Farm has opened its gates to offer the Glastonbury festival. How much longer? In his book *Temporary Autonomous Zone*, Hakim Bey traces the fear of the death of festival back in time.

> The ancient concepts of jubilee and saturnalia originate in an intuition that certain
> events lie outside the scope of 'profane time', the measuring-rod of the State and
> of History. These holidays literally occupied gaps in the calendar – *intercalary intervals.*

By the Middle Ages, nearly a third of the year was given over to holidays. Perhaps
the riots against calendar reform had less to do with the 'eleven lost days' than with
a sense that imperial science was conspiring to close up these gaps in the calendar
where the people's freedoms had accumulated . . . The death of the festival.

For an event like Glastonbury, so associated with a single family and their private
land, the future of festival can appear even more precarious. Each year rumours
spread that this one will be the last. In 1995 there was a big scare for Glastonbury's
future when news came out that Michael Eavis was diagnosed with cancer. The
1999 festival was overshadowed by the death a few weeks earlier of his wife and
co-organiser Jean Eavis. The couple had often talked of retiring after a festival in
2000, since, as Michael put it at the 1999 press conference, 'You want to retire
when you're on top, when it's going well.' He added, 'but it's not much fun retiring on
your own, is it?' If Eavis stops organising the event, will it continue, organised by
another family member perhaps, or organised by a commercial festival promoter like
Virgin or Mean Fiddler? If it continues without Michael Eavis, will it manage to
maintain its alternative ethos? The point *SQUALL* made about the festival's absence
in 1996, that it would be 'sorely missed' that summer, can be extended with a
very simple question: if Glastonbury festival stopped happening, would it be sorely
missed? There is a very simple answer: yes.

 By posting an e-mail on a couple of websites, I asked the very active cyber-
community of Glastonbury for any thoughts on the festival. I wanted in particular to
hear from people who were close to it, perhaps because they had been to many, or
lived nearby. Here are three of the responses, fairly representative:

I stopped attending after a wet/muddy festival in '85 or '86. I remember standing
in the middle of a mudbath with someone I had met, surveying the scene, and looking
 at all the litter mixed in the mud, and the devastation. I realised that my generation
was capable of wreaking far more damage than our parents' generation, which was
a shock.

Don't go any more. Far too big. I don't like big crowds. Don't do drugs any more.

I feel that the festival is an inevitable reflection of our culture – it's primarily about non-
responsibility over consumption of music, drink, drugs, festive food and the whole festie

experience. It's about the rebellious youff of today being hypnotised into the idea that they are doing their own free thing. The constant sensory consumption maintains a blocking out and avoidance of any psychological-ethical naggings.

On the other hand, here are three responses to the question of commodification which I put to musicians of different generations, all involved in festival or in pop and politics in some way:

> NIK TURNER OF HAWKWIND *ET AL*: I do think that the whole sponsorship thing, Radio 1, MTV, *NME*, mobile phone companies, takes the festival away from its more idealistic origins. Glastonbury is the acceptable face of commercial festivals. It is pretty cool that it's lasted so long, but the media discovery of it has sanitised it, maybe festivals generally, and it's a pile of crap in that respect. Michael's very open-handed – I'm not critical of him. Although when he's successful, he goes and buys another 500 acres of land in the name of the festival, so he's doing all right out of it, isn't he!

> TOM ROBINSON: Michael Eavis's achievement is extraordinary. It's so easy for other promoters, who are trying to make big money out of festivals, to moan, or for people who used to go twenty years ago to say, 'Oh it's nothing like as good as it used to be.' Eavis's genius is to keep it renewed, refreshed. Glastonbury festival is a gift to the nation, I really think that!

> JEREMY CUNNINGHAM OF THE LEVELLERS: Yeah, we do rather regret calling Michael Eavis a cunt on the Pyramid Stage, broadcasting live to the nation [in 1992]. It wasn't even me, it was [our singer] Mark, but he ran off afterwards and Eavis cornered me instead. It was all bound up with the banning of the Travellers' Field, the fact that the police were getting more money than the Green campaigns, the fact that just before we were going onstage someone said, 'Now please don't use any bad language.' And to be honest we were nervous – it was our first time on the big stage as a name band. But it was still a stupid thing to say: Glastonbury is the best of all the commercial festivals, no doubt about it.

Finally, you see, the thing is, I have a confession to make. My political background is in anarchism, my cultural background in punk's contumacy, I'm a Glaswegian boy whose birth home was destroyed in the 1960s for an urban motorway, so we lived in railway cottages and caravans later in deepest Norfolk. When I started writing about Glastonbury, before that, started thinking about it seriously, I began either to have or maybe to remember these dreams. Well, one dream – a scene actually, a series of old buildings with arches, a market or meeting place, that I increasingly suspected of being in Glastonbury, a town at the time I'd never visited – and one childhood memory of countryside: a secret well in north Norfolk I used to go to sometimes, gaze at the water, gentle spring, plunge my hands in, near the ancient ruins opposite my primary school.

But you don't want to hear about that. And besides, what on earth am I doing? What has been happening to me writing this book? My reputation (such as it is) as a cultural historian of radical politics, of cultural anarchism, is in danger of tattering. Is this me suffering from, succumbing to what the venerable Arthurian historian Geoffrey Ashe has called 'the Glastonbury Madness, the unbalance of scholars'? When I interviewed Tom Robinson for the book, he apologised for one reply being 'woolly and fuzzy', and put it down to 'the Glastonbury effect, the suspension of everyday rules'. Remember I quoted the spiritualist and founding Avalonian Dion Fortune writing brilliantly (why did I insert that word?) about Glastonbury that 'the veil is thin'? The curious thing is that when the festival is on round each summer solstice, *the veil thickens*. And me, I don't believe in veils, anyway!

But, you know, Glasto plc, the selling out of idealism, consumerism in an anti-materialist world, that's too easy a conclusion, too glib, and I don't want to end on a negative note, I really don't. Michael Eavis is one of the good ones, as was his wife Jean. Glastonbury is basically a sound festival, especially in the Green Fields. The causes it supports are right on. The town, the idea of Glastonbury itself is extraordinary, well, its claims and legends are anyway. Forty years of pop festival culture, thirty of Glastonbury, are worth championing. The histories of its related radical visions and actions need telling. 'How, then, shall we define the valuable tradition [of festival]?' asked Lawrence Whistler in *The English Festivals* in 1947. 'It is one with a green end,' he answered himself. I'm sitting on the thin bank of the River Whitelake near Worthy Farm, Pilton, Somerset, a paperback in my hand. It's Forster, *Howards End* again. I remembered the detail of the boar's teeth tapped into the old tree, and that made me pick up that book. I don't even read novels any more. I'm not even English.

'In these English farms, if anywhere, one might see life steadily and see it whole, group in one vision its transitoriness and its eternal youth . . . The present flowed before them like a stream. The tree rustled. It had made music before they were born, and would continue after their deaths, but its song was of the moment. The moment had passed. The tree rustled again. Their senses were sharpened, and they seemed to apprehend life. Life passed. The tree rustled again.'

ACKNOWLEDGEMENTS

I owe thanks to Emma, Ailsa and Dora, of course. I missed you at Glastonbury in 1999.

And then I owe thanks to my agents, Malcolm Imrie and Martina Dervis.

At Worthy Farm, thanks to Michael Eavis, and to workers in the Festival and Press Office, including Jason Holmes, Sheelagh Allen, Hilary White.

Nik Turner, Tom Robinson, Jeremy Cunningham all spared time to talk with enthusiasm and interest about festivals and music, and I appreciate that. Thanks too to Tony Myers of CND in London and Lord Montagu of Beaulieu who found time to be interviewed.

On other festival-related things, I thank Gonnie Rietveld, Mike Weaver (gonna get out your way one day!), Alan Lodge (Tash), Alan Dearling, Andrew Blake, Lisa McKenna, Lucy Watton, Margaret Greenfield, David Trippas, Palden Jenkins, William Bloom, Steve Charter, Sig Lonegren, Tom Cahill, Bruce Garrard.

At University of Central Lancashire, I owe thanks to Ian Sheridan and other library staff, Michael Doherty for clearing up a legal query, Jane Darcy for her story about why she missed the Stones in Hyde Park in '69, as well as to Will Kaufman and Eithne Quinn. Thanks too to my Popular Music students for their festival stories and for introducing me to their good music.

Thanks to Ian Brownlie for the pre-Glastonbury-festival hangover in Norwich: sitting in a candlelit willow bender in a garden in the middle of the Larkman estate after giving a paper on the East Anglian fairs to a Utopia conference at the concrete UEA – I remember that bit.

In and around Glastonbury itself, both Alister Sieghart and Stephen Abrahall of Mid-Somerset CND spared time to offer much appreciated opinion and to comment on drafts. At Avon and Somerset Constabulary I need to thank David Jones, Caron Smith.

Finally, at Gollancz, thanks to Ian Preece for commissioning the book in the first place, and to Bryony Newhouse, Helen Ewing and Vicki Traino.

BIBLIOGRAPHY

Preface: **Festival culture** / Chapter 1. **Histories of festival culture**

Barnes, Richard. 1983. *The Sun in the East: Norfolk & Suffolk Fairs*. Kirstead, Norfolk: RB Photographic.

Beam, Alan. 1976. *Rehearsal for the Year 2000 (Drugs, Religions, Madness, Crime, Communes, Love, Visions, Festivals and Lunar Energy): The Rebirth of Albion Free State (Known in the Dark Ages as England): Memoirs of a Male Midwife 1966–1976*. London: Revelaction Press.

Berger, George. 1998. *Dance Before the Storm: The Official Story of the Levellers*. London: Virgin.

Blake, Andrew. 1997. *The Land Without Music: Music, Culture and Society in Twentieth Century Britain*. Manchester: Manchester University Press.

Booker, Christopher. 1969. *The Neophiliacs: A Study of the Revolution in English Life in the Fifties and Sixties*. London: Fontana, 1970.

Bord, Janet and Colin Bord. 1972. *Mysterious Britain*. London: Granada.

Boswell, Gordon. 1970. *The Book of Boswell: Autobiography of a Gypsy*. With John Seymour. Harmondsworth: Penguin, 1973.

Bunce, Michael. 1994. *The Countryside Ideal: Anglo-American Images of Landscape*. London: Routledge.

Cashmore, Ernest. 1979. *Rastaman: The Rastafarian Movement in England*. London: Unwin, 1983.

Chambers, Iain. 1986. *Popular Culture: The Metropolitan Experience*. London: Routledge, 1990.

Cohen, Abner. 1982. 'A polyethnic London carnival as a contested cultural performance'. *Ethnic and Racial Studies* vol. 5:1 (January 1982): 23–41.

Dearling, Alan, with Brendan Hanley. 2000. *Alternative Australia: Celebrating Cultural Diversity*. Lyme Regis, Dorset: Enabler Publications.

Downing, David. 1976. *Future Rock*. St Albans, Herts: Panther.

Elstob, Lynne, and Anne Howe. 1987. *The Glastonbury Festivals*. Glastonbury: Gothic Image.

Fairlie, Simon. 1996. *Low Impact Development: Planning and People in a Sustainable Countryside*. Charlbury, Oxfordshire: Jon Carpenter.

Farren, Mick, and Edward Barker. 1972. *Watch Out, Kids*. London: Open Gate Books.

Fountain, Nigel. 1988. *Underground: The London Alternative Press 1966–74*. London: Routledge.

Gorman, Clem. 1975. *People Together: A Guide to Communal Living*. St Albans, Herts: Paladin.

Hopkins, Jerry, Bob Cato, Baron Wolman and Jim Marshall. 1970. *Festival! The Book of American Music Celebrations*. London: Collier.

Malyon, Tim. 1998. 'Tossed in the fire and they never got burned: the Exodus Collective'. In McKay 1998: 187–207.

Marks, J. 1973. *Mick Jagger*. London: Abacus, 1974.

Marwick, Arthur. 1998. *The Sixties: Cultural Revolution in Britain, France, Italy, and the United States, c. 1958–1974*. Oxford: Oxford University Press.

McKay, George. 1996. *Senseless Acts of Beauty: Cultures of Resistance since the Sixties*. London: Verso.
——. ed. 1998. *DiY Culture: Party & Protest in Nineties Britain*. London: Verso.
Melly, George. 1965. *Owning-Up*. Harmondsworth: Penguin, 1970.
——. 1970. *Revolt Into Style: The Pop Arts in Britain*. Harmondsworth: Penguin, 1972.
Monbiot, George. 1998. 'Reclaim the fields and country lanes! The Land is Ours campaign'. In McKay 1998: 174–86.
Montagu, Lord. *The Gilt and the Gingerbread*. London: Michael Joseph.
Phillips, Mike, and Trevor Phillips. 1998. *Windrush: The Irresistible Rise of Multi-Racial Britain*. London: HarperCollins, 1999.
Reclaim the Streets (RTS). 1996. 'Reclaim the Streets'. *Do or Die: Voices from Earth First!* no. 6: 1–14.
Sandford, Jeremy, and Ron Reid. 1974. *Tomorrow's People*. London: Jerome.
Shapiro, Harry. 1988. *Waiting for the Man: The Story of Drugs and Popular Music*. London: Quartet.
Whistler, Lawrence. 1947. *The English Festivals*. London: Heinemann, 1948.

Chapter 2. **Old hippie slogan: 'You're never too old for a happy childhood'**

Beam, Alan. 1976. *Rehearsal for the Year 2000 (Drugs, Religions, Madness, Crime, Communes, Love, Visions, Festivals and Lunar Energy): The Rebirth of Albion Free State (Known in the Dark Ages as England): Memoirs of a Male Midwife 1966–1976*. London: Revelaction Press.
Benham, Patrick. 1993. *The Avalonians*. Glastonbury: Gothic Image Publications.
Blake, Andrew. 1997. *The Land Without Music: Music, Culture and Society in Twentieth-Century Britain*. Manchester: Manchester University Press.
Clarke, Michael. 1982. *The Politics of Pop Festivals*. London: Junction Books.
Eavis, Michael. 1998. 'The Glastonbury Festivals'. www.glastonbury-festival.co.uk/history/gfeavis.htm
Farren, Mick, and Edward Barker. 1972. *Watch Out, Kids*. London: Open Gate Books.
Fortune, Dion. 1934. *Avalon of the Heart*. Revised edition published as *Dion Fortune's Glastonbury: Avalon of the Heart*. Wellingborough, Northants: Aquarian Press, 1989.
Garrard, Bruce, ed. 1986. *The Children of the Rainbow Gathered in the Free State of Avalonia at the Christian Community of Greenlands Farm*. Glastonbury: Unique Publications.
——. 1994. *The Alternative Sector: Notes on Green Philosophy, Politics and Economics*. Glastonbury: Unique Publications.
Hobsbawm, Eric and Terence Ranger, eds. 1983. *The Invention of Tradition*. Cambridge: Cambridge University Press, 1994.
Holdsworth, David. 1976. *The New Society: A Report on the Development of Pop & 'Free' Festivals in the Thames Valley Area 1972–1975 by the Chief Constable*. Thames Valley Police Authority.
Hopkins, Jerry, Bob Cato, Baron Wolman and Jim Marshall. 1970. *Festival! The Book of American Music Celebrations*. London: Collier.
Lowe, Richard, and William Shaw. 1993. *Travellers: Voices of the New Age Nomads*. London: Fourth Estate.
McKay, George. 1996. *Senseless Acts of Beauty: Cultures of Resistance since the Sixties*. London: Verso.
Melly, George. 1965. *Owning-Up*. Harmondsworth: Penguin, 1970.
——. 1970. *Revolt Into Style: The Pop Arts in Britain*. Harmondsworth: Penguin, 1972.
Montagu, Lord. *The Gilt and the Gingerbread*. London: Michael Joseph.
Morgan, Ann, and Bruce Garrard. 1989. *Travellers in Glastonbury*. Glastonbury: Unique Publications.

Morgan, Prys. 1983. 'From a death to a view: the hunt for the Welsh past in the Romantic period'. In Hobsbawm and Ranger 1983: 43–100.

Report of Working Party Following Illegal Invasion of Castlemorton Common nr Malvern, Hereford and Worcester, May 22 to 29, 1992. Hereford and Worcester County Council. 1993/1994.

Sandford, Jeremy, and Ron Reid. 1974. *Tomorrow's People*. London: Jerome.

Shapiro, Harry. 1988. *Waiting for the Man: The Story of Drugs and Popular Music*. London: Quartet.

Stone, C.J. 1999. *The Last of the Hippies*. London: Faber.

Stonehenge '88: News Cuttings. 1988. Glastonbury: Unique Publications.

Whistler, Lawrence. 1947. *The English Festivals*. London: Heinemann, 1948.

Chapter 3. **Misty, mysterious Avalon: Glastonbury legend and festival**

Ashe, Geoffrey, ed. 1968. *The Quest for Arthur's Britain*. London: Paladin, 1971.

——. 1982. *Avalonian Quest*. London: Fontana, 1984.

Benham, Patrick. 1993. *The Avalonians*. Glastonbury: Gothic Image Publications.

Blake, Andrew. 1997. *The Land Without Music: Music, Culture and Society in Twentieth-Century Britain*. Manchester: Manchester University Press.

Boughton, Rutland. 1998. *The Immortal Hour: A Music-Drama*. Hyperion Dyad Records. Cat. no. CDD22040.

Cashmore, Ernest. 1979. *Rastaman: The Rastafarian Movement in England*. London: Unwin, 1983.

Christian, Roy. 1996. *Well Dressing in Derbyshire*. Derby: Derby Countryside Limited.

Clarke, Michael. 1982. *The Politics of Pop Festivals*. London: Junction Books.

Cooper, Simon, and Mike Farrant. 1991. *Fire in our Hearts: The Story of the Jesus Fellowship*. Eastbourne, Sussex: Kingsway Publications.

Croft, Andy, ed. 1998. *A Weapon in the Struggle: The Cultural History of the Communist Party in Britain*. London: Lawrence and Wishart.

Elstob, Lynne, and Anne Howe. 1987. *The Glastonbury Festivals*. Glastonbury: Gothic Image.

Fortune, Dion. 1934. *Avalon of the Heart*. Revised edition published as *Dion Fortune's Glastonbury: Avalon of the Heart*. Wellingborough, Northants: Aquarian Press, 1989.

Free State: the Journal of the Free State of Avalonia. Various.

Garrard, Bruce. 1994. *The Alternative Sector: Notes on Green Philosophy, Politics and Economics*. Glastonbury: Unique Publications.

Garrard, Bruce, and Lucy Lepchani, eds. 1990. *Glastonbury Green Magazine*. Glastonbury: Unique Publications.

Glastonbury: The First 25 Years: A Celebration of the Festival. Glastonbury Festival: 1995.

Hanlon, Richard, and Mike Waite. 1998. 'Notes from the Left: Communism and British classical music'. In Croft 1998: 68–88.

Harmonic Convergence: Press Cuttings, August 1987. Glastonbury: Unique Publications.

Harvey, Graham. 1996. *Listening People, Speaking Earth: Contemporary Paganism*. London: Hurst.

Hurd, Michael. 1962. *Immortal Hour: The Life and Period of Rutland Boughton*. London: Routledge and Kegan Paul.

Michell, John. 1969. *The View Over Atlantis*. London: Abacus, 1973.

——. 1990. *New Light on the Ancient Mystery of Glastonbury*. Glastonbury: Gothic Image, 1997.

Saunders, Nicholas. 1970. *Alternative London*. London: Nicholas Saunders.

——. 1972. *Alternative London 3*. London: Nicholas Saunders.

Spangler, David. 1975. *Festivals in the New Age*. Findhorn Foundation: Findhorn, Scotland.

Stewart, Bob. 1977. *Where is St George? Pagan Imagery in English Folksong*. Bradford-on-Avon, Wiltshire: Moonraker Press.

Stone, C.J. 1999. *The Last of the Hippies*. London: Faber.

Wallis, Mick. 1998. 'Heirs to the pageant: mass spectacle and the Popular Front'. In Croft 1998: 48–67.

Westwood, Jennifer. 1985. *Albion: A Guide to Legendary Britain*. London: HarperCollins, 1992.

Whistler, Lawrence. 1947. *The English Festivals*. London: Heinemann, 1948.

Young, Malcolm. 1993. *In the Sticks: Cultural Identity in a Rural Police Force*. Oxford: Clarendon Press.

Time-line of festival culture

Berger, George. 1998. *Dance Before the Storm: The Official Story of the Levellers*. London: Virgin.

Clarke, Michael. 1982. *The Politics of Pop Festivals*. London: Junction Books.

Cobbold, Chrissie Lytton. 1986. *The Knebworth Rock Festivals*. London: Omnibus.

Cohen, Abner. 1982. 'A polyethnic London carnival as a contested cultural performance'. *Ethnic and Racial Studies* vol. 5:1 (January 1982): 23–41.

Croft, Andy, ed. 1998. *A Weapon in the Struggle: The Cultural History of the Communist Party in Britain*. London: Lawrence and Wishart.

Downing, David. 1976. *Future Rock*. St Albans, Herts: Panther.

Elstob, Lynne, and Anne Howe. 1987. *The Glastonbury Festivals*. Glastonbury: Gothic Image.

Farren, Mick, and Edward Barker. 1972. *Watch Out, Kids*. London: Open Gate Books.

Festival Eye magazine, various.

Fountain, Nigel. 1988. *Underground: The London Alternative Press 1966–74*. London: Routledge.

Glastonbury: The First 25 Years: A Celebration of the Festival. Glastonbury Festival: 1995.

Gorman, Clem. 1975. *People Together: A Guide to Communal Living*. St Albans, Herts: Paladin.

Henderson, Hamish. 1998. 'The Edinburgh People's Festival, 1951–54'. In Croft 1998: 163–70.

Heslam, David, ed. 1992. *NME Rock 'n' Roll Years*. London: BCA.

Hinton, Brian. 1995. *Message to Love: The Isle of Wight Festivals, 1968–70*. Chessington, Surrey: Castle Communications.

Hopkins, Jerry, Bob Cato, Baron Wolman and Jim Marshall. 1970. *Festival! The Book of American Music Celebrations*. London: Collier.

Hutnyk, John. 1996. 'Repetitive beatings or criminal justice?' In Sharma et al 1996: 156–89.

McKay, George. 1996. *Senseless Acts of Beauty: Cultures of Resistance since the Sixties*. London: Verso.

——. ed. 1998. *DiY Culture: Party & Protest in Nineties Britain*. London: Verso.

Minnion, John, and Philip Bolsover, eds. 1983. *The CND Story: The First 25 Years of CND in the Words of the People Involved*. London: Allison & Busby.

Montagu, Lord. *The Gilt and the Gingerbread*. London: Michael Joseph.

Porter, Gerald. 1998. '"The world's ill-divided": the Communist Party and progressive song'. In Croft 1998: 171–91.

Report of Working Party Following Illegal Invasion of Castlemorton Common nr Malvern, Hereford and Worcester, May 22 to 29, 1992. Hereford and Worcester County Council. 1993/1994.

Rimbaud, Penny. 1999. *Shibboleth: My Revolting Life*. Edinburgh: AK Press.

Sandford, Jeremy, and Ron Reid. 1974. *Tomorrow's People*. London: Jerome.

Shapiro, Harry. 1988. *Waiting for the Man: The Story of Drugs and Popular Music*. London: Quartet.

Sharma, Sanjay, John Hutnyk and Ashwani Sharma, eds. 1996. *Dis-Orienting Rhythms: The Politics of the New Asian Dance Music*. London: Zed Books.

Stansill, Bob, and David Zane Mairowitz, eds. 1971. *BAMN: Outlaw Manifestos and Ephemera 1965–70*. Harmondsworth: Penguin.

Veldman, Meredith. 1994. *Fantasy, the Bomb, and the Greening of Britain: Romantic Protest, 1945–1980*. Cambridge: Cambridge University Press.

Widgery, David. 1976. *The Left in Britain: 1956–68*. Harmondsworth: Penguin.

——. 1986. *Beating Time: Riot 'n' Race 'n' Rock 'n' Roll*. London: Chatto and Windus.

Wolfe, Tom. 1968. *The Electric Kool-Aid Acid Test*. New York: Bantam, 1976.

Chapter 4. 'Fields are our lost history': countryside and landscape

Adorno, Theodor W. 1947. 'Theses against occultism'. In Crook 1994: 128–34.

Ashe, Geoffrey, ed. 1968. *The Quest for Arthur's Britain*. London: Paladin, 1971.

——. 1982. *Avalonian Quest*. London: Fontana, 1984.

Booker, Christopher. 1969. *The Neophiliacs: A Study of the Revolution in English Life in the Fifties and Sixties*. London: Fontana, 1970.

Bord, Janet and Colin Bord. 1972. *Mysterious Britain*. London: Granada.

Bunce, Michael. 1994. *The Countryside Ideal: Anglo-American Images of Landscape*. London: Routledge.

Chambers, Iain. 1986. *Popular Culture: The Metropolitan Experience*. London: Routledge, 1990.

Cloke, Paul, and Jo Little, eds. 1997. *Contested Countryside Cultures: Otherness, Marginality and Rurality*. London: Routledge.

Cobbold, Chrissie Lytton. 1986. *The Knebworth Rock Festivals*. London: Omnibus.

Common Ground. 1997. *Field Days: Ideas for Investigations and Celebrations*. London: Common Ground.

Crook, Stephen, ed., 1994. *Adorno: The Stars Down to Earth and Other Essays on the Irrational in Culture*. London: Routledge.

Delgado, Pat, and Colin Andrews. 1989. *Circular Evidence: A Detailed Investigation of the Flattened Swirled Crops Phenomenon*. London: Guild Publishing.

Eavis, Michael. 1998. 'The Glastonbury Festivals'. www.glastonbury-festival.co.uk/history/gfeavis.htm

Fortune, Dion. 1934. *Avalon of the Heart*. Revised edition published as *Dion Fortune's Glastonbury: Avalon of the Heart*. Wellingborough, Northants: Aquarian Press, 1989.

Free State: the Journal of the Free State of Avalonia. Various.

Glastonbury: The First 25 Years: A Celebration of the Festival. Glastonbury Festival: 1995.

Halfacree, Keith. 1997. 'Contrasting roles for the post-productivist countryside: a postmodern perspective on counterurbanisation'. In Cloke and Little 1997: 70–93.

Harrison, Fraser. 1986. *The Living Landscape: The Seasons of a Suffolk Village*. London: Pluto.

Harvey, Graham. 1996. *Listening People, Speaking Earth: Contemporary Paganism*. London: Hurst.

Maffesoli, Michel. 1988. *The Time of the Tribes: The Decline of Individualism in Mass Society*. Trans. by Don Smith. London: Sage, 1996.

Merrick. 1996. *Battle for the Trees: Three Months of Responsible Ancestry*. Leeds Godhaven.

Michell, John. 1969. *The View Over Atlantis*. London: Abacus, 1973.

——. 1990. *New Light on the Ancient Mystery of Glastonbury*. Glastonbury: Gothic Image, 1997.

Neville, Richard. 1970. *Playpower*. St Albans: Paladin, 1973.

Rahtz, Philip. 1968. 'Glastonbury Tor'. In Ashe 1968: 111–22.

Sandford, Jeremy, and Ron Reid. 1974. *Tomorrow's People*. London: Jerome.

Stewart, Bob. 1977. *Where is St George? Pagan Imagery in English Folksong*. Bradford-on-Avon, Wiltshire: Moonraker Press.

Stone, C.J. 1999. *The Last of the Hippies*. London: Faber.

Watkins, Alfred. 1922. *Early British Trackways, Moats, Mounds, Camps and Sites*. Hereford: The Watkins Meter Co.

Chapter 5. **Let me entertain you!**

Berger, George. 1998. *Dance Before the Storm: The Official Story of the Levellers*. London: Virgin.

Blake, Andrew. 1997. *The Land Without Music: Music, Culture and Society in Twentieth-Century Britain*. Manchester: Manchester University Press.

Clarke, Michael. 1982. *The Politics of Pop Festivals*. London: Junction Books.

Croft, Andy, ed. 1998. *A Weapon in the Struggle: The Cultural History of the Communist Party in Britain*. London: Lawrence and Wishart.

Elstob, Lynne, and Anne Howe. 1987. *The Glastonbury Festivals*. Glastonbury: Gothic Image.

Garnett, Robert. 1999. 'Too low to be low: art pop and the Sex Pistols'. In Sabin 1999: 17–30.

Garrard, Bruce, ed. 1986. *The Green Collective: The Best from the Mailing 1984*. Glastonbury: Unique Publications.

Glastonbury: The First 25 Years: A Celebration of the Festival. Glastonbury Festival: 1995.

Hopkins, Jerry, Bob Cato, Baron Wolman and Jim Marshall. 1970. *Festival! The Book of American Music Celebrations*. London: Collier.

Huq, Rupa. 1999. 'The right to rave: opposition to the Criminal Justice and Public Order Act, 1994'. In Jordan and Lent 1999: 15–33.

Hurd, Michael. 1962. *Immortal Hour: The Life and Period of Rutland Boughton*. London: Routledge and Kegan Paul.

Jordan, Tim and Adam Lent, eds. 1999. *Storming the Millennium: The New Politics of Change*. London: Lawrence and Wishart.

Kalra, Virinder J., John Hutnyk and Sanjay Sharma. 1996. 'Re-sounding (anti)racism, or concordant politics? Revolutionary antecedents'. In Sharma et al 1996: 127–55.

Marwick, Arthur. 1998. *The Sixties: Cultural Revolution in Britain, France, Italy, and the United States, c. 1958–1974*. Oxford: Oxford University Press.

Melly, George. 1965. *Owning-Up*. Harmondsworth: Penguin, 1970.

Phillips, Mike, and Trevor Phillips. 1998. *Windrush: The Irresistible Rise of Multi-Racial Britain*. London: HarperCollins, 1999.

Porter, Gerald. 1998. '"The world's ill-divided": the Communist Party and progressive song'. In Croft 1998: 171–91.

Rietveld, Hillegonda. 1997. ''Marshall Jefferson and the Lumpheads'. In Sarah Champion, ed. *Trance Europe Express 5*. Catalogue number: teexcd005.

Rushkoff, Douglas. 1994. *Cyberia: Life in the Trenches of Hyperspace*. London: Flamingo.

Sabin, Roger. 1999. *Punk Rock: So What? The Cultural Legacy of Punk*. London: Routledge.

Sharma, Sanjay, John Hutnyk and Ashwani Sharma, eds. 1996. *Dis-Orienting Rhythms: The Politics of the New Asian Dance Music*. London: Zed Books.

Thompson, Ben. 1998. *Seven Years of Plenty: A Handbook of Irrefutable Pop Greatness 1991–1998*. London: Gollancz.

Whistler, Lawrence. 1947. *The English Festivals*. London: Heinemann, 1948.

Widgery, David. 1986. *Beating Time: Riot 'n' Race 'n' Rock 'n' Roll*. London: Chatto and Windus.

Chapter 6. **A green field far away: the politics of peace and ecology at the festival**

Abrahall, Stephen. 1995. 'Worthy's causes'. In *Glastonbury: The First 25 Years*: 20–21.

Barnes, Richard. 1983. *The Sun in the East: Norfolk & Suffolk Fairs*. Kirstead, Norfolk: RB Photographic.

Blake, Andrew. 1997. *The Land Without Music: Music, Culture and Society in Twentieth-Century Britain*. Manchester: Manchester University Press.

Eavis, Michael. 1998. 'The Glastonbury Festivals'. www.glastonbury-festival.co.uk/history/gfeavis.htm

Elstob, Lynne, and Anne Howe. 1987. *The Glastonbury Festivals*. Glastonbury: Gothic Image.

Farren, Mick, and Edward Barker. 1972. *Watch Out, Kids*. London: Open Gate Books.

Festival Eye magazine, various.

Fortune, Dion. 1934. *Avalon of the Heart*. Revised edition published as *Dion Fortune's Glastonbury: Avalon of the Heart*. Wellingborough, Northants: Aquarian Press, 1989.

Garrard, Bruce, ed. 1986. *The Green Collective: The Best from the Mailing 1984*. Glastonbury: Unique Publications.

——. 1994. *The Alternative Sector: Notes on Green Philosophy, Politics and Economics*. Glastonbury: Unique Publications.

Garrard, Bruce, and Lucy Lepchani, eds. 1990. *Glastonbury Green Magazine*. Glastonbury: Unique Publications.

Glastonbury: The First 25 Years: A Celebration of the Festival. Glastonbury Festival: 1995.

Harford, Barbara, and Sarah Hopkins, eds. 1984. *Greenham Common: Women at the Wire*. London: Women's Press.

Hopkins, Jerry, Bob Cato, Baron Wolman and Jim Marshall. 1970. *Festival! The Book of American Music Celebrations*. London: Collier.

Minnion, John, and Philip Bolsover, eds. 1983. *The CND Story: The First 25 Years of CND in the Words of the People Involved*. London: Allison & Busby.

Roszak, Theodore. 1969. *The Making of a Counter Culture*. London: Univerity of California Press, 1995.

Veldman, Meredith. 1994. *Fantasy, the Bomb, and the Greening of Britain: Romantic Protest, 1945–1980*. Cambridge: Cambridge University Press.

Conclusion. **Glastonbury plc?**

Ashe, Geoffrey. 1982. *Avalonian Quest*. London: Fontana, 1984.

Bey, Hakim. 1991. *TAZ: The Temporary Autonomous Zone, Ontological Anarchy, Poetic Terrorism*. Brooklyn, NY: Autonomedia.

Clarke, Michael. 1982. *The Politics of Pop Festivals*. London: Junction Books.

Dean, John. 1997. 'The bohemian transformed: America, the malcontent and the alterations of the 1960s'. In McKay 1997: 89–103.

Garrard, Bruce. 1994. *The Alternative Sector: Notes on Green Philosophy, Politics and Economics*. Glastonbury: Unique Publications.

Hopkins, Jerry, Bob Cato, Baron Wolman and Jim Marshall. 1970. *Festival! The Book of American Music Celebrations*. London: Collier.

Marwick, Arthur. 1998. *The Sixties: Cultural Revolution in Britain, France, Italy, and the United States, c. 1958–1974*. Oxford: Oxford University Press.

McKay, George. 1996. *Senseless Acts of Beauty: Cultures of Resistance since the Sixties*. London: Verso.

——. ed. 1997. *Yankee Go Home (& Take Me With U): Americanization and Popular Culture*. Sheffield: Sheffield Academic Press.

Melly, George. 1970. *Revolt Into Style: The Pop Arts in Britain*. Harmondsworth: Penguin, 1972.

Ross, Andrew. 1991. *Strange Weather: Culture, Science and Technology in the Age of Limits*. London: Verso.

Shapiro, Harry. 1988. *Waiting for the Man: The Story of Drugs and Popular Music*. London: Quartet.

SQUALL magazine, various.

Turner, Nigel G. 1974. *Makin' It: A Guide to Some Working Alternatives*. Petersham, Surrey: Paper Tiger Productions.

Whistler, Lawrence. 1947. *The English Festivals*. London: Heinemann, 1948.

LIAM BAILEY

p.vi, xi, 112 (comedy tent), 143, 144 (×2), 150, 151, 155, 157, 171, 175.

STEVE DOUBLE

p.ii, iii , iv, 104 (bottom left), 110 (Noel Gallagher & Daddy G), 111 (Chemical Brothers), 112 (Beck & the Prodigy), 192, 210, 211.

ALAN LODGE

p.i, viii, xii, 28, 35, 36, 40, 44, 54, 58, 75, 76, 85, 86, 102 (top right), 104 (bottom right), 106–107, 109 (top left & right), 118, 125, 136, 158, 163, 173 (×2), 182, 197.

OTHER SOURCES

Hulton Getty: p.3, 10, 17, 18, 66, 69, 70, 88, 89 (×2), 91, 92 (×2), 93 (×2), 95 (×2), 96, 98, 99, 100.

p.101 (top right) Mick Young/Retna; 104 (top left) Brian Walker; 105 (right) Marcus Cole, (bottom right) Jeremy Hooper; 108 Ed Sirrs/Retna; 109 (right) Mick Young/Retna; 110–111 (Jarvis Cocker, Damon Albarn & Johnny Cash) Michael Putland/Retna, (Richard Ashcroft) Scarlet Page/Retna; 113 (×2), 114 (bottom ×2), 115, 116 all Antonio Pagano/Retna; 114 (top left), 123, both Howard Denner/Retna; 147 Scarlet Page/Retna; 163 Jeremy Hooper.

Every effort has been made to trace all the copyright holders, but if any have been inadvertently overlooked the publishers will be pleased to include a full acknowledgement in any future edition.

'Fields are our lost history'

The right of George McKay to be identified
as the author of this work has been asserted
by him in accordance with the Copyright,
Designs and Patents Act, 1988.

First published in Great Britain in 2000
by Victor Gollancz
An imprint of Orion Books Ltd
Orion House, 5 Upper St Martin's Lane,
London WC2H 9EA

A CIP catalogue record for this book
is available from the British Library

ISBN 0 575 06807 8

Printed and bound in Great Britain by
Butler & Tanner Ltd, Frome and London